Not Just Me

Anxiety, depression, and learning to embrace your weird

Lisa Jakub

ISBN-10: 1548088080

ISBN-13: 978-1548088088

First Edition

Cover photo by Sarah Cramer Shields

Visit the author's website at LisaJakub.net

For you.

Yes, you. The person reading this.

This book is dedicated to you.

Contents

Introduction: Forgetting to Breathe

The restaurant had recently opened to much fanfare about the creative use of basil foam, so the place was packed. Ultra-hip Hollywood people milled about, drinking popular drinks and wearing clothes that had cat-walked right out of that month's *Vogue*. There were whittled waistlines and physical alterations not found in nature. So, it was pretty much a regular Saturday night in L.A.

Something felt strange as we walked into the restaurant—something dark and foreboding that I felt deep in my soul. I hadn't wanted to leave my house, but I couldn't bail on what promised to be a fun evening with a good friend. I should have been okay. So I went. As Ben and I walked in, the walls started rippling like waves. I realized that this was not likely an interior design choice.

Shit.

Not again. This had been happening more and more frequently. I knew what was coming, and it was not going to be pretty.

I was nineteen and at the height of my acting career. I was supposed to be going to places like this; places like this were, in fact, designed specifically for people like me. Or rather, the person everyone thought I was. I'd been working in the film industry since I was four years old and had been in a couple of movies that broke box office records, as well as several dozen more that absolutely did not. I bought a house when I was fifteen; I had a mortgage before I had a driver's license. I was recognized at coffee shops and doctors' offices.

Acting was my life. I was acting on set and when I was not on set, I was still acting. Acting like I was happy. Acting like I wanted this.

But when I walked into that restaurant, I knew instantly that everyone had seen through my act. They all turned to face me, a hundred lips stopping mid-conversation, a hundred pairs of eyes burning with judgment. I knew they were wondering why I was there. Because I clearly didn't belong. I was a fraud, and I was pretty sure they all hated me.

Instantly, my hands went numb. I turned to Ben—but when I attempted to speak, it was like that scene in *Beetlejuice* when Geena Davis suddenly has a metal plate slapped across her mouth. I couldn't breathe. I could feel the blood draining from my face. Ben turned to me, his eyebrows knitting in concern.

"What? What's...happening?"

"I... I can't...They...not...air..."

At least that's what I tried to say.

I turned to look for the door we just walked through, but couldn't find it. The ceiling was where the floor should have been. My field of vision narrowed like I was trying to peer down the wrong end of a telescope.

Ben said, "Fjgkhgk sdjdflkf ksd hjk?" I thought this was a dick move, for him to suddenly start speaking another language while I was in the process of dying.

It then occurred to me that he was probably speaking English, but I was unable to process words anymore. I tensed up my quadriceps so tightly they started to shake. My legs were about to give out, and all these cool people were going to see me fall to the floor on my unworthy face. It was sad that I was dying, but clearly it was inevitable because my heart couldn't withstand this pressure much longer. It would be oozing out of my low-cut tank top at any moment.

I worried about my dogs. Who would take care of them after I died? It was good that Ben was there. He would tell my parents that I perished at that place with the basil foam, and they would take care of my dogs. I hoped I had mentioned that the little one was on joint medicine.

Suddenly, someone turned on disco lights. They were red and white and flashing, but no one else seemed to notice them. They pierced my brain and made me want to throw up. Great. I was going to vomit on this lovely recycled bamboo flooring. I wondered how well bamboo cleans up? I was clearly going to die before I could clean it. Would Ben have to do it?

Ben held my shoulders steady (they had gone numb, too), but he looked scared.

Was he scared for me?

Or of me?

He said something about a hospital. That was silly. I clearly wouldn't live long enough to make it to the hospital. Not in L.A. traffic. I was embarrassed. I tried to say "I'm fine," because I didn't want him to be frightened that he was about to witness my death, but I'm not sure I really said anything. He put his arm around my waist and half-carried, half-dragged me out into the courtyard. I crumpled to the ground next to a ridiculously ornate fountain where wannabe actors threw pennies and wished for speaking parts. I looked up. The palm trees wore glowing capes. Why did trees need capes?

"Breathe. Lisa. Look at me. Breathe." Ben crouched in front of me, his forehead pressed to my forehead. His breath smelled like pretzels.

I looked back up at the palm trees and watched their capes separate into a million individual twinkling string lights.

"Are you with me?"

I remembered how to breathe in and out. One after the other. I looked down at my hands, which were tightly clenched but didn't seem connected to my brain. I didn't feel like I was actually inhabiting my body, but rather existing somewhere up and to the left a little. Ben followed my gaze and gently pried my fists open, massaging my hands. The joints ached as feeling returned. Four little half-moon shapes marched across my palms. I stared at them, wondering what they were until I realized my fingernails had left their mark. I started to sob with humiliation and fear and sadness that I was *this* out of control.

"I'm sorry. I'm sorry."

There was nothing else to say.

"I'm so sorry."

Ben slumped to the cement, littered with cigarette butts adorned with the trendiest fall lipstick colors. He stopped rubbing my hands only long enough to gently brush the hair out of my face. Then he took both my hands again and finally whispered, "Lis? What the fuck was that?"

I knew exactly what it was. It was a thing that would happen to me literally hundreds of times between the ages of 11 and 38. It was something that haunted me, shamed me. And eventually it was something I came to understand.

"That was a panic attack."

A Brief List of Things That Freak Me Out

I am extremely sensitive. The snap of a shampoo bottle flip-cap startles me so severely that I'm forced to unscrew the lid during every shower, which takes forever and spills shampoo all over the place. My husband and I had to install dimmers in every room of our house, because bright lights make my heart race. A couple of years ago, a book about the 1915 sinking of the *Lusitania* left me teary and miserable for a week, and pretty much ruined our whole Thanksgiving holiday. The Christmas before, I was out of commission for 48 hours after an emotional viewing of *Les Misérables*. At restaurants, when the server asks, "What can I get you?" I freeze and have no idea if I intended to ask for the chopped salad or the peach cobbler. If someone takes more than four hours to return an e-mail, I obsessively read through the copy of it in my Sent folder, sometimes aloud, with different tonal variations, wondering if I said anything stupidly offensive. I fear that my husband is dead if his flight status reads "Delayed" — because honestly, what are they going to say if the plane falls out of the sky?

There have been times — there still are times — when I find it really hard to leave my house. I get panic attacks thinking about going to the grocery store. I've thrown up at the suggestion of a future social interaction, my body too riddled with anxiety to manage the digestion of food. I experience night terrors that cause me to leap out of bed at 3 a.m., and even though I am still asleep, I rush to attempt to save the people I love from their impending tragic deaths, which I have unwittingly caused by some thoughtless action. I'm so terrified and scattered in these moments that they sometimes result in me falling down stairs or stumbling out the front door. I get depressed and can do no more than fling myself to the couch in despair for the plight of this dark, damaged, irreparable world. I've hyperventilated while sitting on curbs outside of bars, clubs and art galleries. I always take my own car for a quick getaway from social events that involve more than one other person, in case the overwhelming small talk smothers my will to live.

It's like I have six fewer layers of skin than everyone else. But I've learned that there are actually a bunch of us that feel like this.

And no one wants to talk about it.

Until someone else brings it up.

And then it's all they want to talk about.

Anxiety is real. And in my experience, this stuff is merely managed — not cured like a summertime cold. It takes vigilance to deal with it day after day, and there are absolutely times when it slithers out of my grasp and flails around wildly.

I've learned to accept that anxiety is part of who I am, but it's become a much smaller part as I've learned some things that make life a little less intense. I want to share those things, and I want you to know that if you have anxiety, panic attacks or depression, you are not alone. I would love to tell you I am going to reveal the magic solution to fix it all, but I can't. I will, however, give you some ideas about what might help.

I'll be writing about anxiety and depression, because I've dealt with both, and in talking to many other people — medical professionals and folks with mood disorders — I've realized these conditions are likely two sides of the same coin. Many people with anxiety also suffer from depression, and vice versa. Depression obsesses about the past, while anxiety freaks out about the future. So you can call it anxiety, depression, stress, Mr. Mopey Pants, whatever — it all just means that you don't feel as good as you want to feel. The rest is pretty much just labels and semantics.

Everyone who is alive feels stressed at some point. There's a work deadline looming. The biopsy results came back "inconclusive." Money seems to run screaming out of the bank of its own volition. You have a date with that total cutie pie and the giant zit mid-forehead will not calm itself down. The tools and techniques in this book will be helpful whether you have a significant anxiety disorder or if you just get stressed out by life. We can all learn how to manage better and be more peaceful, compassionate and joyful.

But if anxiety and depression are starting to interfere with the way you live your life, this book is especially for you. Because I was you. I am you. I know how scary it can be to wonder when another panic attack will hit and if you are ever going to crawl out from under that crushing weight of depression.

I want to tell the truth about this stuff, even when it's not so cute.

It's Not Just Me

I do speaking events at high schools and colleges. I'm completely out of my element at these things, which always involve unpleasant intestinal issues and tunnel vision (for me, not my audiences). I often talk about anxiety. Being honest about it is freeing and also explains why I might be trembling and incapable of producing the appropriate amount of saliva in my mouth as I stand on stage. It lowers the bar for anyone who might have been expecting a former actor to come bounding up there, rolling around in the spotlight like a six-month-old golden retriever puppy with a chew toy.

When I finish my talk, the people who approach me tend to be crying.

I have anxiety, too.

I don't know what to do.

Why does no one talk about this?

I'm suffering and I thought I was the only one.

What do I do?

I hug them and tell them about helpful books and breathing exercises, and I say that I get it. What I really want is for all of us to go sit in a coffee shop and talk about our struggles so we feel less isolated, but there isn't a coffee shop in the world big enough to hold us all. So this book is the next best thing I could come up with.

We are arguably more connected than ever, through e-mail, Facebook, Twitter, Instagram — our phones mere inches away, even when we sleep. But somehow, we still feel lonely. We may get likes or retweets, but that leaves us wading ankle-deep in tepid relationship waters. It doesn't satisfy our primal longing for significant connection.

There is really no need to feel alone with your feelings of anxiety or depression. One in five adults in the US is dealing with some sort of mental health issue.[1] America ranks as the third most anxious and depressed country in the world, just after India and China.[2]

As a society, we are free from so many stresses of the past; we no longer need to worry about the Black Plague or roaming packs of beasts who want to devour us. The majority of us have access to food, shelter and clean water. If we have many of our basic needs met, why are so many of us starving for a little peace? Why are 60-90% of doctor visits attributed to stress-related illnesses?[3] The World Health Organization found that people in wealthy countries suffer from depression at rates up to eight times higher than those in poor countries.[4]

Is this simply because "anxiety" is becoming a buzz word, overused and misused, like "literally" or "feminism"? Maybe we're dealing with the paradox of choice: as the options available to us increase, so does our anxiety. Are we nervous wrecks because we have indoor plumbing, and a choice of regular or chocolate-filled croissants?

This is a complicated issue. There are a wide array of chemical, psychological, genetic and circumstantial reasons behind anxiety and depression. I also believe that cultural norms around definitions of success and the constant striving to acquire more money/stuff/prestige is furthering this epidemic. I've known people who seem to have everything—family, money, social status—but it's not enough to keep going, not enough to save them from the pain. No one is immune. The pessimistic perspective is that we're just all brats who don't know a good thing when we have it. We are spoiled and ungrateful and simply need to get over it and chill out. But that is a rather unhelpful way to view something that is literally killing us: 30,000 Americans die by suicide annually. Even more chilling, 500,000 people attempt to kill themselves every year.[5]

That's why we have to talk about this. It's important to reach out if you are struggling, and it's equally important to talk to friends if you see changes in their behavior that concern you. People tend to think that they should avoid asking someone if he/she is suicidal when the reality is that explicitly talking about the subject can save lives.

"Mental illness" seems to be a blanket term that conjures all kinds of unflattering stereotypes and caricatures. We worry that people will think we're crazy, melodramatic failures if we fess up to our feelings. We brace ourselves for rejection and ridicule, tell ourselves we don't deserve the love and belonging that everyone craves. To make matters worse, some people still hold onto antiquated ideas about anxiety and depression, and view it as a weakness. But not only is that incorrect, it's hugely detrimental—a dangerous notion that's partially responsible for why half of the people struggling with major depression don't seek help or treatment.[6] And those of you of the male persuasion are much less likely to report feeling depressed at all.[7]

But just like people finally got on board with the world not being flat, there is increasing awareness and understanding about mental wellness. In the process of writing this book, I met with some brave souls who were willing to open up the conversation and get honest. You'll read about people who come from a variety of cultural, religious, and racial backgrounds. Some have an official medical diagnosis, others don't. Some of them are financially stable, others are just scraping by. They have MFAs and MBAs and GEDs. But they all have significant things in common: they have anxiety and/or depression, and they all are using super secret code names.

Bonnie has always had anxiety, but now she has anxiety plus two young children to care for. She feels pressure to be a perfect mom and a perfect wife who wears perfect lipstick. She worries that her depression will take over, and she'll be a shut-in, incapable of caring for her family.

Mike's social anxiety has been brutal since middle school, and he's still struggling in his 40s. It's hard for him to hold down a job and he feels like a failure. He's trying to get sober and get back into the work force.

Jackie's panic attacks have been getting worse since her divorce. She finds herself curled up on the floor of her shower, filled with anxiety over finances and her future.

Philip has been on "elephant levels" of medication for both anxiety and depression since high school. He found all of his attempts at existing to be unacceptably bad, so he self-medicated in a variety of ways. He wonders why he's not homeless, in jail or dead.

Charlotte has been hospitalized for her suicide attempts. She estimates that she spends about nine thousand dollars a year dealing with her mental health. That's money she doesn't have, so she had to get a second job to pay her medical bills.

Nate is a disabled Army veteran who served in Afghanistan and Iraq. He's only twenty-nine, but he feels like his future plans have stalled. He's got PTSD and flashbacks and has a hard time focusing. He thinks of himself as an empty shell.

Andrew is ten years old. He gets overwhelmed and anxious easily; he feels like he's inside a pinball machine. He gets worked up and needs to hurt himself—crash into something—to calm down. It's hard to get people around him to understand; his school tells him he just needs to behave. His grandparents tell him he should just get over it.

And then there's me. The late-thirties former child actor-turned-writer with lifelong social anxiety, a panic disorder, occasional depression, and a severe aversion to leaving the house.

You'll hear from all those people and more, and I'll be sharing my story, as well. While my issues still show up, I'm at a point where anxiety no longer sits behind the wheel of my life. Instead, it usually hangs out in the backseat. Sometimes, I'm even able to shove it in the trunk, under the reusable shopping bags. When anxiety does kick me out of the way and take control—and it still does that sometimes—I spend less time sitting complacently on the passenger side, staring out the window and hoping we don't crash into a tree. I have tools to help change the situation and take back control more effectively, and that's what I want to tell you about. At the end of each chapter will be a Something To Try section, with suggestions and descriptions of some of the tools that have helped me.

But you should also know what this book is not

It's tempting to want to fix everything and find a nice, efficient solution to the problem.

But you are not a problem.

I'm not standing here, wearing overalls with a rusty toolbox in hand, ready to fix you. You're not a refrigerator on the fritz; you are not broken. I'm never going to say that you should "cheer up" or "just relax." (Personally, I think anyone who uses either phrase deserves a swift flick to the forehead.) I'm never going to tell you that you should be someone you are not. I'm not going to say you shouldn't feel the way you do.

This book is not THE answer or the only answer or maybe even the best answer for you, but the techniques I'll cover have been helpful for many of us—so perhaps they'll be helpful in your life. I'll tell you about the ways we found a little more balance in our lives when the world took our knees out. I'll tell you how we managed to keep getting up in the morning and how we rewrote the script we use to deal with the world.

It's easy to think that meditation or working out or eating chia seeds will suddenly make us perfectly un-anxious, carefree little pixies. But if you maintain a deep sense of loathing for your own soul, the suffering will continue through every green smoothie and each moment of High-Intensity Interval Training. You deserve love and understanding even when you're feeling weepy and lost.

Maybe even especially then. Some days, just breathing in and out deserves a Major Award.

So, we'll talk about SSRIs and perfectionism and yoga, but not because these are the keys to becoming the world's calmest, coolest, bravest person. We'll talk about them because they can help us understand ourselves better, and that understanding is the pathway to greater kindness, acceptance, forgiveness and empathy. We all need that even more than we need chia seeds.

Taking an honest look at your issues is scary. After a while, anxiety and depression become a strong part of our identities and we get defensive about our own suffering. We feel entitled to our misery and decide that we are simply broken and nothing will help. We get tired of hearing that we should just get more sunshine, or pray, or how your friend's Aunt Margaret was depressed but she got better when she started crocheting and you should too. I get it. So, if you have decided that there is no hope for you, that the alternatives are silly or too hard or they might work for everyone else but definitely not you (because *those* people have more money, easier lives and are better looking), that's fine, too. It's your life, you get to do what you want.

But if you are reading this, maybe you've decided that there's another option for you. Maybe you don't want to cling to angst as an integral part of your being. Perhaps you can shift that mindset even though it feels like it was engraved on your soul the moment you were born.

Anxiety might be a part of you, but it's not the biggest or most important part. If that part is a little less unwieldy all the time, then your authentic self (which I guarantee is way cooler than depression) can shine through. That single realization is a really big deal. So, congrats — because deciding to investigate other ways of being in the world is seriously brave.

The Brain is Just Doing the Brain's Job

There is nothing inherently wrong with anxiety — the brain is just doing what it's supposed to do to keep us safe. But for many of us, it's doing it in unnecessary proportions and inappropriate contexts. Giving a best man's speech at a wedding is unlikely to be a life-ending event, but it can feel that way because of the stories we create about all the things that could possibly go wrong.

Your anxiety is not your fault. let's be super clear about that. In fact, I'm going to put that in bold and put it on another line so that I'm sure you read it.

Your anxiety is not your fault.

And actually, I'm going to amend that to say:

Your anxiety is not your fault...and you possess the resources to make life better for yourself.

There are ways to help yourself out and bring the anxiety down. You have choices. You can hide from your whole life, clinging to a false sense of control and security. Or you can take some chances, quit the garbage that is not serving you, and accept the fact that you might get roughed up by the world — but it's okay, because you are a warrior and you were built for this. It's not going to be easy, because there are legit challenges in the world and you're tired and can't imaging putting more energy into anything. I know. But as a reward for not hiding, you'll get to see a whole bunch of super cool stuff and potentially feel a whole lot better about basically everything.

I vote for this second option. And even if you don't think you deserve to do cool stuff and have good things, maybe I can get you on board with this baby-step idea: You deserve to not feel like crap all the time.

We tend to think we'll be happy when we meet that adorable person with the great hair, or get that better job, or move to a new place where the heating system doesn't make that annoying knocking noise. But life is a game of Whack-A-Mole: As soon as you get one thing under control, something else pops up and you have to deal with that. We believe that we'll feel peaceful once everything falls into place, but I've found that things fall into place when I'm feeling peaceful, regardless of external circumstances.

I used to feel ashamed of my anxiety. I used to try to hide it and pretend to be someone I wasn't. I felt pressure to be a chipper person with predicaments that could be solved in a 22-minute sitcom timeframe. But when I took off the mask of being "fine" all the time, things started to shift. As a species, humans are built for connection. When we hear others' stories, we actually get a rush of oxytocin, that feel-good hormone our bodies release around new lovers, or when women are nursing their children.[8] It's the natural drug of connection, love and understanding. It's what we all crave. We get a natural high just from hearing stories and connecting on a level of deep understanding.

So let's get high on that shit.

*By the way, nothing in this book is intended to be used instead of care from a medical professional. As if it were not abundantly clear by now, I am not a doctor. I've never even played one on TV.

Chapter 1: "Yeah, no, I'm good" — And Other Lies I Tell My Therapist

"Is this a terrible idea?"

"Tacos? How could tacos ever be a terrible idea?"

"No. Not tacos." I was standing in the kitchen, making tacos, so I could see why he was confused.

"Talking to my therapist to do research for this book. I feel like getting my records and writing about my diagnosis is an important part of the story, but it feels terrifying. Is it a terrible idea?"

My husband stalled, chopping a tomato to bide his time. Jeremy knew this was a tricky question. Agreeing that anything to do with my writing was "terrible" was bound to provoke tears. Blind support was not without risks, either. If the project went badly, there was a good chance I might blame him.

"Well, it's not going to be easy, but I think it'll be interesting. You just have to be prepared."

"Prepared for what?"

"I don't know. That's the hard part. What if you find out that your anxiety was worse than you thought? Or not as bad as you thought?"

I'd considered the first one. What if Louise's notes from our therapy sessions just said CRAZY in red pen across the top? What then? Would it send me down that terror spiral again? But what if her professional analysis said my anxiety wasn't as bad as I thought? Would I feel free? Or like an overly-reactive, whiny little baby?

"I think you should talk to her. It's vulnerable and authentic. Doesn't Brené Brown say all that stuff is good?"

Jeremy knows to invoke the work of Brené Brown when I need courage. It's like calling on a beloved saint or rubbing a Buddha belly. He nodded confidently as he finished demolishing a tomato.

"You should be brave and you should meet with Louise and write about it. It'll give you anxiety street cred. But just be careful."

"Before we do this, I have to ask. Are you in a good place?" Louise covered the stacks of insurance documentation with her hands, like a little kid protecting her spelling paper.

Wow. Everyone was really concerned about this. I laughed because that's what I do when I'm uncomfortable. It did indeed seem like a risky thing; was I actually going to dig up all this stuff again? I thought I was in a decent place, but one tiny misstep could send me back to the days of hiding on the floor of my closet, curled in a ball and sobbing atop a pile of shoes.

It had taken me almost ten years after the Basil Foam Restaurant Breakdown to commit to seeing a therapist. Louise and I worked together for two years before we felt we had made enough progress to stop our sessions. That was almost eight years ago. Louise knew I wanted to write about my experience for this book, and she was supportive but cautious. "Cautious" was now starting to look like full-blown concern. I had been doing a decent job managing my anxiety recently, and I hadn't had a depressive episode in a while. Now I was volunteering to wander back down this unpleasant memory lane. Was I making a huge mistake?

"Personally, I've never looked at my records, and I have no desire to look at them. I already lived it," she said. I tried to imagine my therapist in therapy, which felt like some M. C.

Escher sketch where stairs led into themselves. I noticed her hands still hadn't moved from the stack of paperwork.

Those records contained my clinical diagnosis and numerical ratings, like grades I was getting in a class called Dealing With Life 101. Even if it was going to give me credibility, like Jeremy said, was it worth taking an ice pick to a recently healed wound?

Louise and I sat in her office. It was a different one than where we started our therapy sessions. We'd had little contact since we stopped working together; every once in a while I'd run into her semi-awkwardly at the bagel place, but it was rare. Though Louise had stopped seeing patients in the years since we worked together, she had eagerly responded to my e-mail and agreed to meet with me. There was something natural about sitting with her again, even in the unfamiliar setting of this new space. In a startling coincidence, I noticed the rug beneath my feet was the same one that sat under my desk in my home office. I decided this was a sign from the universe that looking at these records was an okay thing to do. Why the universe talked to me through woven textiles, I'm not totally sure, but I was prepared to take any and all available encouragement.

Louise is tall and graceful. I am neither. Whenever we walked together, I felt like a gawky 12-year-old boy — an impression helped not at all by my preferred uniform of ripped jeans and Chuck Taylors. I had heard a rumor that Louise had been a model in college. While that would be unsurprising, I don't actually know if it's true, and I've never been brave enough to ask her personal questions. It's always been very clear that we talk about me, not her. While my emotional inclination is to cling to people I like with the tenacity of a frightened octopus, with Louise, I always found myself being kept at an extremely professional arm's length. But at this particular moment, Louise's arms were still covering the stack of papers; she was searching my face for what I can only assume was evidence of mental fragility. After I convinced her that I was prepared to see my records and assured her that I had an extensive support system reachable via text at any moment, should I need them Louise slid the stack toward me.

My chest tightened as my eyes skimmed over the check marks next to the boxes for:

- social isolation
- impaired concentration
- phobia
- panic attacks
- generalized anxiety
- eating problems
- sleep disturbance
- school/work problems

Then I saw the number. It was my global assessment functioning level, a scale used by mental health clinicians to determine how someone is managing with the issues of life. Louise had assigned me 45 out of 100. If this really was Dealing with Life 101, I had definitely been flunking out. There was a strange comfort in knowing an objective third party like Louise could see how much I was suffering back then. It was nice to know that someone really heard me.

As Louise went through the papers, gently explaining terms like Axis I, II and III, I realized I couldn't see the words she was pointing to on the page. That's common for me—I can't focus my eyes properly when I get anxious. I wasn't in full-blown panic mode, just unsettled. Fundamentally ungrounded. Like walking down the aisle of an airplane at thirty thousand feet.

"Do you want to read through this stuff now, and I can answer any questions you have?"

"Ummm. I think I'm good to read it at home. Umm. Yeah, I think I'm good, I'll look at it at home." My voice turned high and squeaky. I didn't want to tell her that my fuzzy vision had rendered me temporarily illiterate.

"Are you sure? I don't mind. You can just read now, then we can talk about anything that comes up." Louise sounded like she was talking to me underwater. My hearing was going, too. That happens.

"Yeah, no, I'm good. Thank you." I realized I'd said the phrase "I'm good" three times. It was starting to sound like one of those aspirational affirmations you're supposed to say into a mirror. The phrase "yeah, no" also didn't inspire much confidence in my mental sturdiness. I picked up the paperwork, aligned the edges and tapped them on the table in a way I hoped appeared self-assured and imparted a feeling of finality. Why I was not confessing my dizziness and blurred vision to a therapist? MY therapist? Some things are just still hard to admit out-loud. I was hiding behind the mask again, pretending to be fine in the hope of avoiding the attention and concern of others. It's hard to admit that sometimes I'm not quite okay. It seems that I still have a tendency to fall back into my movie past and just act my ass off.

As I tucked the papers into my NY Public Library tote bag, I remembered those painful old feelings that had brought me to Louise in the first place; a pinch in the center of my chest that took my breath away. For so long it seemed I would never feel better, never understand how to live in a way that didn't feel like I was constantly swimming through shards of glass.

But you did. I silently reminded myself. *You survived your twenties. You made it through. It got easier.*

Labeling is bad. Except When It's Not.

Back at home after our meeting, I curled up on the couch, holding the stapled print-outs of my medical file. I suddenly flashed back to one of my first therapy sessions with Louise, so many years earlier. I had been in college at the time, and my anxiety had become paralyzing and unbearable.

"On a scale of one to ten, with ten being the absolute worst, where is your anxiety level most of the day?"

I thought about it.

"Nine."

"Nine? What makes you say that?"

"Well, I assume that things can get worse than this, but I find it hard to imagine how."

I shook off the memory, took a deep breath, and flipped open the paperwork. There it was, right on the top of the page:

Axis 1: 300.23 Social phobia.*

I'm afraid of society.

That's like a fish being afraid of water. It's all around me, I can't escape it—and it's also the thing I most need for my survival. I turned to the next page.

"Lisa was neatly groomed and casually dressed." (I hadn't realized my Chucks were also going for analysis.) "Speech was normal for rate, tone and volume. Her flow of thought was spontaneous, linear and logical. There were no indications of delusions, hallucinations or other psychotic symptoms."

As I read down, there were uncomfortable quotes from me about how stupid I was and how I would never fit in. I talked about my crippling anxiety, my unusual child-actor past and how I worked so much that I never got my high school diploma and I fundamentally didn't belong anywhere. Louise commented on my admission that I had bad stomach cramps and it was hard to eat. She noted I was sleeping more than ten hours a night but was constantly exhausted. She didn't sense that I was suicidal or violent. In the documentation to my insurance company, she reported that we were going to use cognitive behavioral therapy techniques to help me realize that it was actually thoughts, not other people or situations, that determined how I reacted. She would help me learn to recognize and change negative thoughts about myself. We'd work on limiting distorted thinking and make behavioral changes to adjust the reactions that had become almost automatic when I'm faced with anxiety. We'd focus on cognitive restructuring — which sounded like she was going to take apart my brain and put it back together again like some 3,000-piece jigsaw puzzle.

Actually, what we did was much harder than that. And it saved me.

*The Diagnostic and Statistical Manual of Mental Disorders (DSM) terminology has since changed, and my diagnosis is now called Social Anxiety Disorder.

Hello, I'm 300.23

We hear it starting in grade school: Don't label.

And it's true — labels can be useless or downright dangerous. But there are situations in which labels can be helpful. It's valuable to know which can is creamy tomato soup and which one is dog food.

It's up to you to decide how much importance you give this idea of a label or category. Putting words to something is powerful. For me, it's helpful to know that I have a social anxiety disorder and a panic disorder. If I was the only person who had ever felt this way, it wouldn't have an official name, right? When I Googled my symptoms, the search results would just say "That Freaky Thing Lisa Jakub Does." The label makes me feel less alone.

Then again, labels can get dangerous when we look to them to define us, or others. Mental health issues are not a defining quality of who we are. This is not a brand on your forehead, identifying a permanent situation. It's merely a starting place. A road map. It can help you understand where you are and find a way to get where you want to go.

As we look at some definitions, please keep in mind that this book is not intended as a tool for self-diagnosis. Let a doctor do that. (Dr. Google doesn't count.) I just want to establish some clarity around the types of things I'll talk about in the rest of the book.[9]

Anxiety. Anxiety affects your whole self—causing physiological, behavioral and psychological reactions. Anxiety can fluctuate and come in different forms, but generally it includes avoidance behavior—where your life is altered because you are trying to stay away from the things that trigger you, and "self-talk" in which you are actually encouraging your anxious state by the negative things you are thinking about yourself and the world.

Physical symptoms include:
- Shortness of breath
- Heart palpitations
- Trembling and shaking

- Sweating
- Choking or nausea
- Numbness
- Dizziness
- Feeling of being out of touch with yourself

Generalized Anxiety Disorder (GAD). This is categorized by a sense of vague, looming danger out there that you can't quite see — an acute fear of everything and nothing. It is characterized by unrealistic worry about everyday things and the constant expectation of the worst possible outcome. It is not associated with phobias and often shows up alongside depression. GAD is characterized by a fear of: losing control, death, failure, rejection/abandonment and not being able to cope.

These symptoms last for at least six months:
- Restlessness
- Easily fatigued
- Difficulty concentrating
- Irritability
- Muscle tension
- Sleep problems

Situational Anxiety or Phobic Anxiety. This is defined by feelings of intense panic in response to a specific scenario or stimulus. Triggers can range from blood to elevators to pretty much anything else. People with this type of anxiety will alter their routine to avoid the things they fear. If you freak out just thinking about your trigger, that is called "anticipatory anxiety" or "anticipatory panic."

Panic Disorder. If you are experiencing anxiety that comes in episodes of intense fear and acute apprehension, you might have a panic disorder. The fear you experience is out of proportion to the situation; it usually peaks within ten minutes, but rarely lasts longer than one hour. A panic disorder itself doesn't necessarily require any specific trigger (say, trendy restaurants in Los Angeles), and it can strike for no obvious reason. Often this disorder develops in the late teens or early twenties and commonly occurs with other conditions such as depression, alcoholism or drug addiction.

Here are the symptoms:
- Shortness of breath
- Heart palpitations
- Trembling or shaking
- Sweating
- Choking
- Nausea
- Numbness, dizziness
- Feeling of being out of touch with yourself
- Hot flashes or chills
- Fear of dying
- Fear of going crazy or losing control

Agoraphobia. Agoraphobia is the fear of open spaces, but it often shows up as the fear of panic attacks. Some, but not all, people with panic attacks develop agoraphobia. Those with agoraphobia fear being somewhere without an easy escape route. Crowded spaces, tunnels, bridges, planes or subways tend to be challenging. This is the reason I must always sit in what my husband calls "the Gun Slinger seat." I need to face the room, with my back to a wall, whenever possible. This lets me feel less trapped: If I can see something coming, it's easier to bolt. On the few occasions when I have been forced to have my back to the room, I spend the entire meal looking over my shoulder like I'm on the lam from the elaborate bank heist I just pulled off.

Like all mental health issues, agoraphobia can have various levels of intensity, ranging from feeling mildly uncomfortable in crowded places but not needing to avoid them, to not being able to leave the house at all. I've bounced back and forth between those extremes in my life. (I don't have an official agoraphobia diagnosis, but I fit the criteria.)

Social Anxiety Disorder. This one is pretty common, and involves a fear of humiliation or judgment from others. This is the disproportionate worry that other people will perceive you as dumb, crazy, weak or incapable. It's basically the fear of people looking at you and evaluating you, and it's the reason I only had twenty guests at my wedding.

Post-Traumatic Stress Disorder (PTSD). This disorder was first identified during World War I. PTSD isn't only linked to combat; it can occur in the aftermath of any traumatic event such as a divorce, death, accident, illness or any kind of emotional trauma. Giving birth has even recently been added to the list. PTSD can come from the exposure to an event that involved death, the threat of death, or serious injury to yourself or others.

For a PTSD diagnosis, the following symptoms need to persist for at least one month, and interfere with the normal events of life:
- Repetitive thoughts about the event
- Flashbacks—feeling like the event is occurring again
- Nightmares about the event

- Attempt to avoid the thoughts or feelings associated with the trauma
- Avoiding activities associated with the trauma
- Emotional numbness/detachment
- Losing interest in activities that used to be pleasurable
- Increased anxiety, difficulties falling/staying asleep
- Startling easily, outbursts of anger, difficulties concentrating.

Obsessive-Compulsive Disorder. OCD is often accompanied by depression, but it is increasingly being recognized as distinct from anxiety issues. OCD seems to be a different type of disorder that originates from a different part of the brain than mood disorders, so I'm not going to cover that topic here. There are great resources for OCD, but this book is not one of them.

Live Your Mostly-Better, Most-of-the-Time Life

"I hate to point fingers at our beloved Oprah, but I think that a lot of the blame can be laid at her feet."

I expected that my interviews for this book were going to be intimate and shocking, but I didn't expect this. Oprah bashing?

My friend Elizabeth is a therapist. When we met, twenty years ago, she was an actor and a singer who had toured with bands all across Europe. We were both living in Los Angeles, going to auditions and waiting in line to see terrible plays that our friends had written/directed/starred in and also painted the sets for.

Elizabeth has one of the most beautiful souls I've ever known, and that oozes out of every pore. We were once at the grocery store and the check-out guy spontaneously proposed to her. If such a thing had ever happened to me, I would have been turning purple, giggling and dying to tell my friends, but Elizabeth just smiled sweetly, said she was already married (she wasn't) and took her receipt. This happened to her all the time.

Since the days when we went cereal shopping together, Elizabeth has left L.A. and started pursuing her love for psychology. Now, two decades into our friendship, we talk about the ways it's so easy to blame ourselves for our mental unrest. We forget that we live in a world that in many ways corroborates our anxiety. But I'm still not entirely making the connection.

"Wait, how is this Oprah's fault?"

Elizabeth clarified that she was sure Oprah's intentions were good, but something got lost in translation. "The idea that there is a Best Life and that it's attainable makes you constantly question whether what you have is your Best Life. And how would you know? Well, you compare yourself to other people. And if you find someone who has a life that looks better, then you don't have your Best Life and you've failed. Even if you don't compare yourself to others, you compare yourself to who you were yesterday and that is endless — you always need to be better, you can't be the same. By those rules, if you are satisfied, you're settling, and so you're on a never-ending hamster wheel."

When I was working on an early draft of this book, I wrote about the problem of comparing ourselves to others. But what I literally wrote was how dangerous it is to compare ourselves to *otters*. Otters. Not others. I giggled about my typo, then realized my mistake was exactly right. It doesn't make any more sense for me to be comparing myself to an otter, lamenting the fact that I've never once cracked open a sea urchin while floating on my back, than it does for me to compare my life to Emma Watson's.

Maybe we can leave being like otters to the otters, and realize that each of us has a different path and his or her own version of what a successful life looks like. It's exhausting to feel that everything from our career development to our weekend plans needs to be exciting and Instagram-worthy. We can never rest or feel content, because someone else is going to get ahead in this endless race to who-knows-what. But striving can't be all bad, can it? Do we just give up on trying to improve ourselves?

Elizabeth says, "Don't worry about living your Best Life. Live your Mostly-Better, Most-of-the-Time life."

We should make t-shirts. Maybe start a club for the under-achievers of self-improvement. Because she's right: We have anxiety about trying to have less anxiety. We feel like we're screwing that up, too.

"I think a lot of times, anxiety is better described as angst," Elizabeth told me. "It's existential and it has to do with the way we feel disconnected from nature and each other. I blame the Industrial Revolution for many of our ills, because since then we have had this illusion of disconnectedness."

Before you go to Wikipedia to remind yourself what the hell happened during the Industrial Revolution and why it might be causing your panic attacks, here's a quick historical recap:

The Industrial Revolution changed everything about how we live and work, in the years between the mid-1700s and the mid-1800s. That's when, as a culture, we got really into growth and striving. Generally, that was a great thing. There was significant industrial progress — we got more efficient steam engines and the cotton gin. We transformed from an agricultural society based on small, family-run cottage industries to the rise of the factory system. That was fantastic because fewer people starved to death. So yay, revolution! But the world got a lot bigger, very fast, and with change comes... well, change. We became more separate from one another, more focused on progress and personal achievement as indicators of a life well-lived.

We also got really into independence. Back when there were fewer resources, people were required to live in close communities so they could share them. Societies that are interdependent are only as strong as their weakest link, so it was necessary to be all *Kumbaya, we're all in this together*. The rise of industry caused an increase in wealth, which meant we started living farther apart. We became less dependent on each other for survival. We grew more concerned about our personal property since the well-being of others had little tangible effect on us anymore. This self-sufficiency has led to a feeling of isolation and the deterioration of social bonds. We're surrounded by people, but we're lonely.[10]

For me, thinking that my anxiety is caused by the Industrial Revolution and Oprah feels awful. Because there is not much I can do about those things, and in fact, I really like my sewing machine and *Super Soul Sunday*. Cultural influences are so completely out of my control that I feel doomed. If anxiety and depression are cultural, we're surrounded by poisoned air.

So we need to turn inward, right? That's the answer? While it's nice to think I have much more control over my interior life, Elizabeth thinks I'm fairly powerless there, too.

"The 'New Age' thing made us think we have control over our thoughts. It's sexy and gratifying to say, 'If you just put up a vision board and chant some magic words, prosperity will rain down on your face and you will feel happy all the time.' That book *The Secret* was the preschool version of how the universe works. Yes, you absolutely will have better results if you focus your attention on the things you want. Sure. But that's not the end of the story."

If visualizing our goals and hoping really hard isn't the end of the story, what *is*? What is the less sexy/more effective way to deal with our existential angst? It's that tricky concept: acceptance.

"Emotions happen—all of them," Elizabeth told me. "Anger, sadness, jealousy. The question is, do you dwell on them? Or when they knock on the door do you say *Yes hi, nice to see you, now excuse me, I have other things to do.* We tend to wage war on our emotions because we've been told they are unnecessary, avoidable or undesirable. If we stop trying to have total control over our emotions and just attempt to have some influence over them—that's much kinder. Making peace with your emotions is your best shot at making your interior world more pleasant for yourself. So let's do that. That's much better than saying, *just don't think bad things.*"

Something to Try: What Could Make Your Life Mostly-Better, Most-of-the-Time?

There is a phrase that I use frequently: be an ant.

I stole it from a friend. Susan's husband is a contractor and builder and his passion is renovating houses. He used to practice law, until he realized he didn't like lawyering and wanted to build beautiful things instead.

Sometimes Susan helps her husband out on the construction sites and one day there was this giant pile of bricks they needed to move. It was more like a mountain of bricks. Susan said, "It was like, six feet tall. I remember looking at it and thinking how awful this was. It was going to take forever and it was going to be miserable. I wanted to cry looking at this giant pile. But Frank just looked at me and said 'We'll take it brick by brick. Be an ant.'"

Brick by brick wasn't that bad. When Susan was in the moment, dealing only with the brick right in front of her, it was all okay. It was only when she got ahead of herself and let her mind take over that the task seemed impossible.

Most of our fears and anxieties come from the stories we create around the truth, not the truth itself. We're not scared of the dark. We're scared of all the monsters we imagine are lurking there. But when Susan dropped the story about how impossible and difficult moving these bricks would be, she got the job done. Brick by brick, moment by moment. No drama. No tears. Just be an ant.

Think about what bricks you might want to move in your life. Make a list of things you want to:

Stop: What habits or patterns are feeling unproductive and detrimental? Do you have a short temper? A not-so-great relationship with alcohol?

Start: What do you think you might like to start doing? Being a little more patient with yourself? Incorporating physical exercise into your day?

Continue: What seems to be working? Do you have a good support system? A willingness to really look at your life and consider some changes?

Once we've identified the bricks, we can work each day on shifting just one of them. We can question that one single habit, change that tiny aspect of our lives, examine that one unhelpful knee-jerk reaction. We can take it one brick at a time, and then at some point, we'll look back, and we'll see we moved that whole damn mountain.

Chapter 2 : Let's Start With How it Starts, Which Might Not Really Matter

"**W**hy am I so weird?"

I have flung myself onto many a bed, asking the anxiety gods, *Why me? Why can't I be one of the cool kids who takes things in stride and never trembles at the mention of a tailgate? Why can't I be more like my husband?* Jeremy reacted to the news that layoffs at his job were likely imminent by feeling *less* stressed because the silly work details really didn't matter if he was going to get fired anyway. Why could I not embody a fraction of that easy-breeziness?

When I lamented my anxious tendencies to my hairdresser during my semi-annual visit, he immediately diagnosed the problem as astrological. Since I'm a Capricorn with Sagittarius rising and a major water sign influence and lots going on in my Mercury something-or-other, he informed me that anxiety and crippling empathy for the human race is par for the course. The man was holding scissors, so I humored him with a polite smile until he said, "You probably have knee problems, too, right?"

I peered through the curtain of wet hair that had fallen in front of my eyes. "Um. Yes."

He nodded and untangled the hair drier cord. "Yeah, classic Capricorn."

It's natural to wonder why we are like this and obviously, knowing the root cause of our struggles can be helpful. If your brother used to hold you underwater in your grandma's pool or you served two tours in Afghanistan, it's probably useful to talk to someone about those experiences. But many of us (myself included) aren't exactly sure why we have this anxiety. It's not a straight line from cause to effect.

Luckily, we don't need to know why something started in order to start addressing it. Once the situation becomes a little more manageable, maybe then we can go back and dig deeper into what might have led us there. If there's an elephant on the loose, you can stand there all day and point fingers at who let him out, or you can jump in and do the hard work of corralling that big guy. Once the elephant is safely back where he belongs, then you can figure out who thought it would be a good idea to let Dumbo roam around the middle of Cleveland.

Instead of spending decades obsessing about how it all began, the first step should be scheduling a check-up with your doctor to see if there could be something going on physically. Talking to a health professional can be incredibly beneficial—and totally anxiety-provoking. But your doctor is not going to think you are weird. Trust me. They're doctors. They've seen way weirder shit than an anxious person. My primary care physician assured me that people come in to talk to him about anxiety and depression every single day. It's as extraordinary for him as giving a flu shot.

It's important to see a medical professional to rule out some things: Could the anxiety be caused by something like thyroid issues or a B12 deficiency? My doctor believes in "modifying the modifiable," so at your appointment you might talk about things like sleep habits, diet and exercise. These things might seem kind of frivolous in the face of overwhelming anxiety, but this is just the beginning of a long conversation about how to make your life a little easier. A doctor can offer some different pathways to explore.

This was the case with my friend Becca, who in college experienced intense depression and suicidal ideations really sporadically (or so it seemed). She kept a journal at the time, and one day discovered a pattern: She experienced all these destructive thoughts and negative feelings around the same time every month. A conversation with her doctor led to a diagnosis of Premenstrual Dysphoric Disorder, a severe and sometimes disabling version of PMS, caused by a sharp decline in serotonin production in the week leading up to a woman's period. She and her doctor dealt with that issue, and the depression disappeared. The answer is not always going to be that straightforward, but meeting with your doctor should be the first step, regardless.

Since that process can be stressful, I've included a form letter at the end of this book that you can use as a springboard for figuring out what you want to say. Just rip the page from this book, fill it out and hand it to your doctor. Yes, I'm fully authorizing you to tear pages out of this book. (But don't rip out any other pages. That would just be sadistic.) And if you don't want to rip—go to NotJustMeBook.com to download the letter.

So, start with your doctor.

Wait.

I take that back. The *first* first step should be stopping with the recreational drugs, if you've been doing that. I don't mean to sound like Frances McDormand from *Almost Famous*, but seriously—don't do drugs. They might seem like a handy escape from your panic or depression, but it's only going to complicate things. So deal with that first—cut out the self-medicating so we can start with a clean slate. I understand that might take a while. Go ahead. I'll wait here.

So, have you ruled out drugs or a physical condition that might be causing the issues? Cool. Now we can dive in.

Anxiety: A Brief History

Anxiety isn't a modern problem, and its shady past makes it unsurprising that we have a hard time talking about mental illness. Historically, anxiety has had many names and has been blamed on everything from witchcraft to bad blood or just being the owner of lady parts.

Hippocrates was the first to use the term "hysteria" in the fifth century BCE.[11] He had a clear idea about the root cause of the disease: *hystera* is the Greek word for "uterus." In Victorian times, panic attacks were treated with electric shock therapy or lobotomies. In what might have been the kindest form of treatment, doctors sent nervous women home with vibrators for stress relief. By the early twentieth century, it seemed to make sense to sterilize anyone with mental illness, so they couldn't pass it on to children.[12]

In the 1870s, Dr. Silas Weir Mitchell, a prominent physician from Philadelphia, was considered a pioneer in the field that he called "neurasthenia."[13] He created a Rest Cure especially for the ladies, while men with neurasthenia were told to go work on a ranch. The Rest Cure pretty much meant becoming a recluse, forbidden from doing anything but lying around without books or stimulating conversation. Someone even had to come turn the patient over in bed. If you've ever dealt with anxiety, you already know that this was a recipe for a rapid descent into an even darker place.

One of my favorite short stories ever is "The Yellow Wallpaper" by Charlotte Perkins Gilman. She recounts her experience with the Rest Cure in this semi-autobiographical piece, which ends with a woman reacting to her isolation by peeling off all the wallpaper in her room and chewing on the bed frame. Not super encouraging. With the resurgence of that short story in the 1970s (that's right—a full century after Mitchell started prescribing his "treatment") people started giving the Rest Cure some serious side-eye.

Fast forward to today and there is still no conclusive answer to whether anxiety and depression are rooted in nature (you were born with it) or nurture (you are a product of your circumstances and things you've been through). It could all start from a specific moment, like a personal loss or traumatic event that causes post-traumatic stress disorder (PTSD). Anxiety and depression could be caused by a short-term trigger like a significant life change. It can come from cumulative, long-term stress like caring for a loved one who is ill or feeling trapped in a miserable job. It could be exacerbated by your diet or exhaustion. Or maybe you have no idea what caused it, but blaming your mom for making you go to that sleep-away camp in Maine seems like a reasonable place to start.

One study likes to spread the blame around pretty evenly, reporting that anxiety is 40% genetic, 30% learned experiences and 30% psychological tendencies.[14] A "psychological tendency" means your general perceptions and cognitive patterns, like seeing the world as generally scary or uncontrollable (does that ink blot look like a plane crash or a party hat?). I call it the "Eeyore tendency."

My anxiety certainly could have something to do with learned experiences. When I was four years old, I started working as an actor in an environment that demands perfection. I spent the next eighteen formative years in a job with high levels of criticism, competition and rejection. For the most part, I enjoyed my job, but maybe that pressure was integrated into my brain and caused the panic. Maybe I internalized the stress and became this highly sensitive person with acute levels of anxiety around failure and social interaction. When I was fourteen, I played Robin Williams's eldest daughter in *Mrs. Doubtfire*, a movie that did far better than any of us expected. I was frequently approached, mobbed and grabbed in public, and then there was that one time I got a little bit kidnapped. Getting public attention might seem fun, but in reality, it's a How-To Guide for developing agoraphobia.

But maybe it's the other way around and nervousness is just my nature. Maybe I was good at my job pretending to be other people because my soul is inherently sensitive and empathetic. Maybe I was able to portray delicate levels of emotional trauma as an actor because that was my natural state. Maybe I could cry well on camera because I am perpetually three seconds and a dog food commercial away from tears in my everyday life.

There's something appealing about the idea that anxiety and depression are based on our genetics. That way, we can throw up our hands and blame something completely out of our control. If anxiety and depression are genetic, that negates the assumption that we should just get over it. It legitimizes our struggles and, in theory, should reduce the social stigma. What if having anxiety is no different than having freckles?

There is evidence to back up the genetic theory. Extensive research has been done on the serotonin transporter gene (also called SERT or 5-HTT), which lives in our seventeenth chromosome. It helps with manufacturing the neurotransmitter serotonin—the brain's happy chemical. It's been found that people with the short form of the gene tend to be predisposed to anxiety and mood disorders. People who have the long version are less likely to develop these disorders, even when their lives are highly stressful.[15] But it's not all bad to have the short gene. People with a short SERT score higher on cognitive tests, and although they experience more anxiety on stressful days, they have less stress on calm days.[16]

But the gene theory isn't a slam dunk. Several studies have shown that if one twin has an anxiety disorder, there is a strong likelihood that the other genetically identical twin will have one, too—but it's certainly not a guarantee.[17] So, *might* you be wired for teary outbursts if you have the short version of the gene? Sure. But even if your susceptibility to mood issues is strongly determined by your genetics, biology is not destiny. It can be helpful to know that what is going on with us is real—not something we are making up or exaggerating for the sake of getting attention and being drama royalty. But we also have choices to work with what we've got in both the genetic lottery and the random selection of personal circumstances.

This is Going to be Hard. But it's Possible. And Totally Worth It.

After living in a state of panic for a while, it's easy to constantly expect stress, chaos and disaster. Some people—especially those who have experienced trauma—are likely to look at the world through that veil of anxiety and expect bad things.[18] Consciously or subconsciously, we become hyper-vigilant, seeking out problems and disappointments. These behaviors become chronic.

In many cases, we can't change the specific circumstances of our lives (maybe we have chronic pain, financial problems or a difficult relationship with a family member), but what we can do is start to shift our emotions around those circumstances. We can ditch the story we automatically play on repeat—the narrative that we will never feel better, that we will always struggle, that we are inherently unlovable. Maybe we've been told that's just who we are, or maybe we came up with the stories ourselves. We can cling to these stories for years, and they feel like the essence of our being. But it's kind of like wearing the same jacket for years; at some point, the jacket is not going to fit anymore—it's going to be way too small and unfashionable. We have the power to take off that jacket, and that changes everything. Every time we bypass the fabricated story, we get stronger. We practice looking at the truth of our lives and responding in a new way. When you can find some peace with the difficult stuff without piling on stories about how things shouldn't be like this, life gets less hard.

Easier said than done, right? Why don't I just tell you to go relocate the Empire State Building while we're at it? I know. But while the details of life are often out of your control, you can do something about the way you choose to see the world. This isn't some bullshit about looking on the bright side; no one is saying that anxiety and depression are all in your head and you should be all sparkly and brimming with courage all the time. Life isn't always happy, but neither is it dwelling in misery 24/7. There is no need to delude yourself into thinking that everything is rainbows and unicorns. It's not. Frequently, it's back pain and credit card debt. But it's the way you *relate* to the back pain and credit card debt that starts to change the situation. Don't discount how powerful you are in your own life.

Research by psychologists at Columbia University has shown that self-motivation gets easier if we practice it in a specific way; believing we have some authority over our lives can help motivate us.[19] We tend to work harder and overcome setbacks faster if we think our efforts will actually pay off. So how can we feel like we have some influence over our situation when our emotions can feel so outside our control? We make small decisions, tiny changes, set embarrassingly small goals, and reinforce the fact that we are powerful and free to choose. Instead of getting depressed about our weight, we can focus on making a healthy dinner tonight. Instead of being anxious about dealing with our narcissistic boss, we can carve out thirty minutes to work on our résumé. Instead of feeling isolated and weird like no one gets it, we can text one friend and ask him to meet for coffee. This goes for habits, too. Want to start flossing? Set a goal to floss one tooth.

Dealing with the Demons

If approximately 43.6 million adults in the United States suffer from some sort of mental illness, that's the equivalent of the entire population of Argentina feeling miserable.[20] And for many of the 43.6 million of us, it's tempting to wage a war on our anxiety and depression. We want to crush it, run away from it, bury it at the bottom of a volcano. We want to punch it in its whiny, stressed-out face. But the problem is that the harder you fight it, the stronger it gets. That anxiety will sucker-punch us right back.

Some anxiety is good. We need a little healthy stress; it motivates us to actually take action. Worrying about missing your flight before you leave the house might mean that you get there on time. But then there are the times when anxiety is not at all helpful. It won't listen to reason and it sits heavy on your chest, nailing you to the couch and just generally being an asshole. Pretending it's not there, with its clammy hands around your throat, won't help. Pretending that it shouldn't be there—because you should be over it by now, or because you should be stronger than your anxiety—is even worse.

So we need to start by accepting that this is what it is. And yes, this is counter-intuitive, because why do we want to accept something that is making our lives miserable? But acceptance doesn't mean apathy. It doesn't mean we lie there like a doormat letting our anxiety run (and ruin) everything. It just means we acknowledge its existence. We stop picking a fight with reality.

Pema Chodron is an American Buddhist nun, teacher and author. She tells this story about a guy named Milarepa, one of the ancient heroes of Tibetan Buddhism.[21] Milarepa was a dude who lived in a cave, and one day he came home to find his place filled with demons. They were the extra nasty demons who show up just as you're falling asleep, carrying bulleted lists of all the things you've messed up and everything you should have accomplished by now. The demons had taken over the joint, making themselves as comfortable as you can make yourself in a cave.

Milarepa was a sharp fellow, so he realized that these annoying guys were just projections of his mind, parts of himself that he really didn't want around. He tried to get rid of them. He ran at them, yelling, waving his arms and shoving them in their muscular chests; they laughed at him and made a sandwich. He begged them to leave, bribing them with whatever they wanted; they put their feet up on the coffee table. He talked about compassion and called on their empathy; they wiped their noses on the curtains. Eventually, he said, *Fine. I'm not going anywhere. Looks like you're not going anywhere, either. Let's figure out a way to do this together.* And the demons kind of looked at each other. Now that there was nobody to fight with, the cave got pretty boring, what with a distinct lack of Wi-Fi. Most of them left. Except this one demon.

This really stubborn demon with hollow eyes and long claws wasn't going anywhere. He dug into his corner of the couch and spilled coffee on the cushions and stared Milarepa down. Milarepa had only one choice. He laughed. He went up to the demon, opened up the monster's mouth and shoved his head in there. *Fine,* Milarepa said, *I surrender.*

And with that, the last demon was gone.

I put my head in the demon's mouth by talking about my anxiety. I decided to own the story, instead of letting the story own me. I don't hide it anymore. I no longer tell myself that I'm weak and a failure. I don't exhaust myself by thinking that things should be different, and I don't shame myself because I'm struggling. I decided to be nicer to myself not because I'm some spectacular individual. I do it simply because I'm alive, and because no living thing deserves be bullied into eternal misery. I tell people when I'm feeling anxious and I ask for — and accept — help. There was incredible freedom and power to be found in that kind of surrender. I chose to deal with the reality of the situation and stop running away. And that's the basis of action and lasting change.

My anxiety was raging the other day, and I had already made plans to have lunch with a dear friend. I'd gotten a mean comment on my blog, but I was mostly overwhelmed by a general fear of my life. I panicked about leaving my house. What if I had an anxiety attack in front of my friend? I thought about faking the flu. I considered claiming that writing this book was taking up too much of my time, which would not only get me out of being social, but would also make me look busy and important. But I wanted to see Jen, and even an anxious girl's gotta eat. So instead of lying and diving into that shame spiral that told me what a loser I was for not being able to leave my house, I texted her.

I'm feeling anxious. I am probably going to cry at lunch. Are you up for that?

Yes, she responded simply. *See you at noon?*

I stood next to my car for five minutes doing breathing exercises before I could get in, but eventually I did. You might expect that this is the part where I say it was just great to be with my friend and we laughed and laughed and my anxiety simply vanished. Well, life isn't a movie so, no, that's not how it went down. I cried through the entire lunch. I didn't cry Movie Pretty, either, with one single tear slowly rolling down my cheek. I did the swollen-eyed, hard-to-get-the-words-out, blubbery thing. I'm fairly certain there were snot bubbles.

But when I was able to sputter out what was going on, Jen didn't try to fix it. She didn't say "Don't cry." She said things like, "I'm sorry, that sounds hard"and "I get it." and "Is there anything I can do?" I cried as I ate my soup, I cried as I disintegrated my napkin and then her napkin, and I cried when the check came. I didn't pretend I wasn't crying. I didn't apologize. I didn't say she must hate me because I'm a crazy, annoying loser.

It was incredibly tempting to say all those things, but I took a different tactic.

I thanked her.

I thanked her for listening and for being comfortable with me crying for forty-five minutes. I thanked her for letting me be sad and scared. I looked directly into that deep, hollow pit of shame and I shoved a bunch of gratitude in there.

Sometimes life is super hard. That's okay. There is immense bravery in being authentic and choosing to not shy away from the challenging parts of being alive. If there is one thing I've learned in a lifetime of dealing with anxiety, it's that dragging my feelings out of their shady corner and bringing them into the light always helps me to feel better.

That lunch was an incredible gift Jen gave me, but it was also something she benefited from. Because that experience gave her permission to fall apart with me when her life gets overwhelming. I've sat with her through her tears and if I had said that I was a loser for crying, by extension that would mean I thought she was weak when she placed *her* worries on the table. By embracing our own moments of struggle, we're saying that others are allowed to lean on us. They can have snot bubbles, too.

Something to Try: Embrace Your Weird

I have a new mantra these days: Embrace your weird. It has become my touchstone. It helps me get through all kinds of uncomfortable things. It reminds me that everyone has something that brings up feelings of shame and inadequacy. We all feel weird and we're convinced that no one will accept us if they ever find out. It could be our unusual childhood or our anxiety disorder — the details don't really matter. But that shame holds us hostage and prevents us from living fulfilling lives. It zip-ties our hands to the radiator and keeps us from truly connecting, truly being seen. That gets lonely as hell. Hiding and feeling ashamed just doesn't work. Our desperate desire to fit in only makes us small, feeble and invisible in our lives.

But when we embrace the things we think we need to hide, when we learn to use them, we get so much more powerful. We can be our true selves and bring our own unique perspective and experiences to the world. Not only is this better for us — it's better for the world. When you get comfortable with your weird, you no longer feel the need to pick on someone else for theirs. We notice the things that connect us, instead of our differences.

We sometimes feel we are showing a weakness or asking for something we don't deserve when we open up, but think about it from the other side: When someone reaches out to you, how does it make you feel? If you're like me, it feels awesome. I'm honored when someone trusts me and I'm happy for the chance to help out. So maybe you'll make someone feel good, not burdened, by the fact that you shared with them.

Sometimes it helps to let people know that you don't need them to fix anything. My husband has a tendency to go into fix-it mode; he wants to make it better, which is sweet and admirable and sometimes makes me want to kick him in the kneecaps. Because really I just want someone to nod sympathetically while holding my hand. Saying something like, "You are not required to do anything about this, I just need to vent" lets people off the hook if they feel like they are responsible for your wellbeing. But if you want to talk through your options and get perspectives and ideas, tell them that, too. Be honest about what you need.

If you don't have that go-to person, you should know that you're still not alone. More than 20% of Americans, or 60 million people, say that they are unhappy with their lives due to loneliness.[22] That number almost doubles for older people. This is a big problem; social isolation comes with health risk factors comparable to smoking.[23] And while social media can make this feel worse — seeing all those casual acquaintances frolicking in (likely manufactured) social bliss — it's possible to turn it around and use your screen time for good and not evil. Creating a connection with those you might not meet otherwise is one of the coolest uses of the internet, other than baby goat videos.

A friend of mine had a great experience with a site called patientslikeme.com, where she found incredible support for her depression. People were willing to give her a realistic perspective, reassure her, and work through the cognitive behavioral therapy steps with her. Even Reddit has an anxiety thread that, from what I've seen, can be really helpful. (As with everything online, it can be equally un-helpful. Tread carefully.)

Nami.org also offers all kinds of information and support. They have articles about everything from navigating romantic relationships to finding a therapist, and host active discussion groups.

You. Are. Not. Alone.

Chapter 3: The Science of Stress

I was awake at 4:30am, reviewing everything that could go wrong with the talk I was scheduled to give that morning. It was only my second speaking event as a writer; I was in Toronto to talk to a few hundred people at a conference, and the catalogue of possible disasters was extensive. I had a long career as an actor, but that didn't really help me with this new path I had taken. Pretending to be someone else was easy, but standing in front of people as myself, with no character to hide behind—that was truly scary. I curled up on the bed in my hotel room, mentally organizing the impending catastrophes from Merely Humiliating to Full Blown Life-Ruining. Suddenly, I realized I was holding something wet in my hand. I looked down. It was dark red. Hard but malleable. What was that? It was so gross. Had it been on the bed?

I was holding a human toenail. What could have been reassuring, but wasn't really, was that it was actually *my* toenail. I had just ripped it off my little toe and now I was dripping blood everywhere. I hadn't even noticed I was doing it. I was so entrenched in my anxiety that I mutilated myself without even realizing it. I was operating in pure panic mode; my rational self, who could have realized this sort of worry was not helpful, was nowhere to be found. I was in deep fight-or-flight mode, and apparently I opted for fight and my toenail had lost the battle.

In moments like this, it can be helpful to understand a little about the brain. I'd like you to meet someone named Amy. Amy is my nickname for the part of the brain otherwise known as the amygdala.[24] It's made up of two little almond-shaped clusters of brain cells within the limbic system, which is our emotional brain. Amy the Amygdala is in charge of motivation and processing emotional reactions.[25] She's a nice enough girl, but she can get a little too excited.

You can't really blame Amy — she's just doing her job as the fear center of the brain, tasked with deciding if something is a threat.[26] But at times, the queen of fight/flight/freeze can be over-caffeinated and jumpy. Amy doesn't think things through calmly and rationally. She just reacts. She's terrified of rejection and she makes quick associations about things.[27] She would be great on *Real Housewives*, since she's the girl most likely to throw a wine glass or flip a table instead of asking someone to clarify what they just said.

My Amy looks like this, upon receiving an invitation to a dinner party:

Art by Serena Love

Luckily, Amy the Amygdala has a dear friend I call Cora, the prefrontal cortex. As mammals evolved and became more complex, the pre-frontal cortex developed around the amygdala, to put the brakes on instinctual reactions. Cora is one of those chill girls who always knows what to do. Her job is to soothe Amy's unwarranted fears and make the distinction between safe and dangerous. Cora lives right behind the forehead and she's great at planning ahead, strategizing, managing conflicts and predicting outcomes.[28]

Cora is the kind of girl who can pull off that hat:

Art by Serena Love

For those of us who struggle with anxiety, Amy and her love for drama can sometimes strong-arm the cool-headed Cora. When that happens, the sympathetic nervous system freaks out and brings too much adrenaline to the party. This automatic response was useful when we had to run from saber-toothed tigers all the time; adrenaline gives your body an energy shot, so you can go into fight or flight mode and survive a crisis. But if you are just having a meeting with your boss and not facing off with a tiger, that flood of adrenaline feels less like an energy shot and more like way too many tequila shots. Adrenaline — like tequila — might be okay in small doses, but too much leaves you with a brutal hangover.

For all animals, this system is pretty straight forward. When Amy takes over, our skin gets prickly, the air is snatched from our lungs and we want to run away and hide under our blankets. When we sense a threat, we freeze first, flee if we can, fight if we must.

Cora is supposed to take charge at the point when Amy is going into unnecessary panic mode and insisting on yet another shot. But for people with anxiety disorders, Cora tends to be in the bathroom when Amy loses it. In part, this imbalance between Amy and Cora seems to be caused by our individual serotonin levels. If we have more of the neurotransmitter serotonin, Amy is calmer. Less serotonin? Amy is jumpy as hell and Cora misses out on her chance to hold Amy's hand, slow the heart rate, bring the pupils back to normal and tell her that it's all going to be okay.[29]

But the chemical component isn't the only factor. We can work to train these two to better interact with one another. That's what we are doing when we practice cognitive behavioral therapy (CBT) techniques, meditation and breathing exercises. We're teaching Amy to chill out and we're encouraging Cora to step up and talk some sense into her friend when she is panicking unnecessarily.

(Yes, I am totally simplifying this. The brain is an incredibly complex machine and there is a whole lot going on but it is much cuter — and I daresay more helpful — to imagine it this way.)

The Anxious Crayfish

Science really likes to say that humans are the only animals who *fill-in-the-blank*. I don't know if all scientists love Mad Libs or what, but they keep trying to fill in that blank. In the past, they said things like humans are the only animals who "communicate" and "use tools," and they were proven wrong again and again.

I suppose we like to think we are the only ones who *fill-in-the-blank* so we can feel special, but it seems like our crowning distinction might be that we are the only species to have gone though a parachute pants phase. Recently, scientists have been saying we're the only animals who think about the future. While I'd hate to think that cats stress about retirement planning, I'm not sure I buy this scientific postulation.

The Anxious Crayfish is the name of the '90s alt-rock cover band I want to start, but it also refers to a scientific study about the behavioral inhibition response in cute little freshwater creatures.[30] Crayfish who were given benzodiazepines (like Valium) proved to be less inhibited and more exploratory. They wore more daring outfits and went backpacking through Europe. No, actually, I think they just were more willing to scuttle over to an area of the aquarium where they had gotten a mild shock before. Which is horrible.

Why am I telling you about terrible animal testing? Because it reassures us that anxiety is normal. It's healthy. Even crayfish feel something that can be interpreted as anxiety.

This is yet another reason why waging war on anxiety is the wrong way to go. It's good to worry sometimes. When trying something new or venturing into unexplored areas of our aquarium, we *should* feel anxious. Our anxiety becomes a problem when it interferes with our lives and makes us panic over things that are not panic-worthy.

Getting a hold of this concept in action is like taking control of our most primal instincts. Instincts are great, right? They tell us to throw away the yogurt with the fuzzy green stuff on top and to not wander down that dark alley by the bus station. But it's a problem when our instincts try to take over when we don't need them. Asking for a raise is rarely a life or death situation, but it can feel that way to someone whose instincts are out of control.

So what's an alternative to Amy's offerings of fight, flight or freeze? *Space.* If you can stop and create a space for just a few seconds between the trigger and the reaction, it's possible to take a breath and clear your head. Then you can choose your response: Is it really time for Amy to kick in to this primal fear state? Do I have enough information about what is going on to freak out? Or can Cora step in with a different perspective that might be more helpful? This process can feel like trying to stop a freight train, but with practice and patience, it is possible. Just because Amy tells us something doesn't make it true.

Getting Cozy With Not Being Comfy

When we were little kids, we didn't know how to ride bikes or use toilets, but we learned. And yes, there were accidents at various degrees of grossness that happened along the way, but we got more proficient. And we can learn to deal with our panic the same way. We practice by intentionally making ourselves uncomfortable.

This is not the norm for most of us. We tend to go to extraordinary lengths to be comfortable. We buy memory foam pillows and set our thermostats on timers. We desperately try to avoid confrontation and pay extra to get rid of the commercials on Hulu. Humans are constantly running from the slightest suggestion of pain in search of the delightful, open arms of pleasure.

But the definition of "pain" has gotten a little muddled. Sometimes our brain registers something that is just *uncomfortable* as painful, and we bolt into a chain of automatic reactions. This often ends up being worse for us than just dealing with the uncomfortable thing. But we can challenge that impulse — we can choose to respond instead of react.

It's all about unlearning the connection between a specific situation and a stress response. If you talk to a cognitive behavioral therapist, they are going to call this retraining process by the fancy name "in vivo exposure therapy," and then they'll totally make you do it.

I met a guy named Ridley (we'll hear more from him later) who created his own version of exposure therapy. He told me that on the first day of each semester of school, he's always on the verge of a panic attack. "So, I intentionally do something embarrassing like trip or drop all my papers or spill my coffee all over everything in the first few minutes."

In that moment, he creates some space before Amy the Amygdala kicks in, and quickly sees that he did not spontaneously combust out of humiliation and his important relationships are still intact. He felt icky for a bit, it came to a peak, and then that feeling melted away. He outlived the sensation. While it might have been an uncomfortable challenge, that alone was a revelation. He learned a new outcome.

Now you are probably thinking about this poor college student, just trying to get to his seat at the back of the class and forcing himself to dump his coffee. But here's the thing: Ridley is a college professor. I don't know that there is a profession that I more associate with Having Your Shit Together. I always think of professors as being cool and collected. They stand up there and teach everybody else stuff they know a whole lot about. How can they possibly feel uncertain?

Ridley has had anxiety and depression since he was a teenager. He still struggles with many aspects of it, but getting comfortable being uncomfortable is a tool that helps him. He says if the students laugh at him, he gets that awkward moment out of the way and he can slip into his professor persona and focus on doing his job with less stress. He's not constantly worrying that he's going to humiliate himself. And it works. If he's having another day when he is anxious for whatever reason, he does it again. He'll trip over his own feet.

"I'm in control of the embarrassment."

It also sets up a precedent in his class: We're allowed to make mistakes here. And if anyone is really going to learn and grow, perfectionism can't be part of the curriculum.

Exposure therapy is now considered to be the single most effective treatment for phobias—more than medication or talk therapy—and it's had a good track record since at least 1770.[31] A German poet with the spectacular name of Johann Wolfgang von Goethe had a terrible case of acrophobia—a fear of heights. He wanted to not be afraid of heights, so over time, he slowly climbed to the top of a cathedral until his fear dissipated. In his autobiography he described the anxiety and pain he experienced, but he found that he kept climbing so often that his impression of the experience changed.[32] He trained Cora to step in so that Amy was no longer in control.

You might be thinking, *Yeah, I've got all that anxiety and pain, too. That's why I'm trying to make myself more comfortable, because I'm suffering 102% of the time.*

I get that. But the thing is, the vast majority of pain actually comes from running away from fear—from fearing fear. Actually dealing with the fear and learning to manage the response allows for growth and a better handle on anxiety. When we understand that Amy the Amygdala is overreacting by releasing a massive amount of adrenaline and our bodies are responding normally to that, and it won't actually kill us, we can breathe through it. We can ride the wave and tolerate the experience.

This is why we have to get friendly with our fear. We have to throw an arm around the shoulder of our anxiety and get to know it. We remove an entire layer of panic when we are not constantly feeling ashamed and running away from it. Feeling uncomfortable and uncertain is part of the human condition. So we accept worry. And then we consider whether a different response is possible.

Breaking Down the Breakdown

In the cognitive behavioral therapy process, exposure therapy is done in tiny steps. If you're afraid of spiders, you don't go put a spider on your face immediately (or ever, really).

You go slowly.

This is great to do with someone else—a therapist, friend or partner who can hold your hand.

For me, the grocery store is a place of great anxiety. If we were going to break down the exposure therapy steps, I'd create a hierarchy for my goal of going to the store:

1. Drive to the store with my husband (aka my "support person"—sexy, right?), park in the lot for five minutes, then come home.
2. Go to the store with him, walk around outside for five minutes, then go home.
3. Go to the store with him and get a cart, walk around the produce section for five minutes. Go home.
4. Repeat the first three steps—by myself.
5. Go into the store with my husband and buy a couple of things in the express lane.
6. Go to the store with him and do the whole week's worth of shopping. Eat an enormous amount of free sample cheese as a reward.

Break this down into even smaller steps if necessary, using whatever is a trigger for you. The process is going to feel uncomfortable because that's the point: we're learning how to tolerate the things that scare us in small doses. We're making a new association with safety and confidence, to replace the feeling of unbearable anxiety.

Meeting an Orchid: Why Getting Uncomfortable is Worth It

The fact that I do speaking engagements seems highly unlikely. Between my social anxiety, proclivity for panic attacks, shyness, introversion, and my unreasonable fondness for wearing sweatpants, it's odd that I feel drawn to public speaking.

But I do. And the reason comes back to an idea known as the Free Trait Theory.[33] One could argue that public speaking events would be the most inauthentic thing someone like me could do, seeing as I walked away from the whole Hollywood thing and believe a sweet Saturday night involves listening to Smashing Pumpkins while reorganizing the pantry. But Free Trait Theory explains things this way: We are born with certain inherent or culturally implanted traits — introversion is one of them. But that doesn't negate free will. If an action is in the service of a passion or a professional calling, if it's a "core personal project," then we can step out of our trait for a limited time. (The *limited time* part is also important. After I give a talk I usually need about a week of recovery that involves little more than take-out sushi and seven episodes of *Parks and Recreation*.) But we must believe it is truly worth the effort to overcome our organic trait.

You can approach these kinds of passion project challenges by framing them this way:

I really want to...
That reminds me of how...
Which just proves that I can handle...

For me, when an invitation to do a speaking event shows up, I can complete the sentences like this:

I really want to accept this invitation to talk at this writer's conference, because it seems like an interesting opportunity.

That reminds me of how I gave that little speech at our wedding. I thanked everyone for coming, and even though my heart was pounding the whole time and I stumbled over my words, it was fine. Actually, I felt good when I was done because I had expressed myself.

Which just proves I can handle being super nervous and uncomfortable and it doesn't actually kill me, even when it feels like it might.

So when the offer came to speak in Toronto, I had answered these questions and found myself saying yes. That morning in the hotel room, I had gotten myself together (minus a pinkie toenail), and apparently I went up on the stage and said some stuff. Honestly, it was all kind of a blur. But at the end the audience clapped and no one threw anything at me, so I guess it was fine. Even so, I decided the emotional exhaustion just wasn't worth it. I had done it, I had been brave —now? Never again.

After my presentation, I was in a poorly-lit ballroom with no windows, attempting small talk and counting the hours until my flight home, when a woman came up and introduced herself as Eve. She asked about some of the things that I had mentioned in my talk, specifically yoga and meditation for dealing with anxiety. Since it's a topic I love, I can even talk to strangers about it. I rambled on about how much yoga had helped me get my panic attacks under control.

"I think he'd like that. He's been having a really hard time." She nodded emphatically.

I had no idea who she was talking about. Eventually, she twisted around and peeled a boy off the back of her legs. This was Andrew. He was the visual representation of how I felt at these events: head down, tiny shoulders curled in so tightly they almost met in front of his concave chest. In his hands, he held a well-loved stuffed dog named Abbott.

Andrew was small and pale and looked like he had been plucked from within a cotton ball and placed into the harsh light of the world. I wear sunglasses on the cloudiest of days because the world is too bright, too loud, too close, too much. It was clear that Andrew would agree. I wanted him to be my new best friend because I just knew this kid got me. We talked about dogs.

I was reminded of the Orchid Hypothesis.[34] Most kids are dandelions; they can thrive anywhere. They are tough and resilient and fine with whatever. Highly reactive kids are orchids. They wilt easily, but they can also grow stronger and more incredibly lovely than anyone could ever imagine.

I had just found a worthy reason to exercise Free Trait Theory. And he was an orchid.

"My emotions can turn lethal." – Andrew (age 10)

Eve first noticed her son's anxiety in first grade. Andrew got easily overwhelmed and stressed to the point where he was "louder than a howler monkey." He would get worked up about something, and it would take him up to ninety minutes to calm down. He almost always needed a physical impact of some sort to relax again, like crashing into a wall or hitting himself.

Andrew had a stutter and got very anxious about a variety of things: new experiences, groups of more than six people, writing, the dark, feeling over-scheduled, going into the bathroom by himself, and bugs. Although admittedly the bug things seems justified because, as he told me, "I was mutilated by the sidewalk while running from about 200,000 yellow jackets and now I can't tell the difference between a butterfly and a scorpion with dragon wings that's out for my blood." So, the bug fear is just logical: that's an awful lot of yellow jackets.

It's been a long road for Eve and Andrew. The first specialist Eve saw asked her a few questions and wrote a prescription without ever talking to Andrew. Eve didn't fill that one. They went to see two other therapists before finding someone they were both comfortable with. While Eve seems endlessly engaged and committed, other people in Andrew's life have a harder time coping. His grandparents are in the habit of telling him to just get over it. His school interpreted his tears and frustration as a "discipline issue" and kept saying he needed to behave. Finally, he was diagnosed with anxiety, ADHD, and Sensory Integration Disorder.

Eve said, "I was against medicating him. It was Andrew who finally asked me, after an episode where he cried for about forty-five minutes after a frustrating task, if there was anything I could do to help him not feel that way. I told him about the medicine and said we could try it, but told him he would have to be very honest and open about how it was making him feel so we could make sure it was the right one. That was when he was in first grade."

That medication was not the right one. Andrew became irritable and could only tolerate it for a week. Then they tried another drug which caused him to stop eating. But the one after that did help, and when he would get worked up it would take him only ten minutes to calm down, not his usual ninety. They were both grateful for the reprieve.

His official diagnosis seemed to help the school understand what was going on, and Andrew started getting the support he needed. His teachers came up with some helpful behavioral tools for him, for both home and school. They recommended that he bring Abbott the stuffed dog with him into the bathroom to keep him company so he was less afraid of being alone in there. They also recommended Eve replace the shower curtain in their bathroom with a clear one since it was scary to not be able to see what was behind it. (I can completely relate. You will never find a closed shower curtain in my house.)

The school also worked with Eve, teaching her joint compressions to help Andrew when he felt like he was in a pinball machine. The joint compressions created a way for him to get the physical sensation he'd been creating by crashing into wall and hitting himself, but this version came without injury. Eve would push down gently and repeatedly on each of Andrew's joints, knuckles, wrists, elbows, shoulders, toes, ankles, knees and hips.

"The way I had it explained to me was that it resets the nervous system. We used it on a strict schedule when his sensory issues were really intense when he was younger, but now when we use it, it's more of a calming technique for the anxiety."

As Eve described joint compressions, it occurred to me that I unknowingly do a version of this. When panic strikes, I count my fingers. But I do it in this intense way, bending each finger back and pushing down on the joint. It's amazing to me that sometimes we find our way to exactly what our body needs.

It's nice to wax poetic about childhood as a carefree time when Lego was considered a skill builder and we never had to figure out tax forms. But anxious kids don't see it that way. They have wild minds, too.

"I perseverate a lot," Andrew said. "I get those ideas stuck in my head and think about that and nothing else. I guess if I didn't continue to think and think about those things, that would make the day better. Probably."

When Eve and I talked about yoga at that conference she thought it might be good for Andrew, but she had no idea how helpful it would be. Along with the physical practice, Andrew's yoga teacher taught him breathing exercises that he now uses outside of the yoga studio. Andrew said, "Breathing deeply helps me go back to the logical side of my brain."

Eve said that yoga has been "a blessing." She was worried about the possible side effects of the pills Andrew was taking for anxiety, and within a short time of starting yoga, they were able to consult with his doctor and take him off the medication.

Eve said, "He does use the breathing when he gets worked up, so he is able to relax and self-soothe now when he never could before." Andrew's yoga teacher enforces in him the idea that it is perfectly okay to be who he is. Which, quite honestly, is a big reason I do yoga, too.

Another advantage is a physical one. The yoga postures seem to activate Andrew's joints in similar ways to what the joint compressions were doing for him, and he receives the same relaxation benefits. He just doesn't require anyone else to do the compression protocol for him. Eve says it makes him less dependent on her, "so as he gets older he has his own tools to use when he is upset, whether I'm there or not."

Kids at school sometimes give Andrew a hard time but he says they just don't understand what it's like to be anxious to the point where you can't function. He's not sure why people don't just accept others how they are, but he's very clear on the fact that it's not his fault that people are harassing him: anxiety is just part of who he is.

Andrew and Eve know to expect that he'll worry about new and difficult things, and because of that, the anxiety becomes less debilitating and not such a big deal. She accepts him as he is, and that helps him accept himself. He knows how lucky he is to have such great support. "My mom doesn't tell me to just get over it. Instead she hugs me and tells me she understands me."

It's obvious that Eve is concerned about her son, about the things he might face as he gets older, about what will happen when she's not there to support and protect him. But when you listen to Andrew talk about his life, it's hard to worry too much.

"I don't care what other people say about me. I just use my strategies and then keep on being an awesome person."

Mic drop.

Something to Try: Be the Net

"If you need to fall, fall. But be your own net."
- Kelly, one of my yoga teachers

Some things, like speaking events, will cause inevitable anxiety. But I have found a surprising tactic that helps: scheduling my worry. If I have a looming event on Friday and I start panicking on Monday morning, I commit to setting aside time to worry on Thursday. I promise myself that I can freak out as much as I want on Thursday. When I start stressing about it again on Tuesday or Wednesday, I remind myself it's not time for that, yet. I'm not saying the event isn't worrisome, or that I should be better at this, I just decide to ruin one day over it—not five. By the time I get to Friday, I have more energy to do a good job because I've not spent the entire week melting down.

When I am deep in the worry and my mind is spinning with anxiety, it can be helpful to acknowledge each point of panic one at a time. It's almost impossible to do anything else when we are engulfed by anxiety, so identifying the worries and writing them down makes them more concrete and less likely to swirl around in our minds and distract us.[35] I'm not in control of everything in my life, but when I can clearly see my concerns—and some possible solutions—at least I feel more prepared.

Here's how this goes when I'm panicking about going out to dinner with a bunch of people ("a bunch" in my world means any number greater than two).

I don't want to go. It's going to be terrible. I'll want to leave after ten minutes.

It might be terrible. Or it might not. It's pretty much 50/50. Don't carpool. Drive yourself so that you won't feel trapped and you can leave whenever you want. The environment will understand.

I don't know what to talk about.

Let's make a list of conversation topics. People love talking about themselves. Ask them about upcoming travel plans or what their kids are doing. People will talk forever about their kids. Write some questions down on your phone, so you can look at them if you get stuck. It'll just seem like you're a jerk reading a text during dinner, but that's better than worrying about what to say.

What if I don't know what to order? I get nervous and my vision gets fuzzy and it's hard to read the menu.

Before you go, look at the menu online and pick what you want so you don't have to decide when you get there. Hold on to the menu when you order and keep your finger next to the thing you want so in case you forget, you can reference it when the server asks you what you would like. If you get tongue-tied, pointing and smiling always works.

Everyone will hate me.

Is there any actual evidence for that? Like, real, irrefutable evidence? They're your friends and they invited you to dinner, so their hatred seems highly unlikely. But if they do hate you, they won't invite you again and you won't have to go out to dinner anymore. Win-win!

What if I panic and have to leave?

You have your car. We addressed that already. But take cash so you can throw $20 on the table before you bolt. That's just polite.

What if there is no parking?

Then you get to come home and put on sweatpants. Big win.

Chapter 4: Don't Just Do Something. Sit There.

Sharon Salzburg is a meditation teacher, but she's not some spacey chick, draped in crystals, making you touch your root chakra. Sharon gets annoyed by traffic and flight delays. She has stray threads hanging from the bottom of her pink button-up shirt. She is profoundly normal, which is not what you'd expect from someone who frequently speaks on panels with the Dalai Lama.

When I saw Sharon was leading a silent meditation retreat near me, I literally squealed. Five years earlier, it was the guided meditations from her book *Real Happiness* that got me into a dedicated mindfulness practice. She is a renowned author, meditation teacher and one of the handful of people who originally brought meditation to the West.

Sharon went to India to study meditation in 1970, and returned to America to teach four years later. Along with meditation's other heavy hitters, Joseph Goldstein and Jack Kornfield, she established the Insight Meditation Society in Massachusetts. IMS now ranks as one of the most prominent meditation centers in the Western world, and Sharon offers non-sectarian retreats and study for people from all backgrounds.

I signed up for the event and spent the day with a few hundred other meditators in a drafty church in Charlotte, North Carolina. Sharon shared stories, guided meditations, breathing exercises, and walking meditation. (By the way, a large group of people meditatively walking in circles in the parking lot of a Presbyterian church apparently looks like a zombie apocalypse and causes traffic issues.)

With the exception of Sharon, the rest of us were observing "noble silence" — no speaking to anyone, and no electronics. No small talk, no texting, no Facebook updates about how peaceful we were now. This proved challenging. During breaks, people lined up to read the church's guest book, just for the distraction. Reading about Margo Longfellow's visit from Spokane last month was so much better than being quietly stuck with our own thoughts for one more second.

The Non-Chosen Ones

We were split into two groups for lunch. I was in the second group that would eat later, and was trying to be cool about it even though I was hungry from all that stillness. I was overcome with the pouty inner monologue of the non-chosen ones: *There's not going to be enough for me.*

I watched the first shift saunter past with their lunches, sitting in folding chairs and on the floor against the walls. The attendees were mostly baby boomers, silver hair, lots of pashminas and sensible Dansko clogs. This wasn't a group of maxi dress-wearing twenty-somethings, bouncing around bra-less and tucking flowers behind each other's ears. This was a sensible group. They clipped coupons and went to Rotary meetings.

And now, a bunch of them were eating taco salad, with some sort of vegetarian chili. I spontaneously morphed into an adolescent boy and questioned the wisdom of feeding a couple hundred people chili and then making them sit in a quiet room for a few hours. I quickly chastised myself for being so unenlightened. You're not supposed to think about farting at a meditation retreat, are you?

As soon as the bell rang for the second group, I hurried toward the dining room, trying to look like I was not hurrying. It was 1:30 pm and I was ready to eat my meditation cushion. I walked into the brightly lit cafeteria, glowing with bliss and gratitude: I was going to eat this yummy food and it would fuel me for the life-changing insight I just knew was coming in the afternoon.

I looked at the long tables in the middle of the room...and there was no food.

Well, there was lettuce. Sad, wilted lettuce in the bottom of a bowl. And some corn chip dust. No chili. No guacamole.

I was going to die.

The other meditators in my group looked similarly dismayed. We stayed silent, but people started elbowing each other for a stray chopped tomato that had fallen onto the tablecloth. It was about to become a very quiet version of *Lord of the Flies*. I sent mental death rays to the people in the first group. I eyed their plates to see if they took double portions and that's why I was standing there, sucking on a leaf of romaine. But that just made me unhappier. And hungrier.

Eventually, a staff member popped her head in the room and with a big grin, "Not to worry, folks! We've got more food coming. Just sit tight."

We all nodded, trying to be relaxed and mindful and wondering if we could believe her. Was food really coming? How much was coming? Were we being placated? We stood there, empty plates in hand, silent except for our loudly complaining stomachs. Just waiting. And waiting.

I suddenly wondered if this was an orchestrated part of the retreat. Maybe this was what we were actually paying for: the experience of standing in silence, waiting, watching other people munch on three-bean chili. Maybe this was the lesson. Because it's great to feel peaceful when you are sitting on the floor on a nice soft cushion, but the lunch room is where shit gets real. When you're hangry and someone else has something that you want and can't have—that's when we actually want to feel something close to calm. I took a couple of deep breaths and realized it was silly to be acting like I was grabbing for the last loaf in a bread line. I had an apple in my purse, for God's sake. I could get in my car, drive five minutes and go to a restaurant. But in the moment it felt like such a big deal. Who got what and why wasn't it me?

I took a few more deep breaths. I felt the tightness in my jaw release. I dropped my shoulders away from my ears and felt the knot in my stomach untie itself. After ten or fifteen or three hundred forty-five minutes, more trays of chili, bowls of guacamole and bags of chips arrived. It was all okay. It had always been okay.

How much of our lives do we spend in that restless state of keeping tabs? We feel like that success, that bit of good luck, that piece of happiness was something the universe lobbed straight to us and at the last second, our neighbor leapt up and stole it away. Sitting in that lunch room was the perfect opportunity to breathe and notice what a moment of desperate grasping and clinging really felt like. I could save my energy and wait until there was actually a problem, and then I could deal with it with grace.

I hope I'm always rewarded for my mindfulness with large bowls of guacamole.

Meditation: It's Not What You Think

I've been meditating for years now, but the same thought flashes through my mind every morning when my alarm sings its pleasant little riff at 5:30 am: *Meditation is stupid. Sleep is better.*

But I get up and do it anyway, because my first thought of the day is always wrong. Meditation is not stupid. Meditation pieced me back together when I felt broken. It Tetris-ed me back into being. That's why I do it pretty much every day. I put on my husband's sweatshirt in the dark and stumble down the hall, flip on the twinkly lights and stretch, feeling a gentle resistance from my joints as they slowly wake up. I sit on a cushion and do absolutely nothing, except this really, really hard work.

The word for meditation in Tibetan is translated as "getting used to it." It's not easy to step back from our overly-stimulated lives and focus on the breath. In fact, one study gave participants the option of sitting quietly for fifteen minutes with their own thoughts, or giving themselves a mild electric shock. 67% of men and 25% of women chose to push the button and get a shock[36]. We are so uncomfortable just being still, we'd prefer to be distracted by just about anything. Even self-inflicted pain.

But people who practice meditation decide it's worth it to do the difficult thing. We decide to pay attention and notice our emotions without acting on them. We refocus away from the self-indulgent doom-spiral habit of our minds. Meditation is the equivalent of deciding to stop eating the entire bag of Goldfish crackers, even if we've eaten most of them and there are only about fourteen left. With meditation, we take back control over ourselves.

As you read about meditation, you might be thinking:
- I tried that meditation thing a couple of times, it's impossible and/or boring.
- I've never tried it, but it is totally not going to do anything to help these overwhelming emotions of

mine. It's so wimpy and passive, and hippies smell weird. I wonder if she is going to talk about movies anymore?

• Yes, this is totally the thing that is going to make everything better.

Just for a while, please let go of all the preconceived notions you might have about what it means to meditate, because those are just going to get in the way. Meditation simply means paying attention on purpose to this moment right here, not judging it and not getting caught up in a million thoughts about it. In short, meditation is how I practice the habit of calming the fuck down.

Meditation is not a belief system. No one is asking you to leave coins at the foot of a multi-armed deity if that's not your thing. It's just about strengthening your focus and concentration. A form of meditation called Mindfulness Based Stress Reduction (MBSR) is now offered in seven hundred different medical centers to help patients and health care providers deal with pain and suffering.[37] It can help people regulate the pain response, and can lessen the need for narcotic painkillers even after severe back surgeries.[38] Meditation requires turning toward something we want to avoid: our own minds. It is incredibly brave.

But there seems to be some resistance to the mere *idea* of meditation. People think it's passive or Bohemian woo-woo stuff. They say they don't have time; I say if you can't find two minutes per day, you should probably take a look at your life because that's an issue right there. I've heard the problem is finding the discipline to meditate, which is understandable. But for me, the willpower came when I saw my life improve significantly as a direct result of this practice. It became a no-brainer.

But the biggest misconception pop culture promotes about meditation is that the goal is to think of nothing. People tell me all the time that their brain, being a particularly high-strung and manic brain, will never allow it. No offense intended here, because I'm sure you are an absolutely lovely human being — but your brain is not special. Everyone's mind has a bajillion thoughts a minute, because that's the job of the mind. It has kept us alive by constantly scanning the environment to come up with potential problems and threats. The heart beats, the mind thinks. If either of those things stop, we're in serious trouble.

We're not trying to stop our thoughts; we're just attempting to shift our relationship with them. We're learning to take those unhelpful, repetitive, problem-seeking thoughts less seriously. We want to have this nice, fun, casual dating thing going on with our thoughts. Thoughts are great, they're useful, but we don't need to get super attached to them all the time. The problem for many of us is that we're in this dependent, clingy relationship with our mind, where thoughts are obsessing every moment of life and blowing up our phone with needy texts.

We're training ourselves to use our minds effectively. You don't have to be so locked into the present moment that you never plan for the future. Reminiscing about high school is totally okay, too. We're just trying to become aware of what is happening in our minds, so our planning and reminiscing is more intentional and useful. We're also attempting to put space between a thought bubbling up in our head and our reaction to it. That way, our thoughts aren't stuck on some helpless, repetitive loop, where we replay our mistakes or lie awake all night catastrophizing everything that could possibly go wrong next week.

It's easy to make meditation goal-oriented, and think that we've failed if our mind wanders. But if your mind wanders and you notice it—that's actually the whole point. That's the key moment of the practice, when you transform from someone just sitting quietly to someone meditating. We'll get into specific instructions for meditation soon, but the bottom line is, it's that easy and that hard. You just sit with your mind and notice it thinking. With no judgment.

Meditation is one thing in life that is not about achieving something. The only thing you are trying to do is not get pissed off when you notice your thoughts completely bouncing off the walls. That's your only job. Don't get upset when your mind runs off like a Great Dane puppy every twelve seconds. Just bring that puppy back. With kindness. With love. With no harsh lectures. (Have you ever tried lecturing a puppy? Those cute, dopey puppy eyes just look lovingly back at you. It's pointless.) The problem is never the puppy acting like a puppy. It's how we react to the puppy that makes the difference.

Every time you notice and bring yourself back to the present moment is a fresh start. As long as you're alive, you get to start over. Every day. Multiple times during the day, even. Every new breath is a do-over. You can't fail at meditation as long as you are being kind to yourself, and aware of your experience—whatever it is. If you can sit with yourself for half a second longer than you did yesterday, you are a super star. You win at meditating. Pick up your ribbon at the door.

Meditation Might Look Easy...

I'm not sure where this idea came from that meditation should be easy, or that it must be easy for the people who do it. People say they tried meditation and they're not good at it, which is like saying "You know, I just sat down at the piano for the first time and I tried to play Rachmaninoff's first sonata and it's *really hard*." Well, yeah, it's hard. Meditation seems like it should be easy, because it's just breathing and we do that twenty thousand times a day. But learning to sit quietly with yourself can be brutal. We're re-wiring a lifetime of habits and thought patterns and that can be painful. But like playing Rachmaninoff's first sonata, it's worth it. (I would assume. I don't really know. I can't even play Chopsticks.)

You know what's even harder than meditation? Depression. Anxiety. Panic.

With a consistent meditation practice, we can find flickering moments of space and peace. When the mind stops bouncing around and releases its grip, it's an incredible relief, and that happens more frequently with practice. Then you notice those spacious moments showing up when you are at the dentist or about to yell at your partner for being so crabby in the morning. When I notice that I'm obsessing about why I don't have more Twitter followers or wondering how many years I have left before I develop dementia, I can decide to let that go and pick a new thought. That's my meditation practice in action—and that's when it gets really good.

It doesn't really matter how it goes while I'm sitting there on the floor meditating, because regardless of how peaceful I feel then, the mere attempt to get quiet has a domino effect that makes the rest of my day better. Meditation is like brushing your teeth: not necessarily the most thrilling activity, but it vastly improves the rest of your life. If I don't brush my teeth for a few days, I (and those around me) suffer. And if I don't meditate for a few days, I (and those around me) suffer.

So why does meditation work? One reason is because when our mood starts to spiral downward, it's not just about the mood. The biggest challenge is our *reaction* to the mood. We start thinking that this mood should not be happening and we wonder how bad it's going to get. A meditation practice helps us notice that we're not breathing well or that we're hurt and want to lash out. Our reaction to all those feelings slows down.

My mind often feels like a snow globe that's been thrown in one of those paint can agitators at the hardware store. Meditation calms down the sympathetic nervous system,[39] increases blood flow to the brain, and lets that snow globe stop shaking[40]. When the snow settles, you can see inside more clearly. When someone sends me an aggressive e-mail or I've had a disagreement with a friend, I can stop for a second and let the snow settle. Instead of sending a nasty e-mail back or banishing a friend who dared to have a misunderstanding with me, I breathe. I watch the thoughts settle. I can take more effective action from that clear-headed place.

Meditation: The Science Stuff

There are super cool explanations for why meditation works—it actually changes the structure of your brain. In case this whole section has been feeling a little too conceptual and airy-fairy for you, here's the research:

There used to be this idea that once you reached adulthood, your brain didn't change much. But that's actually not true. Old dogs can learn new tricks. Brain change and growth is a matter of neuroplasticity; basically, "neurons that fire together, wire together."[41] When a part of the brain fires frequently, it becomes the go-to setting. This means that our experiences can program us to feel a certain way about things. If anger and fear are your habit, you'll interpret everything through that lens and tend to feel threatened and helpless. But it's possible to rewire your system and modify the lens, even when life throws some serious crap at you.

Meditation creates new pathways in the brain structure and changes the areas associated with stress, awareness, and empathy.[42] An eight-week study conducted by Harvard researchers found that a consistent meditation practice increases density of the gray matter in the hippocampus — that's the part of the brain that deals with learning, memory, compassion, introspection and self-awareness.[43] Any guesses what other part of the brain undergoes physical changes with regular meditation? Yes, our excitable friend Amy. The amygdala decreases in cell volume and actually gets smaller. There is a reduction in the gray matter of the primal fight-or-flight part of the brain, and an increased thickening in the parts that help regulate those instincts and increase emotional regulation and compassion.[44]

In case you're thinking you need to be a monk to receive such benefits, a recent study had subjects participate in a mindfulness retreat for just three days. These folks were stressed out — they were all unemployed and looking for work. After their meditation training, there were changes in the areas of the brain that deal with focus and calm. Even four months after the experiment, the subjects showed lower levels of unhealthy inflammation in their blood than the control group. It seems that the changes in the brain caused a decrease in inflammation throughout the body.[45]

Meditation can affect issues ranging from asthma and irritable bowel syndrome to binge eating and smoking cessation. It lowers feelings of loneliness among senior citizens and lowers stress among cancer patients.[46] And by the way, it's free, and there are no nasty side effects.

Meditation is essentially concentration training, so focus and memory improve, too. A two-week mindfulness course helped people during the verbal reasoning section of the GRE. Reading comprehension and memory capacity improved— sixteen percentile points, to be exact.[47] So meditation is like brain doping, just without ever having to do a pee test.

It also seems that the longer you practice, the greater the benefits. A study from UCLA found that long-term meditators had lasting impacts on their brains as they got older. They had greater gray matter, not just in one place, but throughout the entire structure, causing their brains to be better preserved during the aging process.[48]

All this comes from something so simple: paying attention. It's not some wacky, esoteric concept; it's weight training for your brain. And just like going to the gym, you don't work out to be good at working out. You work out so that the rest of your life is easier. I meditate because it makes the rest of my life easier.

If meditation did have an unpleasant side effect, it's the fact that self-awareness can be startling. I'd been meditating for a couple of weeks. It had started to open up my world, and that world was scary. I'd sit down to get quiet and it was bloody carnage in there. It seemed like meditation was making my anxiety *worse,* but actually, I was waking up to what had been going on all along. I had become brainwashed to the repetitive, unhelpful, rabid-raccoon thoughts constantly going on in my mind. I had always thought that my brain was so logical, but when I paid attention, I realized it was thinking the same unfounded, negative thoughts approximately 96% of the time. Getting honest about that was unpleasant.

So I sat in my therapist's office and told Louise how chaotic my brain was feeling. My mind was a bad neighborhood where I shouldn't be wandering alone. I needed to shut this down. Louise reassured me that this rough patch was what progress looked like: the best way out is always through. Then she said, "If you can see your thoughts, then you are not your thoughts, right? You as a person are separate from the thoughts you have. You don't have to listen to your mind all the time. You don't have to believe it."

I am not my thoughts. This was revolutionary and empowering for me. I didn't have to act on every thought my brain came up with? That felt like the world's most important life hack. I didn't have to be the victim, berated by the mean things that jerk in my head says.

This was my *Breaking Bad*, "I am the one who knocks" Walter White moment. I am the badass who decides when to listen and when to dismiss. I am the one in charge. I rearranged the power structure. I began approaching my thoughts with curiosity and compassion, and then decided how seriously I wanted to take them. My mind was no longer the master that had me cowering in the corner; it was downgraded to servant status. I could use my mind; it didn't get to use me.

So I meditate every day, like my life depends on it. Because it does.

Here's How: Meditation Instructions

I once dated a guy who didn't like soup.

"Really?" I asked. "All kinds of soup?"

"I just don't like soup."

"So you don't like beef stew or spicy Thai coconut or clam chowder or miso or gazpacho? Not even gazpacho?"

I was a tiny bit obsessed with his reluctance toward soup. With such a wide variety of soups available, how can someone just say they don't like any of them? It's not quite fair to say that soup broke us up. But soup totally broke us up.

I feel the same way when people write off meditation. And yes, I get it, not everyone needs to like meditation and soup like I do, but it's easy to try one kind and decide it's not for you. There is a whole world out there with many types of meditation. And soup.

If you are interested in meditation, I recommend committing to doing it every day for twenty-one days. Lock yourself in the bathroom if you need to, but stop doing stuff for two whole minutes. (If you can work up to longer, even better — twenty minutes a day is when things really start to get interesting.)

Here's what you do:

Get comfortable. Sit on a chair or the couch or the floor. Lie down on the bed or on the coffee table for all I care. This is going to be challenging enough without forcing your body into some uncomfortable position. If you are on the floor, try sitting on the edge of a cushion or blanket, so that your hips are higher than your knees. (It can often be helpful to do something physical before you meditate, so if you know you are the fidgety type, consider tiring out your body before you sit.)

Set a timer — maybe start somewhere between three and fifteen minutes. Don't get too caught up in the number; it's more important to meditate regularly than it is to meditate for a long time. You can close your eyes or keep them open if that makes you too sleepy. Take a deep breath in as you count to three. Puff out your belly as you count. Hold for a moment. Breathe out for six, pulling your belly back in. (If those counts don't work for you, adjust so you are comfortable. But aim for an exhale that is twice as long as the inhale.) Do that for two minutes, then return to a normal, yet deepened breath for the rest of your meditation time. Focus on the sound of the breath, the sensation of the air at the nostrils, or in the chest or belly.

The breath is a key component to activating the parasympathetic nervous system and calming down Amy the Amygdala, but it also acts as a point of focus and a way to be in the present moment. It functions as a double-dose of anxiety prevention. But even with all our good intentions, your brain is going to go to a million other places. Dark places, blame-y places. Places where you hate me for even suggesting this terrible idea that is currently ruining your life. Also, totally mundane places. Your grocery list. The pile of laundry that's starting to smell funky. Wondering who named the state of Idaho. Absolutely anything can seem important when the alternative is just sitting down quietly without checking your e-mail.

That's fine. That's normal. Just observe how you're feeling. There's no need to get lost in the thoughts about how you can't do this and how it works for everyone except you. No need to think that you really should have reached nirvana by now...and man, Nirvana was such a great band...

When those thoughts come, just return to the breath. No judgment. Just breathe. Those thoughts are like clouds on a windy day. Let them come and go. You're bigger than the clouds; you're the sky.

If you feel more comfortable with some company, check out an audio recording of a guided meditation. I recorded a free guided meditation, the link is at NotJustMeBook.com. There are also many app options, such as Headspace, Mindfulness, Calm, and my favorite, Insight Timer. It offers guided meditations, music, ambient noise and bells. It tracks your meditation sessions and offers milestones and cool graphs to keep you motivated. You can also connect with friends and see who else is meditating with the app, all over the world, at the same time you are.

Some days you might rock this meditation thing. Other days you might want to jump out of your skin. But there's no wasted time when it comes to meditation. It's like putting money in a bank account: every little bit helps. And when your timer goes off, let go of whatever just happened. Whether it was your most clear, peaceful meditation session or you were locked in a constant wrestling match with your mind, you have to let it go. That's the last piece of the puzzle: Don't let yourself get attached to thoughts about how you related to your thoughts. Let your meditation practice be the one thing in life you feel no need to judge.

The Latin root of the word "meditation" comes from the word *medeor*, which means "to heal."[49] I heal my heart, my soul, and my mind when I meditate. So do yourself a favor and do it again tomorrow. And the next day. Do it for twenty-one days in a row. See what happens.

Many Kinds of Soup: Meditation and Mindfulness

The word mindfulness refers to a form of meditation that tends to be more Western-friendly and informal since it doesn't require setting aside intentional time to practice. Jon Kabat-Zinn, a molecular biologist and a Professor of Medicine emeritus at the University of Massachusetts Medical School, is probably the biggest influence in bringing mindfulness to the West and making it more accessible through his MBSR program. Mindfulness can be done as a formal meditation practice while sitting on a cushion, or it can be done while driving your car or waiting in line at the post office. It's a way of paying attention and engaging with the world.

Sitting for formal meditation is great, but for those who are in deep distress or have experienced trauma, sometimes stillness just isn't an option quite yet. That's okay because there are other ways to get into that meditative zone in a mindful way. The body and mind are intrinsically linked and sometimes we need to engage the body to gain access to the mind. We are trying to stop the constant jump from one thought to another, and find that bliss where nothing exists but you and this moment. I don't really care how you choose to get there. The following is not an exhaustive list of the meditation menu—there are many ways to tap into the joy of the present moment. But here are some ideas to get you started.

Types of Formal Meditation
• Loving-kindness/Metta meditation. Focusing on developing compassion for self and others. This is a personal favorite of mine—see the next section for instructions.

- Vipassana. Also called "mindfulness meditation" in the West. Focusing the attention to get a clear awareness of what is happening as it happens.
- A body scan. An example of this can be found at the end of Chapter 10. Mentally scanning through the body from the toes to the head to relax every muscle and calm the mind.
- Open awareness. A wide-angle lens form of meditation. Noticing the sounds, sights, and smells in the environment around you and letting your focus remain open to whatever arises from moment to moment.
- Focused attention meditation. Focusing on just one thing —the breath, a physical item, a visualization or a mantra (a positive word/phrase). My friend Carl calls this "committing to noticing the hell out of something."
- Guided meditation. There are many groups and apps that are available to help talk the listener through a meditation. This could include bells, music or visualization. The Insight Timer app is my favorite.

Mindfulness-Based Stress Reduction (MBSR)
- Mostly breath awareness and body scanning, created by John Kabat-Zinn. MBSR helps us to experience life more fully by practicing our ability to return to the present moment, and not get lost in the past or future. That allows for us to make conscious choices, rather than react unconsciously. This program is offered online and in person through many universities. MBSR audio recordings can also be found online.

Meditation-Like Activities That Invoke the Same Positive Changes in the Nervous System

- Pranayama. Deep breathing exercises like alternate nostril breathing (see the end of Chapter 5 for an example), three-part breath or ocean-sounding breath.
- Contemplative prayer. Repetition of sacred words or sentences with focus and devotion.
- Mantra. Words or phrases that act as objects of meditation. Often a powerful sound or vibration in the body that can help deepen the state of meditation.
- Yoga nidra. Commonly known as yogic sleep. This is usually done while lying down, often using props like pillows and blankets to create total physical, mental, and emotional relaxation.

Any Activity to Which You Bring Mindful, Focused Awareness Can Be Meditative

- painting
- coloring
- dance/Nia
- walking
- Tai Chi or other martial arts
- Yoga (much more on this in Chapter 7)

Something to Try: Metta (Loving-kindness) Meditation, Also Known as Compassion-Training

When choosing a focus for meditation, like the breath or a candle flame or a specific mantra/phrase, we're giving our frenetic monkey mind something to do. It's like we have this hyper little monkey in our heads, constantly swinging from one thought to another. That monkey is chattering constantly away, giving his opinion on just about everything, but when we meditate it's like saying, "Yo, monkey, take this pile of buttons and move them one at a time to this other pile." We're giving that wacky little monkey a project, so he doesn't go wild and throw feces everywhere. Loving-kindness is my favorite way to do that.

Pretty much everyone agrees that having compassion for people is good, and we can increase compassion for others by having compassion for ourselves. Because we can think we are really nice people, but if we're beating the shit out of ourselves for something we said three weeks ago, news flash: We're not actually very nice. This practice strengthens our kindness muscles.

Sit to meditate as usual, in a comfy position. Again, if you are on the floor, it can be helpful to place a cushion or blanket under your hips to raise them up higher than your knees. Breathe naturally and repeat the phrases (out loud or in your head):

May I be well.
May I be safe.
May I be happy.
May I be healthy.
May I live with ease.

Now insert the name of someone you love. And yes, of course pets count.
May ____ be well.
May ____ be safe.
May ____ be happy.
May ____ be healthy.
May ____ live with ease.

Insert the name of someone you don't really have any feelings about. Your mail carrier, for example, or your Uber driver.

May ____ be well.
May ____ be safe.
May ____ be happy.
May ____ be healthy.
May ____ live with ease.

Now insert the name of someone you have a... complicated relationship with. Someone with whom things are difficult. The mere mention of this person brings up not-so-flattering feelings in your heart.

May ____ be well.
May ____ be safe.
May ____ be happy.
May ____ be healthy.
May ____ live with ease.

If that last one stresses you out, make sure you circle back to yourself again, because right now, *you* are the one suffering. And remember, dealing with family is super high-level spiritual work.

May I be well.
May I be safe.
May I be happy.
May I be healthy.
May I live with ease.

The last step is to open up all this loving-kindness to the wider world:

May all beings be well.
May all beings be safe.
May all beings be happy.
May all beings be healthy.
May all beings live with ease.

Chapter 5: Social Anxiety, Anxiety and Society

Sometimes I wonder if my social anxiety developed as a direct result of my career as an actor. A significant part of the job requires being cool with people pointing, whispering and surreptitiously photographing you while there is a little bit of mustard on your face. Being recognized was something I was supposed to enjoy; it was supposed to make me feel special, confident, and successful. But I didn't feel any of that and I didn't want to get recognized. I really, REALLY didn't want to get recognized.

Have you ever seen someone with a phobia of snakes be forced to look at a snake? You know how they shake and cry and you can tell they would rather donate a kidney without anesthesia than look at a snake? That's how I felt about getting recognized. It became a phobia.

It's fairly easy to avoid interactions with a snake. It's harder to avoid being recognized from a movie that's on HBO twice a day. There is either a screaming teenager at the other end of the restaurant or there is not—and there is no way to gear up for that. They come out of nowhere.

I cut my hair.

I dyed my hair black. Then red.

I wore glasses.

I got bangs.

I wore only clothes that were grey or brown, so I could blend in with bricks and dirt, and maybe no one would see me at all. None of that helped. I still got recognized.

When I was twenty-two, I was desperately unhappy with my life. I retired from acting and left L.A to search for a more authentic path for myself. The downsides of the film industry had started to weigh on me, and I hoped there was a life out in the "real world" that would have some meaning and purpose for me. I had no plan, very few experiences of life outside of a film set, and had been too busy working to go to high school. But I finally got my GED in my mid-twenties and was attempting to recreate myself in Virginia. I wanted to be something other than The Girl From That '90s Movie You Watched Fourteen Times. I dove into my role of Regular College Student, but shaking the old identity wasn't easy. When I got back my statistics exam, the teaching assistant had written at the top: *Dear Doubtfire Girl, you got a B-.*

I felt like a peacock trying to go unnoticed in a lecture hall. People stared, whispered, and took photos they thought were incognito. There was pointing and squinting. Throat-choking hugs, high-pitched squealing, and pleas to recreate scenes or gossip about my cast-mates. I got a lot of questions about whether or not I liked Dick Van Dyke. (I swear to you, I had no clue why people were asking me that. I thought it was just a coincidence so many people asked me an oddly specific question until I finally Googled it and was reminded of that scene where my character in *Mrs. Doubtfire* fights for her right to watch *The Dick Van Dyke Show*.)

Fame probably seems fun. Shouldn't it be awesome to have people tell you that you're great? For me, it didn't make me angry or annoyed; it made me embarrassed. It made me feel like I was standing there naked, being evaluated. I felt like a failure because I wasn't good at being this quasi-famous person everyone expected. I was awkward, nervous, and shy. I was much more startled than starlet.

While the majority of people were nice when they approached me, some were not. Some were demanding, and treated me like a hired dancing monkey. They were loud, and they felt entitled to a piece of me. Let's not forget that the snap of a shampoo bottle scares me, so a 250-pound man from Oklahoma enthusiastically slapping me on the back is likely to short-circuit something in my brain.

I felt trapped in a life in which I was getting attention that I didn't want and didn't deserve. So, in an attempt to not get recognized, I didn't go out much. And what started as a preference for not being in public developed into a fear of leaving my house: agoraphobia. Even though I get recognized less frequently now, I still sometimes find myself standing in my front hallway, car keys in hand, shivering. It's not just about being recognized; the fear is about being overwhelmed by whatever is *out there*, and my inability to escape it easily.

When my agoraphobia is intense, it mixes together with my social anxiety in one big steaming pile of misery. I obsess about the things that could go wrong, out there with all those *people*. What if I unexpectedly run into a friend, and I can't think of anything to say? (Once, in a moment of social panic, someone asked me my dog's name and I blanked.) I could get recognized, and then what if I can only stammer and blush and look at my feet and I disappoint people who just wanted a good story about meeting someone who used to be an actor? I could have a panic attack at Target and everyone would stare at me. I could get anxious and dizzy and crash my car and kill someone. Sometimes, the rabbit-hole of tragic possibilities causes me to put down my purse and seek safety under a quilt.

Social anxiety: Preparing for Judgment

Social anxiety is the intense and persistent fear of being watched and scrutinized by others, causing extreme self-consciousness. It is essentially pathological shyness.[50] About fifteen million Americans have social anxiety disorder, and more than a third of them report that they had symptoms for ten or more years before seeking help.[51]

People with social anxiety are extremely sensitive to subtle social cues. In a lab, subjects were shown photos of angry faces that flickered by on a computer screen faster than they could consciously register them. For people with social anxiety, their amygdala responded instantaneously to the angry face, and their anxiety levels rose. People without social anxiety didn't register the fabricated social disapproval at all. Those non-anxious folks felt just fine and went on with their non-anxious lives.[52]

But social anxiety is more than just being incredibly sensitive to other people throwing shade. It's a feeling of being constantly embarrassed or humiliated by one's actions. Personal and professional relationships can be negatively affected and the result can be paralyzing — even life-threatening.

Mike: No Safe Place

"I have about ten seconds in the morning when I wake up before it hits. I walk around with it all day long."

While some of us don't know why we're anxious, Mike can pinpoint the start of his anxiety to May of 1982. When he was eight years old, his mom had a massive heart attack. The ambulance arrived and the EMTs got her heart beating again, but she hadn't gotten enough blood to her brain during the time when she was clinically dead. She spent seven months in the hospital before Mike and his father brought her home. The brain damage left her a spastic quadriplegic, meaning she didn't have any control over her body — couldn't move, couldn't talk, but she was alive.

"She was a prisoner in her own body. She had to eat though a tube in her stomach. We had to bathe her, clean her when she went to the bathroom, everything."

That's when the cycle of depression and anxiety started for Mike. For him, the two go hand in hand. He burns with the anxiety for a while, and then the depression kicks in. He's tired of fighting this brutal cycle, exhausted by his habit of always expecting terrible things.

"What happened to my mom screwed up my fight or flight response, because it wasn't like a death where you can deal with it and move on. You walk into the nightmare every day. From that point on, there was this anxiousness in me. This waiting and expecting the worst."

The social anxiety really hit in middle school. Mike was a little overweight and got bullied. So every day, he would wake up to the anguish of his home situation, go to school and get picked on all day, and then return to his challenges at home.

"There was no safe place. Ever."

By the time he reached high school, Mike discovered that he could funnel his negative energy into rage. Somehow, anger felt easier to him. Being aggressive at least made him feel like he was finally not scared. And it kept people away from him, it was easier to isolate that way.

"I kind of walked around simmering. I've always used words more than fists. And words can do a lot more damage."

Mike is now in his 40s. He's divorced with two kids and he's still struggling with the issues that plagued him when he was eight years old. He constantly feels unsafe, with pretty much everyone.

"I'm very insecure walking into a room of people. I'm terrified. I'm very quiet because I'm over-thinking what I say. I don't want to say something wrong or stupid. If I tell a joke and nobody laughs...oh my God...it's the worst thing. I feel removed from the crowd, like there's the rest of everybody and then there's me, standing outside. Separate. In my mind they're all judging me, they don't like me because I'm not good enough to be in this group. I think all the time, *Man, I'm stupid, I hate myself.*"

So Mike withdraws, as many people with social anxiety do. The fear of rejection is brutal, and in an attempt to avoid it, they preemptively reject themselves. Mike feels like a burden anyway, so he assumes other people won't care if he isolates himself. At one point, when it was just all too much to bear, he considered suicide. He found himself wanting to end it all, lingering in that dark and hopeless place.

"I was right there. I was right there."

Suicidal ideations are not uncommon for those with acute social anxiety. The root of the desperation seems to be found in the loneliness that results from the self-imposed isolation[53]. But Mike didn't go through with the attempt to take his life. With the encouragement of his girlfriend, he dragged himself to his father's doorstep and asked for help. By that point, he had lost 45 pounds and says that he looked as if he was "not long for this world." While he no longer feels like a suicide risk, he still can't find a way to be comfortable in social situations.

"I want to be witty, I want to be funny, I want to be engaging. And I'm terrified that I'm not going to be. I read facial tics, I read body language and the inflection of people's voices, and I overanalyze it. I'm critical of everything I say and how I present myself. I'm still thinking about things I said five years ago."

What Mike does is called "ruminating".[54] This is the psychological definition of rumination, so it doesn't mean to simply give something careful consideration. This is thinking repetitively about our distress and its potential causes and outcomes, rather than the solutions. It's what I think of as "getting in the shower and mentally recreating negative events so obsessively that I can't remember if I washed my body."

It's easy to think that ruminating will be helpful. We tend to assume that thinking something through will get us to a helpful conclusion. But that's not what ruminating is, because there is no conclusion to arrive at. Thinking about something obsessively doesn't mean that you gain more control over it. There is no amount of thinking about what Mike said at a party five years ago that will change anything. Ruminating is simply choosing to bash your head against a wall. It's not useful for you and I'm pretty sure the wall doesn't love it, either.

Not only is ruminating unhelpful; it's actively harmful. It reinforces a habit until it's almost subconscious, like biting your fingernails. These repetitive thoughts set up connections in the brain that you really don't want there.[55] It's like greasing a groove so that your mind — when allowed to run amok — will fall into that easy, lubed-up track and just keep ruminating for days, weeks or years. This is what happens when family members have a fight and still aren't talking to each other twenty years later. No one remembers the topic of the original conflict, but those grooves of emotion are so deep they're like World War I trenches no one can see their way out of, so everyone just hunkers down for the long haul.

Nobody wants to live in that trench of pain, but the pattern becomes so habitual that our thoughts slip back there when we're not paying attention. Mike's grooves are that he is unworthy and unlovable, and people are going to abandon him—so when he gets anxious, that's the groove his mind jumps into.

So, how can we notice when we're falling into the groove, and change the detrimental pattern? We practice presence in this moment, even if all we really want is to come up with more reasons that everyone hates us. But that's not easy.

Mike started telling himself that he was stupid, that he doesn't have much to show for the first forty years of his life. He feels like he's an annoyance and wonders if everyone would be better off if he wasn't around.

"I've not been very successful. I wasn't successful in my marriage, I haven't been successful career-wise. To be bluntly honest, I'm flat broke and unemployed. I'm struggling to get back into the work force and it's really difficult. The self-talk escalates and pretty soon, saying *you're stupid* isn't good enough. You're saying you hate yourself. That was my mantra for the last couple of years: I hate myself, I wish I was dead. Struggling to get out of that has been a bitch. Really tough."

In order to deal with legitimately challenging circumstances, Mike had been self-medicating to numb his pain. He sees now that numbing out isn't the answer, and when I interviewed him, he was eleven days sober. Mike credits his girlfriend for showing him his own inner strength and for standing by him when he was at his lowest, and during the painful process of getting clean. But it had been a long eleven days.

"Right now I'm focused on staying sober and putting the crutch down. Even if it's just killing me all day long, I can go to bed at the end of the day and say, *I didn't hide today, today I faced it – all day long*. It kicked my ass, but I'm going to bed sober. I'm going to get up sober and I may face it all day tomorrow, but eventually, it's got to get better. It's not easy, but I'm doing it."

Mike recently went outside and saw that a couple of branches had fallen off a tree in his yard. He didn't have a chain saw, so his took a hack saw and worked for ninety minutes on the trees. And at the end of it? He felt kind of okay. He felt a little lighter. He had accomplished something, and he felt a tiny bit successful. It reminded him of how he felt when he used to train in Taekwondo. It gave him the ability to focus and work though the negativity. "You're exhausted and you don't have the energy to be anxious."

Mike had warned me that his was not a success story. He was treading water, looking for any lifeline to hold on to, any way to keep from going under. But I think he is a success story. Sometimes, any day you can keep breathing in and out is a win.

"I can't control it, but maybe someday I'll have a small victory. That will inspire me to keep going."

So, You're in a Trench. Now What?

Ruminating is common with many kinds of anxiety. That constant negative chatter plasters you to the wall like you're in a Graviton. If you find yourself ruminating – in your shower, your car, as you're supposed to be making thirty cupcakes for the birthday party – acknowledge that you're going down an unhelpful path. I like to say, *I see you, you wild thoughts, but I'm not going to engage with you because I have better things to do.* (I like to throw in a temper-tantrum-esque *YOU'RE NOT THE*

BOSS OF ME, WILD THOUGHTS on really challenging days. I also sprinkle in some pretty filthy profanity.)

Repetitive negative thoughts are not helpful and you are not required to pay attention to them. But deciding to just not think about something rarely works; if I say that under no circumstances should you think about a panda bear, your mind will suddenly become obsessed with pandas. First, we need to notice that the thoughts have started to rule our minds. Sharon Salzburg calls her inner critic Lucy, like the classic bully from Charlie Brown. Her favorite comeback is a simple and sweet, "Hi, Lucy" and Sharon imagines handing her a cup of tea so she'll just sit quietly. Other days require the slightly more assertive, "Chill out, Lucy."

Once you've identified the nasty thoughts, re-focus your attention. You can gently shift your focus away from ruminating about the past and what you should have said, or the future and the ten million ways this might play out, and simply feel the breath in your body. Try actually looking at the face of the person helping you at the store — or in any way you can, just be wherever you are and feel your feet on the floor. Wiggle your toes. This habit of actively being in your life, rather than in your head, can create some new connections and pathways — grease some new grooves — that don't involve trapping you in that trench.

And of course, there is an app for that. Mindfulness apps can be really helpful for triggering present moment awareness. I have The Mindfulness App set so that a sweet little chime rings at 10 a.m., noon and 3 p.m. When that happens, I stop and take three deep breaths and notice where I am. Is my body tense? Is my mind ruminating? Am I telling myself stories about how I'm too shy, too weird, too different from everyone else? What would happen if I dropped those stories?

If your head is in that wild, scared mood, think about your thoughts like a river—a river that is tumultuous and choppy at the moment. You're not trying to stop the flow of that river. How would that even work? You'd just stand in the middle of the river and command it to stop because you said so? Pound your fists on the surface until it obeys? That's impossible and you'd just end up splashing yourself in the face. Rivers, like thoughts, flow. It's what they do.

All you are trying to do is drag your drenched self to sit on the nice calm bank so you don't drown. Just watch the river from there, and appreciate its power without getting carried away downstream. You can choose when you want to engage; you can hop in the river when it's calm and enjoy it on your terms, without being constantly dragged around and pulled under by the currents.

This is mindfulness: the act of being aware of the present moment without judgment. It's a lot like meditating—but this is a spur-of-the-moment kind of mindfulness that doesn't require you to set time aside in your day to make it happen. It's like triage meditation—a way to stop the bleeding when you're in the middle of it all.

As Mike found, physical activity is another great way to retrain the attention. Exercise increases endorphin levels and blood flow to the brain, and when you work your muscles to fatigue, it's hard to expend so much energy on runaway thoughts. One study divided 156 men and women with depression into three groups. One group took part in an aerobic exercise program, another took Zoloft, and a third did both. After sixteen weeks, 60% of the people in all three groups could no longer be classified as having major depression. The group's scores on two rating scales of depression were essentially the same.[56] Those natural workout happy-chemicals are really effective, plus, there is the satisfying high of moral superiority you get when you think about all those lazy lumps who didn't get their hearts pumping. So, you know, whatever works.

It's Not Quite Social Anxiety: Introversion and Shyness

I hate talking on the phone. In a classroom or conference scenario, I always sit in the back of the room, right by the door. I duck out of group photos and find eye contact challenging. Social encounters exhaust me and I love being alone. People say, "Don't be such an introvert," but they might as well be saying, "Don't be so short." I am 5'3 and I am an introvert. And while introversion doesn't necessarily mean social anxiety, there can be some overlap.

Introverts don't hate people, we just prefer them in smaller doses with a significant period of time to recover from them. Introversion is also different from shyness. Shyness tends to be a fear of judgment, but introverts simply prefer less stimulation.[57] I am mostly introverted, but I tend towards shyness as well. Many introverts tend to prefer engaging in a less-stimulating, more focused way. At parties, we often linger in the quieter corners with just a few other people, or else you'll find us sprawled out on the kitchen floor engaged in a deep discussion with the dog. This doesn't mean that you could never see an introvert standing on the coffee table, destroying "Livin' on a Prayer." It could happen. But don't expect to see her for the next three days.

Introversion: A Brief History

Introversion doesn't tend to be considered a particularly charming trait, and many of us have had that awkward encounter in which someone commands that we "come out of our shell." But it wasn't always this way. Around the turn of the twentieth century, America decided it needed a new kind of hero. In the wonderful book *Quiet: The Power of Introverts in a World That Can't Stop Talking,* Susan Cain discusses a theory about the shift away from the "culture of character" towards the "culture of personality."[58] Basically, the culture of character valued someone who was thoughtful and introspective. Quietly honorable. The perennial Good Guy of the early 1800s was an introvert—think Atticus Finch in *To Kill a Mockingbird.*

Once again, the Industrial Revolution changed everything. The world opened up. Social and professional success was no longer about working with your family on the farm or with your neighbors at the corner store. People were working with strangers from other towns. It was important to sell these strangers not only on your business, but on you. The ideal person became more extroverted, oozing showmanship and congeniality. He or she was bold and entertaining, a charismatic leader and an enthusiastic team player. The focus was now on making a good impression when presenting yourself to others. The model personality changed; suddenly, if you were talking about a guy who was a shy, lone wolf, you were likely referring to someone who just tried to assassinate a president. The social norm shifted: Extrovert = Good. Introvert = You should become an extrovert.

Just like with our anxious crayfish, we can turn to the animal kingdom for reassurance that, like anxiety, introversion is natural. Studies have found that about 20% of any particular species are slow to warm up, while the rest of them charge boldly into their penguin/lion/sloth lives.[59] It's just part of natural chemical make-up.

Introverts still accomplish impressive things that require them to engage with the larger world. Bill Gates, Abraham Lincoln, Albert Einstein, Rosa Parks, Audrey Hepburn and Mahatma Gandhi all identified as introverts. In fact, Gandhi considered his shyness to be the root of his greatest asset: it gave him restraint. If Gandhi had been an extrovert, Indian independence, and a whole lot of other civil rights activism, would have looked very different.

Please Like Me. Social Acceptance and the Primitive Brain

The problem is that there is a part of my brain that says if I'm quiet and blend into the background, I can avoid criticism, pain and suffering. But that's impossible, because no one is immune to those things. By diving too far into my introversion and hiding from others, I might be avoiding a little bit of pain, but I'm inadvertently hiding from joy, too.

Evolutionarily, it makes sense that we would have this deep awareness of what other people expect from us.[60] A few thousand years ago, attentiveness to human interaction was vital to survival. Back then, if you pissed off the leader of your community because you accidentally flirted with her husband, that was a big problem. You were excommunicated and thrown out of your society and you died alone in the forest without food or shelter and you probably *should* lie awake all night obsessing about the way you touched his shoulder inappropriately because it would literally be the death of you.

It was also probably good to stay awake all night because of the roaming packs of wolves.

This kind of dramatic social control is still how it works for apes, but it's not so true for humans anymore. A lack of social acceptance isn't awesome, but it doesn't mean automatic death. Still, the primal part of the brain gets triggered and it legitimately feels like the end of the world.

And while we tend to be great at noticing that something is off with a social interaction, we are notoriously terrible at interpreting the cause. It's incredible really, how little other people are actually thinking about you. We are *always* on our own minds. It's hard for us to think of anything other than ourselves and what we like or don't like—our personal preferences, our fears and joys. We like mountain bikes and hate conference calls. Our hair looks good and our arms look flabby. But it always starts with us. It's easy to imagine that everyone else's brain is filled up with us, too. But really, other people are thinking about themselves and wondering if they can get a babysitter for next Wednesday night. And burritos. You'd be shocked at how often people think about burritos. Everyone else is just as self-absorbed as you are; they don't have time to be thinking about you, too. They're busy looking at their phones.

Bonnie: Social Stigma and Perfect Lipstick

My friend Bonnie has two of the cutest little kids in the world. And yes, I'm totally biased, but they both have fiery red hair, so I stand behind my statement completely. Bonnie struggled with mood disorders before she had children, but after the birth of her first kid, everything intensified. She had postpartum depression and thought she would never be able to leave her house again.

When I interviewed Bonnie, she prefaced the conversation by doing the thing that all parents do when they are about to get honest and vulnerable. She made sure I knew how much she loves her kids. She said it three times, in various ways. And then she said the things that are hard to say.

"There is this gripping exhaustion, and it's so easy to lose yourself in it. You are supposed to be just as good at everything you did before, but now 3/4 of your brain is being used up and 90% of your body is being used up, but you are supposed to go on and not miss a beat. It's hard to make peace with who you are."

To anyone else it would seem like she really hadn't missed a beat. When my last book came out, Bonnie sent me a printed collage of her entire family holding up hand-decorated signs saying "Go, Lisa! We love you! We're so proud of you!" as if I were coming around the bend of a marathon. Seriously? This incredible show of support is what "missing a beat" looks like?

It's still hard for me to think of Bonnie as a mom. We met in our early 20s. Back then, our husbands were just our boyfriends, and while they were in their grad school study groups, she and I would get drunk on cheap red wine while watching *American Idol* and yelling our opinions at the screen. Unlike mine, Bonnie's opinions about *American Idol* were actually educated; she's a singer. I'd watch her sing in clubs, thinking I'd never seen a more impressively self-assured person than the woman standing up there, belting out Ella Fitzgerald to sophisticated New Yorkers drinking Manhattans in Manhattan.

But even though for me she will eternally remain twenty-two, Bonnie is actually the mother of two entire people. She told me she felt a shift: suddenly she was not important anymore because it's all about the kids. She knows it's better for the children when parents include themselves in the equation, too, but it's hard to do in practice. If Bonnie does something for herself, she feels like she is taking something away from her family and misses them, but when she's spending all her time with her kids, she gets bored and wants more. It's a tug-of-war in which she feels like she is constantly failing because she should be doing something different than whatever she is doing.

This feeling isn't limited to parenthood. I heard similar stories from non-parents, parents of grown kids, pretty much everyone. We've created a culture that tells us we're never living up to our potential; we're always coming up short. If we're working, we should be having more fun. If we're relaxing, we're lazy. If we're at home, we should get out more. If we're out, we should have downtime. Artists should get real jobs. 9-5ers aren't living passionately.

The pressure is omnipresent, and Bonnie feels the constant judgment. "You should never show signs that you're frustrated. Never be angry. Always look perfect. You have to be doing great professionally, putting healthy meals on the table, getting your kids to actually eat those meals while everyone is sitting at the table and you're looking beautiful with your perfect lipstick. But that's the fantasy. In reality, there are times you feel like a legitimate shit show. There are times when I am my own personal nightmare."

Bonnie tried to keep going through her depression, assuming she just needed to toughen up and get over it. After all, she had great kids, a healthy marriage, she was booking cool gigs singing with her band. What right did she have to be depressed? Things changed one day when her husband said, "It doesn't need to be this bad, you can get help."

"It made me realize how much my depression was impacting him. You tend to make your loved ones more important than you, so when it's affecting them, it's time to do something about it. I wouldn't have taken the medication on my own, but when it impacts others you love, that's the straw that breaks the camel's back."

She started taking a low dose of Zoloft. She found it empowering; she felt like she was taking action, doing something about the problem and not just letting depression happen to her. Bonnie doesn't know if the medication is just a placebo because it's such a low dose, but she really doesn't care. It's not numbing her out, and she feels like it just sheds a light on the situation. It makes things a little easier.

When Bonnie talks about her kids, it's obvious that she is madly in love with them. She loves the way they look at the world, the way she sees both herself and her husband in them. It cracks her up that they like '80s hip hop. I was curious to know if becoming a parent caused her more anxiety or less, and the answer, unsurprisingly, is "both."

"I feel like day-to-day I have more anxiety: I'm running and running, it's very busy and you're constantly doing things for your kids and they're screaming and there is a lot more stimuli. It's loud. But the other stuff, outside my kids, I worry about less. My anxiety is probably a little more, but it's shifted to my children, which is freeing in a lot of ways, because some of the things I worried about before have evaporated. It makes my music more joyful because I don't put as much stock into it now. I'm not wondering, *am I going to make a career out of this? Is anyone going to come to my shows?* I just feel excited because I get to sing."

Bonnie's husband is one of those happy-go-lucky guys, who seems to always be okay in every circumstance. It seems so much easier to go through life like that.

"I know being a rollercoaster personality, being someone who feels so deeply and passionately about things, has benefits—but it also has significant drawbacks. I have pain and anger that other people don't have to deal with. I want my children to be like my husband and not like me, because I don't want them to have to deal with that."

When I thank her for being so open with me, Bonnie says what I hear at the end of pretty much every interview: She feels ashamed of her depression and anxiety, but she wants to speak more freely and honestly about it.

"It's so hard, but I'm trying to talk more about it. Most people think that everyone else is better, and no one else is struggling to the extent that we are. Facebook gives us this whitewashed concept of life. It seems like everyone else is doing all these great things. It can be really detrimental, because people think it's real."

Something to Try: Nadi Shodhana (Alternate Nostril Breathing)

If you catch yourself getting lost in ruminating, or perfect lipstick pressure, here's something to help stop the negative spiral. I like to do this breathing exercise first thing in the morning, or whenever I'm feeling anxious, but you can try it at any time. Nadi Shodhana helps improve focus and concentration. It also supports lung and nervous system function, and can help with blood pressure issues.[61] Personally, I feel like trying to keep track of which nostril I'm breathing with requires so much of my attention that my mind has less time to wander. The end result is that I feel calmer and more peaceful. Just keep in mind that if you have allergies or a cold and your nose is stuffy, this is going to be more challenging.

• Sit comfortably, but sit up tall—that will help the air flow more easily.

• Breathe in and out through your nose, slow and steady. Try to match the length of your inhales and exhales. Pause for a moment before you start each inhale and exhale.

• Take your right hand, and tuck your peace fingers (pointer and middle) into the palm of your right hand, so your thumb, ring finger and pinky finger are sticking up. Rest your ring finger next to your left nostril and your thumb next to your right. (And if that is feeling too complicated or uncomfortable, just rest the index and middle fingers in the center of the forehead.)

• Take a deep breath in through both nostrils. Use your thumb to close your right nostril gently and exhale through your left.

• Inhale through the left nostril, then switch so that your ring finger closes your left nostril and exhale through the right side.

• Inhale through the right side, and switch, closing the right side and exhaling left side.

• Continue for five or ten cycles, or however long feels comfortable for you. Keep your attention on the breath, bringing your mind back whenever your thoughts wander.

• When you're finished alternating the breath, release your right hand into your lap and take a few deep breaths through both nostrils.

I like doing this breath on airplanes to relax, but it tends to look like I'm picking my nose. That's an excellent time to practice the "hands-free" version - simply imagine the air flowing through the left nostril, then the right. It still works and people stare less.

Breathing exercises like this have been immensely helpful for my anxiety, but it's not going to be a magic cure for everything. If your anxiety reaches a peak you can't come down from on your own, consider the Crisis Text Line. It's a not-for-profit that offers free, 24/7 support for anyone who needs it. And it's a gift for anyone who hates talking on the phone as much as I do. Check it out at crisistextline.org or text HOME to 741741.

Chapter 6: "Can you make it?"

I was nineteen, and I should have been okay. My parents' separation wouldn't impact my daily life the way it would have when I was younger. I wasn't a grade-schooler destined to be pulled in two by a custody battle, splitting time between parents, setting up two different bedrooms and trying to remember whose turn it was to pick me up at school.

Nevertheless, I was not at all fine. Our family life had quickly deteriorated into an unrecognizable mess of lying and fighting. We had always been The Three Musketeers (I'm an only child), and I was overwhelmed by the equal parts love and outrage I felt towards both my parents. Drowning in the guilt of not being able to keep my family together, I locked myself in the bathroom and punched the tile until my knuckles bled.

Six months earlier, my dearest friend had gotten sick. Christine was fine, and then she wasn't. Doctors couldn't figure out what was wrong, so I sat by her hospital bed, massaging her aching hands and making plans to go get frozen yogurt as soon as she came home. But she never came home. She was diagnosed with lupus, and then, what seemed like twenty minutes later, her mom and I were picking out the shoes we would bury her in.

We decided on the pair with white flowers on them. Those were Christine's favorite; when my boyfriend had made fun of them, she launched a campaign for me to dump him. She decided anyone who would be such a dick about flowery shoes could never be my soul mate—she didn't care how deep his dimple was. But suddenly Christine was gone, and so was my sense of teenage invincibility. I'd lie in the grass next to her grave in Forest Lawn Cemetery, wondering how I'd ever get up again.

The t-shirt I always wore to auditions had belonged to Christine. It was nothing special: a dark grey crew neck from the Gap. She had gotten too busty for it and, with a smirk, she had given it to me, saying it would fit me just fine. So I put on my dead friend's shirt and went to auditions amidst the incessant thoughts that I needed to leave my job as an actor. I could no longer find any joy in my work. I didn't like acting. I didn't like the life, the criticism, and the competition. My body ached with emptiness.

I wanted a new job. A new identity. I had been working as an actor since the age of four, but now it seemed I had wasted my life. I had nothing but this prestigious job I didn't want, and my safety net was disintegrating. My parents and I were in free fall—the three of us too shocked at what we had so quickly become to even think about saving each other.

I clung to my acting career because it was all I had, but it was like a hot potato I was dying to fling out of my hands. My friends assumed my complaints about the film industry were the result of a bad day that could be cured by a night out and a fruity cocktail. But this movie life had destroyed my happiness and slaughtered my parent's marriage. I had split up my family; my mother traveled with me to film sets when she should have been spending time with my father. The whole thing was my fault. I was still in my teens, but clearly my life was over. The darkness was staining my mind. "You're crazy" was no longer a throwaway line. It felt like a clinical diagnosis. And a death sentence.

While I understood it was natural to feel grief about my parents' separation and the loss of my dear friend, it felt like I had hit the bottom of grief, found a trap door, and tumbled down another thirty floors. One night, as I sat on the edge of my bathtub, a purple Bic razor seemed to be offering a fucked up kind of salvation. If I could remove my skin, I could feel something different than all the emotional agony. I could at least make my outsides match my insides. My inner self was shredded, a painfully pink, pulsing mass shuddering at the slightest breeze blowing on exposed nerves. Why did I look okay on the outside? How could I be this functional mass of ruin? I wanted people to understand the aguish I carried daily. Blood might do it.

Exhaustion seeped into my bones. I had been tired before. Actor's hours can be brutal. I'd worked on a movie that demanded nineteen-hour days on the freezing plains of Saskatchewan, scantily dressed in corsets and bloomers as a prostitute in the 1850s — yet this was an even more soul-sucking tired than that. I kept drifting back to how easy it would be if that razor just slipped sideways. I wasn't sure that I wanted to die, but I was desperate for something to hurt in a way I understood.

I couldn't be trusted, but I didn't want to trouble anyone with my silly problems. I had no right to be this miserable. I didn't have cancer. I had a fridge full of food. I was the recipient of white privilege and clean drinking water. I wasn't worth someone else's time. But it was 10 p.m. and I needed help. Putting on shoes was beyond my capabilities, so I staggered across our lawn in my socks and banged on the neighbor's door.

I wondered momentarily if this was weakness, this plea for help I was about to make. But even in this moment of crisis, it was clear to me that the real weakness was pretending I was okay. Weakness was being too scared to reach out and admit that I no longer knew how to be alive. This thing I was doing — pounding on my neighbor's door late at night — was the bravest thing I had ever done in my whole damn life.

It was raining. I don't know if it was actually raining, but it felt like it was raining. Our neighbor came to the door, looking sleepy and confused. The flickering blue of the TV cast the hall behind her in an eerie glow; she must have been drowsing while watching the news. Her husband padded to the door behind her, wrenching up his forehead at the sight of the teenager from next door in her grass-stained socks and stringy hair. I'm not sure if I looked very old or very young. Maybe a disconcerting combination of both. I was an old woman, haggard by this world that had caused so much pain. At the same time, I was a toddler lost in the mall, pulling on passing pant legs, desperate for someone to help me find my way home.

They guided me into their living room. I didn't know either of them very well, but I knew they were both doctors, so I assumed they would know other doctors. I was terrified of going to counseling because of the awful stuff in my brain, but I knew I couldn't survive myself on my own. I begged them for the name of a therapist and tripped on the rug as they made me sit on the couch. I felt bad that I was going to get it wet, either from the rain that might have been outside, or the spigot of tears that gushed from my face.

They looked at each other, concerned. I saw myself through their eyes, and it was scary. She went to the kitchen and got on the phone, turning her back to me and casting quick glances over her shoulder while covering her mouth with her hand.

He looked at me like I was an injured rabbit they were trying to nurse back to health. Should we feed it something? Will it try to bolt? He smiled at me, a tentative, weak smile through squinted eyes; it was hard to look at me. I laughed and it sounded meaner than I intended. I just didn't know what to say. I felt awful for making him look at such a sad thing in his living room.

She came back with a piece of paper she had ripped off the back of an envelope. It had an address on it.

"Doctor Salvatore. Nine o'clock tomorrow morning. Can you make it?"

I blinked at her. My head was swimming and I wasn't sure what she was asking. Was I available to go at that time? Or was I capable of breathing in and out until then?

I nodded yes and wiped my face with the sleeve of my sweatshirt. It was mostly true. I was available at that time. And I really hoped I could breathe in and out until then.

"Thank you."

More tears exploded onto their expensive couch.

I made it to the appointment. And I began the long road back to who I was.

Hello, Darkness, My Old Friend

Depression is on the rise in America. Even with the increase in anti-depressant use, suicide rates in the US are higher than they have been in thirty years.[62] The overall suicide rate jumped 24% from 1999 to 2014.[63] Depression is also striking younger people more than ever before. Forty years ago, most people who suffered from mood disorders were in their 40s and 50s. These days, the average age is mid-20s.[64] A devastating exhibition by an advocacy group called Active Minds places 1,100 empty backpacks on college campuses around the country, representing the number of undergraduates who kill themselves each year.[65] Seventeen percent of Americans will suffer a major episode of depression at some point in their lives,[66] and women are twice as likely to be diagnosed as men.[67]

It can be easy to overuse the term depression: *OMG, my frizzy hair situation is depressing!* (No. That's not depression. That's just life. Go buy a better conditioner.)

So what does depression really look like?

When depression is brought on by loss, a traumatic event, or a medical issue, it is called *situational depression*. It is considered to be an issue of coping with adjustment, and it shares many of the symptoms of clinical depression. Clinical depression is also called major depressive disorder and that's when sadness just wallops you out of nowhere, regardless of circumstances.

Major depression is diagnosed when someone experiences either:[68]

- Feeling depressed or sad most of the day
- Loss of interest or ability to derive pleasure from all or nearly all activities that were previously enjoyed

And four or more of the following over at least a two-week period:

- Unintended weight loss or gain
- Sleep troubles — sleeping too much or too little
- Feeling slowed down or agitated though the day
- Fatigue or loss of energy
- Feeling worthless or extreme, inappropriate guilt
- Having a hard time thinking or concentrating
- Obsessing about death or suicide (with or without a specific plan)

While mostly I've had situational depression triggered by difficult emotional circumstances, there have been other times when the cause is not so clear-cut. When all seems well and I'm in a happy relationship, doing work I love, sometimes the cloud still settles in and covers my heart in sludge. I find myself stuck in a hollow hopelessness, trapped in a darkness I can't name. I feel like a burden and a disappointment, and that voice inside repeats that I am a failure. Over and over and over. That voice says people are laughing at me, pitying me, wondering what I am doing with my life and assuring me that the very core of my being is worthless. And the guilt over "nothing being wrong" pounds my spirit into the ground.

When this happens, I lay on the floor of my room and pray —to someone, I don't even know who—to please make me like everyone else. Make me a person who can be happy with a cup of tea and a patch of sunshine. Someone who can see tragedy and suffering in the world and still manage to go on, making oatmeal cookies and jokes and plans to pick strawberries with friends. Please just make me someone who can cope. Please just make me okay.

I am not saying that I've been the most depressed, most anxious person in the world. It's not a competition. Depression is not shameful, but I also don't see it as a badge of honor, either. It's not romantic. The whole "tortured artist" thing isn't even interesting anymore. But I figure if I'm going to be sharing other people's stories, I should suck it up and tell you mine, too. Mental health issues can be not as bad as mine. They can also be much, much worse.

Philip: Zero Problems. Total Depression.

Just as I began doing research for this book, I got a message from someone whose name called out an echo from my teens.

You probably don't remember this, but we went to a movie in 10th or 11th grade. There were a few of us, it was like Ace Ventura or Congo or something. I worked as an usher and I got everyone in using passes. But later in college I might have claimed that "I took Lisa to a movie once." I totally made it sound like a date. But it was technically and grammatically somewhat truthful.

We hadn't really spoken since our faux date, and I only slightly remembered Philip from my patchy high school days in Canada. Mostly my memories involve him wearing a backwards baseball cap and snickering outside 7-Eleven. The rest of Philip's confessional message was about his struggles with depression and anxiety. Since I instantly adore anyone who is voluntarily honest about things that make them sound dorky, I called him up to ask incredibly intimate mental health questions after not speaking for twenty years. That's not weird, right?

Philip answered the phone and hearing his voice instantly sent me back to that 7-Eleven, sitting on the hood of a rusty K-Car sometime in the mid-'90s. That's right about the time when Philip's story with depression started.

He realized it was an issue for him around girls. He just couldn't like the girls who liked him. But it wasn't as if he was only falling for people who were way out of his league.

"I just had an inability to understand why anyone would like me. I resented people who thought I was any good, because I didn't. That also applies to my family. I didn't get along with my family and a lot of it was because even when I was at my meanest, they always insisted that I had potential. I was terrible to anyone who had feelings for me."

Philip dealt with this deep emotional discord the way lots of people do: He popped bottles. The only time he felt happy was when he was drinking. So he drank. A lot. He went to work one morning and someone thanked him for his help the night before. Philip had actually gone into work, helped fix a machine and went home again. He was so drunk that he had no recollection of it.

Along with depression and alcoholism, he struggled with anxiety, too. He was once in his office and started having a panic attack.

"I decided I was going to die. I drove to the hospital and I told them I thought I was having a heart attack. They rushed me in and hooked me up to a lot of electrodes and an hour later they told me that there was absolutely nothing wrong."

After some trial and error, he settled on medications for both depression and anxiety. "I feel kind of numb all the time. Never angry, never happy, never sad, never frustrated. But I'm very functional and it doesn't stop me from loving my kids or loving my wife. For years I felt like taking medicine was a false way of fixing things, like I wasn't truly addressing what the problem was. But I eventually decided that these things were what saved me. When I see a homeless person, I honestly wonder if that's what I would be if I hadn't gotten this treated. I would be in jail or dead or homeless or something."

If there is an upside that comes with mood disorders, it might be that they tend to come with a greater sense of compassion. It changes how you move through the world and how you see the people around you. We see people who are

119

written off as "crazy" and it's not so easy for us to dehumanize them. Some of us feel like we've been two inches away from that. Just one detail—a strong support system, good insurance, an understanding boss—can make all the difference in the world. Yet that closeness to the fringes of society tends to send us back into hiding, intensifying the shame and the fear of rejection. We go silent about our struggles.

Philip called depression a life-ruining experience. "And so many people fix it by just killing themselves. It's so vicious and yet no one talks about it. Including me."

The Problem With the Gorilla

Depression creates a connection between a sad mood and negative thoughts. It creates a negative attention bias—we focus our attention on the bad stuff to the exclusion of all else.[69] This means that for someone who has experienced depression, normal feelings of sadness can trigger majorly negative thinking. It isn't necessarily the events themselves that spiral us into a depression, but it's the way we interpret the events. A minor annoyance (like getting stuck in traffic or dealing with customer service) can feel like a massive problem. Significant setbacks can become entirely debilitating. We believe that whatever happens is going to make us depressed again, and this can ignite thoughts that make a crummy situation even worse. Our reactions to our moods dig us deeper into the pit of depression.

I once saw a video that asked the viewer to count how many times a group of people passed a basketball back and forth. I was convinced I got the right answer. Fifteen! I had won! That was so easy! But then they asked: had I seen the gorilla?[70]

The what?

While I was busy obsessing about counting the passes, a person in a gorilla suit had entered the frame and danced around while everyone else passed the ball around him. I hadn't even noticed it. I had been so hyper-focused on the basketball that I hadn't noticed a freaking gorilla. That's called "selective attention," and that's what happens with depression. It pulls everything into a vortex where sadness eclipses everything else, even if there are a whole bunch of not-sad things happening in world, like a gorilla sauntering around an office building.

We expect critical thinking skills will help us out of the mood, so we try to think our way through our emotions, dissect them and figure out what went wrong. But we end up ruminating, consumed by our thoughts and feeling worse. What could have just been a passing moment of reasonable sadness, disappointment or loneliness becomes a cycle. Instead of just feeling the natural sadness that comes as a consequence of being a human, we decide it shouldn't be that way and we super-size it.

Learning to Deal With the Arrow

There's no need to throw on giant suits of armor in an attempt to protect ourselves from our emotions. Instead, we can sit with the fact that we are sad because there was yet another bombing, or we're disappointed because that challenging work project completely fell apart. We can actually feel those things without trying to numb it so it doesn't hurt. If we don't pile on the feeling that we are sad and weak and we'll always be sad and weak, the legit emotions can eventually pass through.

The Buddha told a story about two arrows. The first arrow comes flying at us out of nowhere, and represents the inevitable pain of the world. Illness, loss, unexpectedly high utility bills. The second arrow we shoot at ourselves as a reaction to our pain, and we cause more suffering as we blame and obsess and let our mind run wild. So maybe we can decide to just deal with that unavoidable first arrow. We can choose to not shoot ourselves with the second one.

Those of us who have had experience with depression have some go-to arrows that are just waiting to take aim. Things like, *no one understands me, I'm stupid, I'm a failure, I'm crazy, I don't matter, I'm a fraud, my life is a mess, it's always going to be like this and it's never going to get any better.* We walk around like Eeyore. The biggest problem with walking around like Eeyore, other than the inherent difficulties of navigating life as a cartoon donkey with a bow on our tail, is that every time we get depressed, the connections that exist in our brains linking our mood, thoughts, body and behavior get stronger.[71] We build up those muscles so that next time, we get depressed even more efficiently. Depression becomes a habit that our mind and body automatically revert back to when challenging issues come up.

It's like when I went back to visit my grandma after having been away for a while. I could only find my way to her house via the George's House of Spuds Food Truck. Since I was a kid, this rusty old truck has been selling soggy, delicious French fries doused in malt vinegar and three pounds of sea salt in the traditional Canadian way. Since that was always where I went first when I visited my grandma, I literally had no idea where to turn to get to her house without going to George's House of Spuds first. That had been my habit for so long.

What if I didn't want fries one day? (Unlikely scenario, but stick with me.)

The French fry truck is depression. Those thoughts and feelings that may have started because of a specific circumstance, or because of something going on in our bodies biologically, become a habit we think we can't break. But that deep-fried French fry grease hasn't been cleaned out since 2007 and it's terrible for me, so it's worth reconsidering its place in my life. Rerouting our moods is rarely as easy as turning left instead of right, of course, but it is possible to carve out a new path — one that allows for the possibility of getting where we want to go without stopping at that greasy, depressing place.

Ridley: When the Person Hurting You is You

"For the most part it's always been razor blades. Well, I think early on it might have been a kitchen knife. But for the most part, it's been razor blades."

I imagine Ridley in his teens — a scrawnier version of the man in front of me — waiting until the kitchen is clear, then searching the drawers for a knife, the right knife, the correct size and weight, to draw along his arm. To carve up his thighs. I can feel the searing cut and my chest gets tight.

While the image is brutal, it's not uncommon, especially for young people between the ages of 15 and 25. Approximately 15% of teens report engaging in self-injury. That number goes up to 35% among college students.[72] Cutting is an incredibly sensitive topic, one that caries crushing amounts of shame. I've interviewed people who talk openly about suicide attempts, sexual dysfunction and substance addiction, but they all start to fidget when the discussion turns to cutting.

"So, what did you find satisfying about it?" I try to tread lightly, but I feel like an elephant in a rose garden. Ridley had rolled up his sleeves to show me his scars. There was clearly shame there, but it was mixed with this endearing eagerness. He presented the thin, raised white lines to me, like finally he recognized another anxiety-prone soul who might understand. It was like grade school show-and tell. Show the scars. Tell the pain.

"I have never been a person who cut on a regular basis. It was only when I was at a breaking point and I couldn't deal anymore. I couldn't go on. I couldn't deal with the everyday pain and couldn't take another step. That's when I would end up doing it. It's never been from a place of suicidal thoughts; the function of it was always to be able to control the pain in some way. I had no control over the circumstances of my life and how I was reacting to the stress and anxiety. I could decide how much or how little physical pain to inflict on myself. And at what time. As stupid as this sounds, I was in control of the pain. Which I'm so often not. I rarely feel like I'm in control of life."

I remember that feeling from when I used to punch bathroom tiles. I couldn't handle looking okay when I felt so broken. The physical pain offered a break from what was going on in my head. It's not something I love remembering, and I felt an itch to change the subject, but I didn't.

"Do you still do it?"

"Did it once a year and a half ago after Emily and I broke up. I was just doing whatever I could to get through every day. I've probably done it once in the last seven or eight years."

"What made you stop?"

"It was probably the self-consciousness of it. Being afraid of people seeing the scars. All my scars are hidden. I did it on my arm, but most of the time I did it on my thighs so it was always covered by shorts or whatever. I was afraid of people knowing. It's why I wear all the bracelets on the one arm, so that it covers the scars."

Ridley has been anxious for as long as he can remember, and his depression intensifies every winter. He's always felt like a loner and has turned to self-medication to cope with everyday life—drugs and alcohol numb him out. He's been on a variety of prescribed medications, most of which work for a little while but don't offer long-term improvement. He started some new meds that make him feel listless and indifferent to his life. "I'm not approaching life from a place of courage," he tells me. "I'm pulling away."

He thinks he's ugly and is dismissive of his girlfriend when she calls him handsome. (Which, unequivocally, he is. When we first met I found myself looking at my feet a lot. I find eye contact challenging under the best of circumstances, and with good-looking dudes it probably seems as if I have some sort of neck injury that prevents me from raising my head.)

I hadn't really considered that men might struggle with body dysmorphia, too. I think about women with eating disorders, exacerbated by tiny pixies with bony hips frolicking on magazine covers. Ridley's frustrated that it's not something people talk about.

"Men have body image issues, too. Every pack of underwear at Target has a guy with a six-pack. It's never a flabby, hairy guy over thirty."

Exercise offers him a healthier form of self-abuse. "I ride my bike until I feel like I'm going to puke, or go to the gym until I feel like my arms are going to fall off. That helps a lot." Ridley's constantly putting himself down, even in his attempts to take care of himself. He put a note on his mirror that said "Go to the gym, fatty." He thinks he should have accomplished certain things in his life; he feels like a failure. He negates his career in higher education, waving away the writing he has published. He's mean—not to others—but he's pretty terrible to himself. He's been mean for so long that it doesn't seem mean anymore; it just seems right.

Self-talk is a problem for most people who struggle with anxiety or depression. And it feels justifiable. When we are in a situation that feels particularly helpless, judging, complaining and narrating the scene makes us at least *feel* like we're in control. We're creating the story, so we must be in control, right? But this constant barrage of judgment actually distracts us and prevents us from accomplishing things. There's actually nothing beneficial about it—as a friend of mine says, "There is no cheese down that tunnel."

When it comes down to it, we're not in control of much of anything, really. Not the stock market or acne flare-ups or other people's behavior. No matter how much we obsess about it, the world just keeps on happening around us. Once you get over how terrifying that is, it's pretty freeing.

We can examine the automatic assumptions that we are unlovable, ugly, useless, stupid, weak—whatever comes up as part of our story about what's happening. When we go into a tailspin of negative self-talk, we can choose to practice "cognitive reprisal" and investigate kindly, with the goal of reframing our perspective. We can get a new view of the situation, which can change everything without changing anything. We can ask questions like:

- Is it really true that I fail at everything? What is the factual evidence for that? Are there examples that contradict that claim? Are there things I haven't failed at? Write those down.

- Okay, so that awkward thing happened in the meeting when I got that information wrong in front of everyone. I'll take a look at that so I'm more prepared next time. But, did anything else happen in the meeting that was not terrible? Can I recognize that even if I'm super well-prepared, sometimes people make mistakes?
- If this were a friend dealing with this issue, how would I feel about them? What would I say to them? Write that down.
- So, if this issue that I'm feeling anxious about is true, then what? Would that be the end of the world for me? Or could I survive it? Could I be more resilient than I think I am?

These questions can help combat catastrophizing — turning molehills into mountains, seeing total disaster where it doesn't exist. I once whined to a friend about how things in my life seemed to be going well but I was still anxious because "what happens when the other shoe drops?" She said, "You'll do what we all do. You pick up the damn shoe and keep going."

Questioning the legitimacy of negative self-talk can bring us back to the reality that we are stronger than we think. Writing down some counter statements is a great idea, as is putting them somewhere you'll come across them regularly.

- I can handle this, it will pass.
- I'm okay the way I am.
- It's okay to make mistakes — everyone does.
- "Life is too important to be taken seriously." - Oscar Wilde

There are so many versions of self-harm: cutting, hair pulling, punching, burning, or just the general emotional shit-kicking that many of us dole out to ourselves on a daily basis. It feels like maybe if we beat someone else to the punch, if we smack ourselves in the face rather than wait for the world to do it, it will hurt less.

Not true.

You deserve to be in your own corner. You don't need to do anything to earn that—it's true simply because you exist. Because you are a person, you deserve a chance not to be kicked when you are down; you deserve the benefit of the doubt that you are trying your best, and you get a second chance, or even a third. I know that is hard to believe, because we've been spending our whole lives being our own tailor-made nemesis. But that doesn't make it okay.

All forms of physical self-harm can be overcome with treatment. If this is something you have been doing, or even considering, please reach out and talk to a professional about it. You don't have to deal with this on your own.

Something to Try: Make it Rain

The acronym RAIN[73] can be great for those early moments of realizing you are engaging in some brutal self-talk. It has four steps:

Recognize what is going on. *Hey, look, I'm freaking out about this thing that happened and I'm saying a whole lot of unhelpful things to myself.*

Allow the experience to be there, just as it is. *It's okay. Glad I noticed what was going on. I am feeling really sad about how this whole thing went down.*

Investigate with kindness. *I wonder what this is about? Can I do something to be a little extra kind to myself right now, since I'm having a hard time? Can I stop piling on all those other emotional things that are not actually part of the sadness I'm feeling in this moment?*

Non-identification with the experience. *This kind of thing happens sometimes. I'm not destined to be sad forever. These mean thoughts I keep thinking about myself are just chatter, not the truth. I don't have to believe them. This too shall pass.*

Chapter 7: Yoga — It's Not Just for Liberals Anymore

I started my journey with yoga when I was thirty years old. That's also when I started using the word "journey." I was in college, still struggling with my status as a non-traditional student and dipping in and out of my terrible dance with depression. But there was a thing called study abroad that combined my two favorite things, traveling and reading books.

During the summer semester of my third year, I went to study at Oxford, the fanciest of fancy institutions in England. Here I was, a former actor with just a GED, and I would be sweeping down the same halls that housed T.S. Eliot, Margaret Thatcher and Lewis Carroll. I would eat in the grand rooms where Oscar Wilde and Stephen Hawking had dined — not together, although that would have been fantastic. My time in those hallowed halls was going to fulfill every pretentious academic fantasy I'd ever had.

Except it was horrible.

I pictured candle-lit gatherings with my classmates, where we'd play gin rummy in the aforementioned grand halls. I didn't factor in the eighteen-year-olds being so psyched that they could legally drink under England's laws that they spent most of the time passed out in ancient rose gardens. I didn't have a single friend; nobody seemed to like me. Once they found out I used to be an actor it seemed I was put behind some sort of plate glass window, to be stared at but not engaged with. Also, since I was a decade older and didn't drink much, I think they all suspected I was some sort of narc. I'd hear a conversation about people going out to a pub that night.

"Cool! Which one?" I'd ask.

"Oh. We're not sure yet." Their eyes would dart around under lowered eyelids.

"Uhhh. We'll come get you."

They never, ever came to get me.

So I'd go to the ramen place by myself or I would eat another egg salad sandwich out of a cellophane package from Woolworth's, alone in my six-foot by ten-foot dorm room. My social anxiety raged and I cried because I would never fit in anywhere.

One day, as I was wandering the streets of Oxford alone, I noticed there was a meditation place just around the corner from the school. I'd been meditating on my own for a couple of years by then. It had such a positive impact on my anxiety, could it help to ease this crushing sense of isolation, too? The center offered a free public class every day at 12:15 p.m. I finished up at Oxford around noon, so if I ran, I could throw my books back in my cell and make it just in time.

Every single day, I climbed the spiral staircase to the meditation room and saw the same faces smiling with silent kindness. I'd tuck into a chair in the back, my legs folded under me, and I'd breathe along with the meditation teacher's gentle guidance. I kept returning my attention to this moment. The sensation of just being me. As painful as that was.

Trying to do this impressive-sounding Oxford thing had been a mega fail, but for that forty-five minutes, I connected to something deeper than rejection and loneliness. The experience reminded me that I'd be okay. It actually reminded me that I was already okay, even when I didn't feel like it. The loneliness wasn't going to kill me.

When the semester was finally over, I went home. I assumed my mood would lift as soon as I cleared customs, but the sadness lingered like a burned grease smell you can't get out of your hair. I had also gained weight. I won't be so cliché as to bash English food, but the vegetarian options weren't great and I had packed on several pounds of buttered potatoes. I had wanted this fancy credential to prove to...someone....that I was smart and educated. All it did was leave me feeling like an outcast with a puffy belly that I tried to hide under an overpriced Oxford sweatshirt.

I shuffled around my house, lamenting the fact that I'd never be able to have this nice, normal, non-Hollywood life that I longed for. I'd always be weird, the one left behind while others laughed and played croquet.

Jeremy dragged me to a neighborhood block party, noting that I needed to put on real pants and get some sunshine. After awkward small talk that made me want to crawl back under my bed, I noticed that my neighbor was wearing a t-shirt featuring a stick figure in a yoga posture.

Yoga was connected to meditation somehow, wasn't it? If meditation had been my lifeline, maybe yoga could help me in a way that would also get rid of these jiggly love-handles.

"Do you do yoga?" I asked, pointing at her shirt.

My neighbor lit up and told me all about a wonderful studio in our town. "It's hot yoga."

"Oh," I said. "No. I'm Canadian. I'm no good in the heat."

"It's pretty amazing," she said.

"Well, I am pretty desperate," I admitted.

The First Class

"I want to go to a yoga class," I announced, flopping on to Louise's couch.

"Interesting. Say more about that." She was such a therapist.

"Well, it's hot yoga so it's sweating in a hot room with a bunch of bendy strangers, even though I'm out of shape and still have issues and pain from when I fractured three vertebrae in my spine eighteen years ago. Actually, now that I say it out loud, it sounds like a terrible idea. Never mind."

It's hard to get away with saying "never mind" in a therapy session, so we devoted the next fifty minutes to discussing the likelihood of me surviving a yoga class. What if I had a panic attack? What if I sucked at it, which I totally would because I couldn't even touch my toes? What if everyone laughed at me?

We decided it was just one class, just ninety minutes, and I never had to go back again if I didn't want to. I had significant doubts, but in the back of my mind I thought maybe the healthier, less miserable version of me was a person who did yoga.

So, I went to my first class.

I hated it.

It was hot and the people there were good at yoga. Yes, they were nice and welcoming and supportive but they were making me do something that was hard. This was no simple little stretching class; it was heart-pounding, sweat-pouring brutal. I wasn't good at it, and doing things I'm not good at makes me want to move to another state and change my name. After class, I thought, *that is for crazy people. No, thank you.* But it said something on the yoga studio website about how you should try three classes before you make a judgment. Not judging something immediately? Who the hell were these people?

Jeremy was on a work trip to California, and he called to check in that evening.

"Hey, how was that yoga class?"

"Horrible. Hated it. Never going back."

I explained that I had spent the day limping around, feeling like a rag someone had left on the bathroom floor of a cheap hotel. I had clearly broken myself.

"I'd like to try yoga," my traitor of a husband said.

He had a hangover. Jeremy grew up in California, so after his meeting he had gone out to a bar with his old friends from high school, and had tried — and failed — to keep up. Now he was suffering. His voice was husky and I could hear him squinting.

"I'm going to be all healthy now," he said. "I want to be one of those healthy people who does yoga."

So all because Jeremy went on an ill-advised bender, he talked me into going back to that sweaty place. And this second time was sort of okay. It was fun to have him there; I could show him how to set up his mat and where the towels were. I felt better knowing what to expect. That class made me want to cry less, and I felt pretty good after.

I noticed the challenges I faced in the yoga room would come, they would peak, and then they would fade. When I was in triangle pose, my body bending at an angle that made me resemble a broken starfish, my mind started going wild. Why was this teacher guy holding us here for an eternity and why did he need to be such a sadistic jerkface? But I stayed and I chose to breathe instead of swearing at him. And then when we came out of the posture, suddenly, it was over. I had lived. That wave hadn't drowned me after all. I felt victorious.

It reminded me of all the emotions we have in the course of a single day. A single hour. They all came and then they all went. Think about all those things in your past you thought you'd never get through. But you did. Your broken heart healed, you got a new job after you got fired, you went to that funeral. That day that was the worst day of your life? You got through that, too. It was hard, but you did it. And you eventually noticed that you could laugh at Paul Rudd movies again. Yoga reminded me that this too shall pass, and I'm a hell of a lot stronger than I think. Whenever I wanted to fight or run away, I learned to face that resistance with breath, instead.

Jeremy loved yoga immediately and a few days later we returned for my third class. It was like the gates opened and there were angels singing. It's not like I had gotten good at yoga. I wasn't flexible or strong or coordinated. I fell down and I often stayed down because I was too exhausted to get up again. But when I walked out of class, there was this internal stillness mixed with personal triumph that felt like a shot of champagne bubbles to my brain.

This was why people came back. They came back *because* it was hard, and the challenge got them out of their heads. And yes, it was a little bit about trying to get Michelle Obama arms, but it was mostly because yoga gave my brain a hug. It didn't matter that I couldn't balance on one foot; my mind got a break, a moment to be still and spacious because I was so incredibly focused. I was more connected and whole than I had ever felt. After class, I was essentially a more sparkly, open version of myself. It was like I was at the eye doctor and someone just clicked the refractor machine lens to a clearer disc.

If I could get peaceful and quiet in the middle of a yoga class, where it was hot and hard and there were lots of sweaty people, maybe I could get peaceful in other places. I could practice doing hard things in the room I knew was safe, then I could take that skill and confidence out into the world. Maybe this wasn't just yoga; maybe it was life training.

Yoga: A Brief History

The word "yoga" is derived from the Sanskrit word *yuj,* meaning to yoke, join, or attach.[74] It's not merely exercise; it's about union, connection and directing one's attention. Some of us are alienated from ourselves, distracted by the chaos of life, unable to self-soothe and be our own champion. Yoga is in the business of reminding us who we really are — it's a search for the truth. When we drop the extraneous drama, the connections become more clear: the union between heart and lungs, body and spirit, muscle and bone, you and your community, you and you. It's about pulling together while expanding outward. It's about grounding down and reaching up. Strength and flexibility. Power and surrender.

Embracing these opposite ideas is really helpful for general life. Both things can be true at once: we can be scared but still brave, strong but still soft, open but still firm with our boundaries. We're evolved; we can hold two ostensibly different ideas simultaneously. It's the fluidity with which we shift between them that allows us to be flexible in the world.

It's not either/or. It's both/and.[75]

The Bhagavad Gita is an ancient yogic text from about the second century BCE.[76] It says that the meaning of yoga is to act as a deliverance from pain and sorrow. Sounds pretty good, right? So does that mean that you need to ditch your belief system and become Hindu to practice yoga? No. Definitely no. Yoga is not a religion. It's a philosophy. Yoga can be practiced with spiritual elements or not. Saying you're bowing to Hindu gods just because you do yoga is like saying you're worshipping Jesus by singing Jingle Bells.

You don't need to have a polytheistic image of the divine, the latest in sticky mat technology or a Sanskrit tattoo on your shoulder. Prefer to worship the Flying Spaghetti Monster while doing yoga in your PJs on a beach towel? Awesome. Welcome to yoga. It's the process of connecting to the stillness at the core of every human being. Once you locate that direct connection, you can use it to create a more authentic, powerful, and awake life.

When you can find that stillness and ease the whirling tornado of the mind, you get to be yourself. You get to be the person you are when you feel the most comfortable in your own skin. You get to be the dancing-in-the-kitchen you. The laughing-at-stupid-puns you. The owning-it-in-those-killer-jeans you. It can be rare to get glimpses of that self, but yoga is a way to see a lot more of that person. Yoga helps us ditch the self-brutalizing, so that person can show up in the rest of life off the mat.

Yoga: The Science Stuff

Admittedly, yoga has a reputation. It can seem a little too trendy and like it's only for pale, super-bendy girls in overpriced stretch pants. But in reality, the practice of yoga was designed for men more than 2,000 years ago, and the goal has never been to show off your asana. A 2016 study shows over 36 million Americans practice yoga; that number is up from 20 million in 2012.[77] It's showing up in public parks, ads for painkillers and in dedicated yoga rooms in many airports.

With increased public interest comes increased funding for studies on yoga's effectiveness for various health issues. One study split participants who suffered from anxiety and/or depression into two groups. One group added in a yoga program, the other continued with their regular treatment for anxiety and/or depression. The yoga group reported an increase in resilience (a super important outcome for people with depression), an increase in positive experiences, and a decrease in the frequency of negative experiences. Participants experienced a significant reduction in overall psychological distress. All this came from doing an average of twelve minutes of yoga a day, on most days, for six weeks.[78]

Another study found that a twice weekly yoga class plus a home practice was enough to reduce the symptoms of major depressive disorder. The key seems to be in targeting the parasympathetic nervous system with the combination of intentional breath work and physical movement.[79]

Yoga also seems to change the brain. When yoga was compared to a metabolically matched walking program, the yoga group had increased GABA levels by 27%.[80] GABA is an amino acid that acts as a neurotransmitter in the central nervous system. It calms nervousness by inhibiting nerve transmission in the brain. Since medications that increase GABA activity are often prescribed for anxiety and low mood, this is a pretty cool thing.

Yoga has also been found to be beneficial for people who are under high levels of stress, like police recruits. After a six-class yoga intervention, trainees experienced significant improvements in perceived stress and mood and reductions in tension, fatigue, and anger.[81] Increasing numbers of schools are implementing yoga programs for their students, in the hope of achieving similar results.

Yoga also seems to offer ways to manage sensory inputs and emotional reactions. People who practice yoga will tell you that it helps them manage the emotional pain of life, but it seems to help with physical pain, as well. Yoga practitioners were able to tolerate pain more than twice as long as a control group.[82] This test group also had the same kind of increased grey matter (the stuff in the central nervous system that helps process information in the brain) that was found in the meditation study from Chapter 4. So it's not just about the benefits derived from yoga-as-exercise; it's the combination of movement, breath, mindful attention and relaxation. Yoga programs are being offered in increasing numbers of hospitals and medical facilities, to help people who suffer from chronic pain. And it seems to be proving what yogis have known for more than two thousand years.

Ariel: Hold On. Pain Ends.

Ariel was an escape artist. She had a loving family and two parents who worked hard to give her everything she needed, and most of the things she wanted. Still, she could never get comfortable in her own skin, so she searched for a way out. When she was four or five years old, she'd drink the beers her dad would set down on the coffee table. By junior high she was drinking every weekend, and she started huffing cleaning supplies, glue and paint—whatever she could get her hands on. At fourteen she realized sex offered another way she could escape herself. She preferred grown-up men to boys—men could buy her alcohol. Those men eventually introduced her to pills, cocaine, and meth.

Ariel was in and out of behavioral health centers for years; when she was nineteen she started dipping in and out of marriages. She'd straighten out for a little while, then fall back into the world of drugs and alcohol.

"I learned how to manufacture methamphetamine. How I lived through this, I'll never know. I saw the most horrible things in the two years this went on. I hated the things I was doing, the people I was doing them with, and mostly, I hated myself."

During another stint in rehab, she met her next husband. They married, had two babies, and she got healthy. But when he relapsed and left, she was alone and turned to alcohol again.

"After having a complete breakdown and ending up in a state mental hospital — which is one of the scariest things I've ever done — I decided to go into another rehabilitation center."

This treatment center had a lot of extras, like yoga, art therapy, meditation, and dialectical behavioral therapy, which is a combination of cognitive behavioral therapy and mindfulness.

"The problem was that I hated myself so much, I didn't think I was worth saving. I was failing as a wife, failing as a parent, and failing as a human. My anxiety was through the roof."

Ariel has a tattoo that says "HOPE," an acronym for Hold On Pain Ends. So, she did whatever she could to hold on through the pain. She went to yoga and art therapy. She started meditating every day, even though she could only sit for two or three minutes at a time.

"I sat and I stayed with whatever happened to me. I was taught that all alcoholics have to learn how to be comfortable in their skin. I wasn't special or unique. That little voice in my head? Everyone has one. It was so uncomfortable, but it also felt good to begin to get healthy again."

After her time in the rehabilitation center, she was still attending yoga classes, but not loving them. She went anyway.

It gave her something "wholesome" to do during the day and it distracted her from her desire to get outside of herself.

"What it did was put me directly inside of myself. Inside of my body. It was moving meditation! For the first time in my life I was able to be in my skin, in my body, with no distraction. I learned how to breathe deeply. I learned how to let go of my thoughts. I learned how to create space in my body by letting go of the years of torture I had put my body through. I learned to invite love and light into that space. I started to grow and to thrive."

Ariel is now sober—and a yoga teacher. She believes that yoga is for everybody because we're all recovering from something. "It doesn't have to be addiction or mental illness. We don't make it into our grown-up years without some sort of trauma, grief, or loss. All yoga is recovery yoga. I teach yoga to help people heal. I always incorporate a few minutes of meditation into my classes. I had to learn how to stay with whatever came up. Until I did that, my yoga practice couldn't grow. The two work together for me."

I met Ariel at the meditation retreat where I had my Lunch Room Epiphany. She was so full of joy and lightness that her story was truly shocking to me. She had gone through such darkness and yet she found a way to course-correct. Ariel's daily practice of yoga and meditation takes her deeper into herself, and further away from the story about her wounds and pain. In times of chaos, she turns to yoga and chooses to create her own peace. She throws herself into a handstand instead of into a bottle of Maker's Mark.

"My body and my mind are both aware of what they need. It's a beautiful place to be. I have so much gratitude for all of it. What matters to me is that I know how to cope with life today."

Something to Try: Here Comes the Sun

Before you tell me you can't do yoga because you're not flexible, let me reassure you that as long as you are breathing, you can do yoga. Yoga is completely modifiable. It meets you wherever you are. Saying you can't do yoga because you're not flexible is like saying you can't eat because you're hungry. Yoga is how you get flexible.

A Sun Salutation is a great place to start as a beginner to yoga, so here are the basic instructions and some photos of me doing the postures to get you started. (Please talk to your doctor before starting a new exercise routine, just to make sure you're good to go.) Just a couple of these Sun Salutations in the morning is a lovely way to wake up.

Sun Salutation A

1. Stand with your feet about hip's width distance apart, your hands at your heart, palms together. Inhale, stand tall, reach up to the sky.

2. Exhale and bring your hands through the midline of your body and fold forward (bend your knees as you go down).

3. Inhale as you lift half-way up with a flat back, bring your hands to your shins or thighs.

4. Exhale to fold all the way down again, bending your knees if the backs of your legs feel tight.

5. Inhale, put your hands on the floor and step your feet back to a plank position.

6. Exhale and drop your knees, lowering yourself into a low push-up (6a). If you want a little more challenge, don't drop the knees as you move into a low push up with your

elbows tucked in close to your body. Make sure you are being kind to your shoulders (6b).

7. Inhale, pulling your chest through and lifting your upper body into a slight back bend, pushing the tops of your feet into the floor. This is called Upward Facing Dog (7a). You can also keep both legs firmly pressed into the floor and just lift your chest a little, which is called Baby Cobra (7b). In either pose, pull your shoulders away from your ears and keep your neck long.

8. Tuck your toes under and lift your hips up with an inhale, into Downward Facing Dog.

9. On a smooth, long exhale, walk your feet to your hands in a forward fold, bending the knees as you approach the front of your mat.

10. Inhale, half-way lift with a flat back, again bringing hands to shins or thighs.

11. Exhale and fold down again.

12. Then inhale and reach all the way up to the sky. You can either lift in a reverse swan-dive with a flat back, or slowly roll up through the spine, imagining each vertebra stacking one on top of the other. When you exhale, release your arms down by your sides. Look! I brought you right back to the beginning because I'm tricky like that. Do the whole thing over three to ten times.

(If the inhale and exhale cues feel a little too fast for you, feel free to slow the whole thing down and take a few breaths in each posture. The cues are just there to get you thinking about coordinating the breath with the movement.)

While a home practice is great, if you have the time and resources, I highly recommend going to a yoga studio. A yoga teacher can offer personalized instruction so you don't injure yourself, and it's great to connect with a community. There are a billion kinds of yoga classes and teachers, so give yourself the chance to experiment and find what works for you.

Chapter 8: The Balance Found Me

"I've seen the light in people that had been hidden
for so long." - Carl Salazar

Carl Salazar is the founder of Expedition Balance, a non-profit organization that offers yoga and meditation retreats for military Veterans with post-traumatic stress disorder. He had read some of my writing and sent me an e-mail responding to a post on my blog about yoga and anxiety. Carl asked if I was interested in joining them to teach a therapeutic writing class and see how the yoga excursions were beneficial for Vets.

It was sort of a random e-mail to get, but after some research to make sure it was not an elaborate yoga-based scheme to kidnap me, I was totally in. Typical yoga retreats are great, but they tend to be a bunch of lithe people traveling to some exotic, tropical locale, drinking coconut water and down-dogging at every picture-perfect sunset. This was different. This was the heart of yoga in action. This was yoga as service.

And where would we be going for this retreat? Should I pack my bikini for the beaches of Costa Rica? Would I need some antibiotics to prepare for back-bending in Bangalore?

Nope.

I booked a flight to a little oil town called Abilene, Texas.

It took me three flights to get to Abilene, and on one of them, it occurred to me that I knew absolutely nothing about the military. Not good. I had been so focused on the yoga and PTSD aspects of the retreat that I had largely overlooked the military part. I didn't even know enough to know how to ask questions.

Where did you go to do your soldiering work?

What...ummm...part did you play in the Marines?

I had stopped watching *Saving Private Ryan* within the first ten minutes because I was crying so hard I couldn't breathe, and therefore I have zero military education. I know that there is the Army and Navy and something about Seals and Green Berets, but all I can think of is sea life wearing sassy little French hats and I'm an idiot. Shit.

Was this my in vivo exposure therapy? Was this me putting myself in a social situation where I was a total outsider so that I could practice managing my anxiety around judgment and rejection? Or was this just a situation in which I was doomed to fail miserably, say something stupid and trigger some military hero's PTSD symptoms?

No one was going to talk to me.

And there was no Wi-Fi.

This was going to be a total waste and a humiliating disaster.

I was consoled by the fact that there would be yoga. Yoga, I knew. And from the e-mail exchanges I had with the guy who ran the program, he liked yoga, so I liked him. Carl was in the Navy for eleven years, and he was deployed in the Persian Gulf during Operation Desert Shield/Storm.

"The time I spent in service was mostly great, and I walked away without any major physical or mental scars. After leaving the Navy, I got married, had kids, got an MBA, and went to work in the 'normal' world. After a long time chasing jobs, I realized I missed doing service."

Carl saw that many other Vets didn't get out so easily. They struggled with their battle wounds. He wanted to help those with "invisible" injuries like PTSD to find balance in their lives.

Post traumatic stress disorder is not easy to remedy. Trauma-focused therapy has been the most common treatment for PTSD, wherein people directly confront their memories and past experiences in order to realize that they're no longer in danger. But this type of work can be incredibly painful, often too painful, and sometimes people aren't willing or able to face the trauma head-on. So they get stuck.[83]

Carl looked around for an organization that was doing what he felt would be the best support for those suffering from PTSD — offering community, mindfulness, yoga and outdoor excursions to Vets. He couldn't find anything like that in Houston, so he created Expedition Balance. It's a small organization, just Carl and a few volunteers; they are totally dependent on donations to keep the programs going.[84] As much as he loves the work and loves sharing the things that are important to him, the organization isn't just about helping others. "It sort of saved my life, too. I wandered without a mission for a long time."

PTSD has gone by many names: shell shock, battle fatigue, soldier's heart. But it finally made its way into the official diagnosis of the American Psychiatric Association in 1980.[85] About one quarter of those who serve in war zones are likely to have major post-traumatic effects,[86] which fall into four categories of symptoms:

- Reliving the event: nightmares and flashbacks
- Avoiding situations that remind you of the event, such as crowds or driving
- Negative changes in beliefs and feelings: relationship problems and feeling that no one can be trusted
- Being jittery or hyper-alert: insomnia, being startled by noises[87]

Through Expedition Balance weekend retreats and community events, Carl has seen that life-affirming, non-clinical experiences with peers in a natural environment is an effective way for Vets to deal with lingering issues. He's seen raw vulnerability transform into profound healing. But not everyone is convinced.

"Sometimes the Vets say to me, 'Sorry Carl, I forgot my tutu, I can't practice yoga today.' But those are mostly the older guys, Vietnam era. The younger ones don't tend to think of it as a girl thing or a hippie thing. But they're all scared of not being good at it. They know there are going to be some things they can't do. They have a hard time with that. They're afraid of their own limitations."

While it helps people with PTSD to talk about what they've experienced, that alone is rarely enough. Someone with a traumatic past can be triggered by almost anything, suddenly feeling as if they are flung back into past danger. So while expressing what happened in the past is good, it's vital that the body and mind learn to come back to the present moment where there is not currently a risk. That's what Carl is trying to facilitate with these trips.

"Who are you?"

Woefully underprepared as I was, I eventually found myself on a three-thousand-acre ranch in central Texas. I walked into the huge house where we'd be staying for the retreat and I was alone. I had arrived early; the rest of the retreat group was delayed. I wandered around the massive, shiny industrial kitchen attached to a great room with various sitting areas and dining tables. I found a long hallway that led to eight bedrooms. I read and reread the directions posted on the bathroom door telling me we were on a septic tank, so no "paper products" may go in the toilet. Does that mean toilet paper, too? What do I do with that? There was a little open trash can — do I put used toilet paper in that? Gross.

My room was covered in Texas stuff, should I momentarily forget what state I was in. A ceramic cowboy boot attempted to contain a dozen American and Texas state flags. Decorative pillows informed me that the stars around here were both big and bright. There was a mural of Texas on the wall and a cross stitch said that there was a special place in heaven for a Texan mother. I was also advised to check my sheets before getting into bed. Because scorpions.

Where the hell was I?

Then I heard something instantly comforting: the scratchy rhythmic tick of a dog's paws on tile. My heart settled. Dogs have long offered salvation for the overwhelmed introvert. Those furry, non-judgmental souls will happily lick our faces regardless of our social ineptitude. I'm the one at the dinner party who is curled up under the table with a canine if at all possible. I looked excitedly out my open door into the hall and saw a pit bull walk halfway past, then snap his head over as he sensed my presence. The dog was wearing a camouflage vest with a sign on it that said "Do not pet me. I'm working." I wondered how necessary that was. Are many people tempted to cuddle a pit bull wearing camo?

"Who are you?"

Another figure had filled my doorway. I took my eyes from the dog and looked up, way up. This dude was about 6'3 and his shoulders seemed to touch both sides of the doorframe. I looked at this giant man and this uniform-wearing pit bull that I wasn't allowed to touch and decided this trip was starting off very poorly.

"Umm. I'm Lisa."

"What are you doing here?"

"Oh, I'm teaching the writing class?" (I'm not sure why I said it like a question.) "I got here early?" (Also not a question.) "I flew into Abilene so I didn't come in the van from Houston with everyone else."

As I scrambled to justify my mere existence, he squinted at me, aggressively sizing me up, and said nothing. I knew I was making a pitiful first impression, so I tried to mirror his posture and make all 5'3" of me look confident and tough. "And who are you?"

"I'm Aryeh," he said flatly. He gestured to the dog, who sniffed the air and stared me down. "This is Bandit."

With that, they were gone. I wanted to flush myself down the toilet and disappear, but I was pretty sure the septic system couldn't handle it.

Because life is strange, after Aryeh's unwelcome welcome, he became my best friend on the trip. But it took a while. I was a civilian. An outsider. I felt it. I didn't have PTSD, so I could never truly understand, but eventually, something shifted. I listened a lot. I didn't ask too many questions. I dropped F-bombs with abandon to let them know I could. Very slowly, Aryeh and the other Vets let me in. They told me their stories.

Aryeh is in his late forties, and he's a twenty-three-year Veteran of both the Army and the Navy. He has one of the kindest hearts I've ever met, but it's wrapped in seven layers of asshole. He's cagey and sardonic but also incredibly thoughtful and he gives exceptionally good hugs. His service dog can sense the change in body chemistry when Aryeh is about to have a PTSD flashback or an episode of anxiety. Bandit helps him focus and get through it. Aryeh has physical problems with his back and knees, in addition to the emotional trauma. He has four different medications on his kitchen counter and was warned that all of them could cause suicidal thoughts, tendencies and actions.

There were eight other Vets on the retreat, from different branches of the military, who were struggling with a variety of physical and emotional scars. One had a heart attack at age 35; many have destroyed knees, shoulders, backs. Another tells me about the injury he got in Iraq—he takes my hand and runs my fingers over the deep scar on his forehead, showing me the place where he should have skull, but doesn't. His traumatic brain injury (TBI) means he has blackouts that last for hours, and when he comes to he has no idea where he is or what he has done. Once he woke up in jail.

Some of the physical pain has obvious roots, but not all; this is common for those who have experienced trauma. It's widely understood that challenging experiences have a negative effect on immune system functioning.[88] Kids with traumatic histories have fifty times the rate of asthma as those who had regular childhoods.[89] It's hard to live in a body that is constantly on alert for threats. It gets worn out, and that shows up in unexpected ways.

I might be 100% civilian, a pacifist vegetarian Canadian who trembled uncontrollably the one time I held a gun, but it eventually became clear that I fit in just fine here. The jokes were plentiful and filthy, and the irreverence delightfully palpable. During yoga classes, many students worry about passing gas, but with the Vets, it became less of a concern and more of a competition. Stories circulated about a disabled friend who got into a fight at a concert and ended up removing his prosthetic leg to beat someone over the head with it. Someone came to a class about the importance of good nutrition with a super-sized bag of gummy bears to pass around. In quieter moments, they talked about their time in service:

"We were in the middle of nowhere and we ran out of supplies, so we were pretty much starving. I lost fifty pounds."

"I was raped by another soldier."

"You can lose a lot of buddies if you can't pull the trigger."

"A tribal leader got executed. We thought we should take him back to his village, so we dragged this body ten miles through the mountains."

"I'm so embarrassed to admit it, but I wanted to end my life."

"After active duty, I went to work at the VA. You'd be amazed at how many people walk in there to kill themselves. And the VA is good: You'll hear about it on the eighth floor and by the time you get down to the second floor to check it out, the blood will be cleaned up, the bullet hole in the wall patched and painted."

Veterans Affairs reports that twenty Vets commit suicide each day.[90] *Each day.* While that number is helpful to make this crisis tangible, it needs to be said that some people I talked with don't love this stat. The number comes from the death records from only twenty-one states, so they don't feel it's truly representative of the situation. This brings us back to the problem with studies and statistics: they can give us an indication of what's going on, but they're never the full picture.

But the numbers do tell us that our Veterans need more support when they come home, for both PTSD and moral injury—the inner conflict that comes from doing things that may have violated a person's core ethical and moral beliefs. In a high-stakes situation when someone else holds legitimate authority, morality can get incredibly complicated, causing feelings of guilt and shame. As with all issues of shame, what helps is community.[91]

And this is why we have come here—to heal through connection. Focusing on a shared history of trauma helps with the horrible feelings of isolation and loneliness that come with PTSD.[92] Replaying the experiences creates a bond that alleviates the suffering to some extent but physicality plays an important role, too. Since trauma imprints on both the mind and body, it makes sense that effective treatment would involve both. We hold our issues in our tissues.

In pretty much every culture, for as long as people have felt the need to express themselves, dancing, singing and movement have been part of bonding, healing and transforming anger. Dancing was a part of the Truth and Reconciliation court proceedings after the deadly oppression of apartheid in South Africa: Nelson Mandela danced at the presentation of the summary report.[93] Indigenous societies in Canada overwhelmingly choose to include practices of dance in their community-based healing programs.[94] Movement therapy is now used in hospitals, prisons, mental health clinics, women's shelters, and special needs schools.[95] This kind of body engagement can encourage health and promote social and emotional functioning in all kinds of different communities.[96] So moving together was part of what we did in Texas. There wasn't much dancing, but we moved by hiking, horseback riding, and practicing yoga.

Every morning, we went outside and set up our yoga mats in a circle. Blocks, straps and blankets were nearby to help make postures more accessible to everyone. We were all still sleepy with stiff muscles and a severe lack of caffeine, but we put our bodies into yoga postures. We focused on the breath and worked on yielding to the stillness of the posture. Stillness can be challenging for everyone, but many Vets have an especially hard time because they need to move to feel safe. But Carl reassures them, "Pay attention to how much stillness moves. How much our breath causes movement in our bodies, the rising and falling of the chest, the motion in our bellies."

At the end of class we rested in *savasana,* the relaxation period at the end of a yoga class that looks like a group nap time. My friends really rested. They looked like they were finally unguarded, melting into their mats and letting go. I listened to them take slow, deep, belly breaths, and matched my breathing to theirs.

The mindfulness/meditation thing was a pretty soft sell throughout the weekend. Carl didn't want to spook anyone by shoving it down their throats. There was already some resistance about "Buddhist stuff" and how that fits in with personal faith. Carl reassured everyone that this had nothing to do with religion. No one was being asked to buy into anything. We were just talking about a scientifically proven method of dealing with stress. When we did eventually sit down for a talk about mindfulness, Carl made it clear that it was about waking up to our day-to-day choices, not just sitting on the floor doing some breathing exercises.

"When you feel like a victim, you give up your power. Everyone has the power to make choices. Getting mad is a choice," Carl told us. "Our brains are trainable, thanks to neuroplasticity. That's great news because it means you're not stuck with what you've got. Your brain is still growing. And yes, it's hard work, but it can make things better."

One afternoon, the Vets all gathered in front of the fireplace, but this time it was to listen to me. I was nervous, but I had gotten more comfortable with this crew, so I wasn't in a state of removing-my-toenails panic. I was supposed to stand at the front of the room and give my presentation, but instead I settled in on the floor with everyone, my feet curled up underneath me. I talked about the fact that I didn't have PTSD, and I was not comparing my struggles to theirs. But I did have some demons. I discussed my experience with the catharsis of writing and the ways that words had helped me come to terms with those demons. Writing was how I externalized the things that haunted me and found some peace. Writing was where I could pin down that voice in my head that was constantly chattering, and I could see it for who it really was: a scared little kid with no rational grasp on what was real and true.

I sent the Vets off on their own to write, about anything, for fifteen minutes. They didn't need to write about their darkest days; they could have written a shopping list. All I asked was that they withheld judgement, no editing or worrying about spelling and grammar. They just needed to dump the words out onto the page. After fifteen minutes, many of them were still buried in their notebooks, scribbling a few final thoughts. When we came back together, I asked them about the process of writing and how it felt to express themselves that way. No one was required to share what they wrote, but many of them wanted to read their work.

No one had written a shopping list.

They wrote about the many ways they felt empty and lost, uncertain about how to be a civilian again. They wrote about the ways their parents hadn't supported them, their friends had died in front of them. They purged the words from their hearts and sent them out in the world, hoping that someone might understand. They read and we cried and hugged each other. We acknowledged that there is your family of origin and the family you choose. We created a family and felt less alone because we knew we'd have a hand to hold when we needed it.

Nate: Jenga and PTSD Flashbacks

Methods that often work for regular depression and anxiety can fall short for Veterans. Cognitive behavioral therapy doesn't work as reliably for them as it does with the civilian population. Only about one in three combat Vets see any improvement in PTSD symptoms from CBT, and many end up dropping out of therapy programs because of adverse reactions.[97]

What appears to work is community. Social support isn't just a warm fuzzy feeling—it's a biological necessity and the starting point for treatment. Community acts as a way to integrate the past event into your life, transforming it from a continual, lingering threat into a memory of something that is part of your history. That happens more easily when you know you are not alone.[98]

Loneliness is piercing for a lot of Vets. Aryeh told me about a cartoon he saw of a soldier in combat gear in the desert thinking, "I just want to go back." In the next frame, that same guy in jeans on his couch was thinking, "I just want to go back." Vets often miss the sense of community, of brother/ sisterhood, of service and excitement. It can be hard to come home.

Nate wanted to go back. At twenty-nine, he was having a hard time adjusting to life as a civilian. He enlisted in the Army at age seventeen, choosing to get his GED instead of finishing high school. His friend lost a parent in the attack on the Pentagon on 9/11 and Nate wanted to do something. He was deployed to Afghanistan in 2006, then later to Iraq. Just a few of his injuries include several hernias, a broken ankle, and significant hearing loss. He had to jump into a trench during a fight, and although he sustained serious injuries, he had to wait two weeks until it was safe enough to get medevacked out. In 2008, he retired with a 100% disability allotment. He put my hand on his shoulder to show me how it loudly pops out of the socket from years of carrying so much gear.

Nate told stories I couldn't even understand. Literally. About 25% of the words he used were unknown to me; he talked about the VFW, DD214, IEDs, the Korengal Valley, and told jokes about the Air Force that I didn't get. He talked about walking five thousand miles in five months. Nate was most animated when he told stories filled with death and trauma. This is common with PTSD. The events that caused so much pain also take on an enormous amount of meaning, and people often feel fully alive only when recreating the past.[99]

Even though it seemed like Nate and I spoke different languages, somehow we bonded. Nate was stationed in Italy for a while, so we talked about Rome. I filmed a mini-series there and for several months I lived around the corner from his favorite church, which was one of my favorites, too. It was decorated with the bones of more than three thousand church friars, their skulls and femurs arranged in elaborate patterns that were more exquisite than macabre.

One morning, while brushing away the tiny red ants crawling on his yoga mat, Nate said, "You know the thing about fire ants, right? They're not native to Texas. They were accidentally imported from South America." When someone made a joke about pirates: "You know the thing about pirates, right? They wear that patch over one eye so that when they go down into the dark hull, one eye will be adjusted to the low light conditions."

Nate knows the thing about everything. He can also cook, draw and play every instrument that exists. It seems the only thing he can't do is golf, but he's working on it. Even with all that knowledge, talent and the mop of adorably cow-licked dirty-blond hair, he called himself a broken shell. Going back to college after service was hard for him; he struggled with writing papers. He dropped out, frustrated by his inability to concentrate. Many Vets return to college post-service on the GI Bill, but it's estimated that over 80% drop out.[100] When Nate came to Expedition Balance, he felt like his life was falling apart. One morning he couldn't get out of bed until late in the afternoon. When he finally joined us and shuffled into the living room, he was pale and quiet.

Nate tried anti-depressants but they left him in a fog, numb and unable to function. Research backs him up on this. While studies have shown some modest improvement for combat Vets on medications, most have not benefited at all.[101] It seems they just don't respond very well to meds, while traumatized civilians fare slightly better. And yet, over the last decade, the Departments of Defense and Veterans Affairs combined spent over $4.5 billion on antidepressants, antipsychotics, and anti-anxiety drugs. Approximately 213,000 people (20% of the 1.1 million active-duty troops surveyed) were found to be taking some form of psychotropic drug: antidepressants, antipsychotics, sedative hypnotics, or other controlled substances.[102]

I asked Nate if there was anything that did make him feel better. He said fishing helps, he finds that very peaceful. Marijuana helps, too. He wasn't the only Vet to tell me this. Someone else said his anxiety is so intense that every morning, as soon as he wakes up, he immediately starts vomiting. The only thing that stops it is cannabis. "I'm getting fond of plants," someone else said, quietly. This was definitely not part of the ExBal program, but the topic kept coming up.

Nate said, "When I got out of the military, I was anti-weed. I thought it was the devil. But I went to the VA and they gave me prescription after prescription. I didn't like feeling like a zombie and not having control of myself. And then if you forget to take the medication, it all comes back full force. I had no support system, so I wanted to take all of the pills, if you know what I mean."

I knew what he meant. The U.S. Department of Veterans Affairs now acknowledges that they overprescribed pills and created a large population of addicted Veterans — a complicated and sometimes fatal situation.[103] In 2013, the VA curtailed prescribing practices and many Veterans started buying pain pills, or the cheaper versions, heroin and fentanyl, illegally. The VA is now working to increase its rehabilitation programs and using alternatives to painkillers, such as acupuncture. Some Vets are turning to cannabis to get off the pills and manage the symptoms of their trauma. This comes even with the blessing of some medical professionals — one woman told me that every time she had an appointment, her doctor asked if she had tried cannabis yet. Several other Vets chimed in that they had similar encouragement from their doctors. In fact, the Drug Enforcement Administration recently okayed a study on the effect of medical marijuana on post-traumatic stress disorder.[104] The study will include seventy-six Veterans who have treatment-resistant PTSD. But to say this is a controversial topic is an understatement.

One evening, Nate and I were sitting on the couch talking while everyone else was devouring leftover snickerdoodles and playing Jenga. It had been a long day, and we were all tired from being out in the Texas sun. Nate and I were ranking our favorite documentaries when across the room, Jenga did what Jenga does. The wood pieces clattered loudly to the tabletop. Nate startled and jumped. His eyes darted around the room and then glazed over. He said something I didn't understand. He shivered. He panted. His face turned crimson. He looked as if he had suddenly found himself in the Korengal Valley.

If we could have opened up Nate's brain at that moment, we would have seen his Amy the Amygdala lit up like a Christmas tree. Amy was not making the distinction between the mountains of Afghanistan and this ranch in Texas.[105] She was telling Nate that he was in terrible danger; Jenga pieces had become rocket propelled grenades. Nate's stress hormone system was completely failing him. Instead of quickly realizing that the crash was just someone losing at Jenga, the panic lingered, his body trying to defend against a threat that was no longer there. This is the precise definition of traumatic stress: the inability to live fully in the present moment.

I had gotten paperwork about this. Before the retreat, Carl had sent me some information on how to assist someone during a PTSD flashback. I tried to make eye contact with Nate and encouraged him to take a deep, slow breath. I gave him space, and then I totally did it wrong. I put my arm around him. I should have asked permission first, but it was almost automatic, and as my hand touched his back I knew there was a strong possibility I'd get punched in the face. But I didn't. He started breathing again. When he came back to himself, when the glaze melted from his eyes, he said "Yeah, that's a thing that happens."

And then told me I really needed to watch *Restrepo*.

Saying Goodbye

Throughout the retreat, I watched new friendships form. People were opening up to each other, relaxing and letting their guards down. One Vet said she didn't have a family, until now. Another Vet's wife said that because of these retreats, she'd finally gotten her husband back from war.

Over breakfast the day we were leaving, Nate shrugged and said he didn't think that yoga was going to be his thing.

"That's okay," I said. "It's not a mandate."

"I mean, the yoga was fine, I guess. I definitely felt relaxed. Just not my thing." He said in general the weekend was pretty good. It was very different than the other Veterans' events he had attended.

"What were those like?" I asked.

"We pretty much just sat around and got drunk."

We packed our stuff and the Vets loaded up the van. Everyone else was driving back to Houston while I was flying out of Abilene. Carl gathered everyone up and said, "We gotta go. Let's love on Lisa."

They lined up with military precision and each gave me a hug. I cried harder and harder with each one. I tried to say things that were encouraging but nothing felt sufficient to express my love and gratitude for being allowed into this community.

It felt like the end of a film shoot. We had this intense experience and now everyone was going their separate ways. They were leaving, leaving me, and who knew when we'd see each other again? It was a repeat of this painfully heart-wrenching feeling that was so pervasive in my childhood. A feeling of deep connection followed by decimating loss.

I threw my arms around Nate and made him promise to keep in touch. I made him promise to keep writing and drawing and cooking and telling everyone the thing about pirates. I wanted to make him promise to stay in the world [106]

Aryeh loitered, waiting to say goodbye last. I couldn't reach up tall enough to put my arms around his shoulders, so I went for the waist. Somehow we had gotten past our rocky beginning and now I had a hard time letting go of him. As we walked to the van, Aryeh took something off his wrist and put it on mine. It was a black metal cuff, engraved with a name, K-I-A, Somalia, and an American flag.

"Wait, what is this?" I asked him.

"You know *Black Hawk Down*?"

I nodded. As it happened, my ex-boyfriend had been an assistant director on that movie. I had never been able to watch it. I looked down at the bracelet that was four times too big for my wrist. I rubbed my finger over the engraved name.

"So, this is a friend of yours?"

"Was. He was a friend of mine."

I finally understood: It was a memorial bracelet.

"Aryeh. You can't give this to me. You can't."

"Too late, ma'am. Already did."

Aryeh called for Bandit and they got in the van and left. I stood alone in the kitchen again, but this time I knew I belonged. This was my tribe. And even though they were driving away, they were deeply embedded in my heart.

Having a good support system is the single-most important factor in determining whether or not you suffer from lingering trauma.[107] In the aftermath of World War II, children who stayed in London with their parents, suffering through nightly bombings, were less traumatized than those who were sent away to the peaceful English countryside.[108] A lack of support has been shown to be twice as reliable at predicting the likelihood of PTSD as the severity of the experience.[109]

Suffering is the one great equalizer. We suffer from different traumas, of varying intensities, but in the process of being alive we all experience suffering. Belonging is how we survive and how we thrive. I feel that as I sit here, writing this, looking down at the memorial bracelet on my wrist. We're one big platoon that has been placed on this planet together. Let's not leave anyone behind.

Jane: EMDR for Trauma

Trauma and PTSD can come from many sources other than combat. Illness, an accident or assault, a difficult childbirth or even witnessing someone else's trauma can cause a lasting impact. Many are turning to alternative treatments to help them cope. A survey of 225 people who had escaped from the Twin Towers before they fell on September 11th, asked what had helped them to deal with the repercussions of their trauma. They said acupuncture, massage, yoga, and EMDR, in that order.[110] I was familiar with—and have tried—the first three, but I didn't even know what EMDR stood for. I needed talk to someone who had done it.

Jane is in her early 30s. She's a writer with a pixie haircut and a retro vibe. She speaks softly, with carefully chosen words.

"The rape happened with someone I knew casually, so afterwards I had a lot of trust issues with myself. I clearly trusted the wrong person, so how could I trust myself now? So there was a lot of anxiety about that, even in my committed relationship, because if I can't trust myself, how can I trust the person I've trusted?"

Seven years after the attack, Jane was still confronted with endless feelings of anxiety and rage. She had always felt she needed to deal with it all on her own, but when she started having ideations about harming herself, she decided to get help. Her doctor offered her the names of several therapists. For various reasons, the first therapist was not the right fit for her, but Jane had a friend who had done EMDR (which stands for Eye Movement Desensitization and Reprocessing), a therapy based in bilateral stimulation of the body that can help change the reactions to memories of trauma. One of the therapists her doctor suggested specialized in EMDR, and Jane went to see her.

"There was a little talk therapy in the beginning. She met my husband because she wants to know all about your support system. I gave her the background of everything that had happened in the past seven years. We first used the headset, which uses a tone in each ear, I think they might be different tones, and it alternates. The alternating is important to get the bilateral stimulation of the body. I had the option of using the headphones or these little vibrating pads that you hold in your hands."

Bilateral stimulation can also be done by simply tapping your fingers on your body at different pressure points, or by moving the eyes from side to side, like a cartoon character trying to hypnotize someone with a pocket watch.

I get it. It sounds ludicrous. But stick with me here. A study in the Journal of Clinical Psychiatry stated that brief EMDR treatments produce substantial reduction of PTSD symptoms and depression.[111] And those benefits seem to last long beyond the treatment sessions. Some police officers now use EMDR to deal with the graphic and traumatic experiences they encounter on the job.[112] While there are different theories about why EMDR works (which means that no one really understands it and some say it doesn't actually work at all), it seems that the bilateral stimulation helps the brain's two hemispheres sync up, and when we can access different areas of the brain, we can release old, unhelpful patterns and think about something a different way.

Another theory is that the back-and-forth movement of the eyes is similar to what happens during Rapid Eye Movement (REM) sleep. People suffering from PSTD tend to spend very little time in that restorative phase and increasing the amount of time spent in REM reduces depression. EMDR seems to give people access to loosely associated memories and images from their past. It then becomes easier to heal and move on because those memories are placed in the proper perspective: the past.

"If you had an attack or rape and you were not able to fight, you are stuck in that response zone. It's hard to break out of that anxious moment and it can occur in other kinds of moments. Your brain is stuck on repeat. For me, I was stuck on freeze." Jane's Amy the Amygdala went through her options the evening of the rape. Fight wasn't working. Flight wasn't possible. So she did the only thing she could. She froze.

Jane's initial therapy visits were focused on getting her more comfortable, then they moved to the deeper stuff. EMDR is an active therapy; you have to be ready to work, which was appealing to Jane's Type-A personality. She was ready to deal with this issue and feel productive. She felt it was time; it had been seven years.

"There was this great article I read about how there is a seven-year cycle with skin cells. So, seven years in, that bastard has not touched my body, I have a whole new body. New skin cells and everything."

Jane told her therapist that she was ready to do the work and wanted it over with. She wanted to be done. And in the softest, most gentle voice, her therapist said, "Let's just get it the fuck over with."

Jane thought, "Yes, that's how I feel. It's been seven fucking years, I want him out of my head and my emotions and my nervous system. I want him out."

The therapist asked her to stand and hold the vibrating pads in her hands as she reenacted the rape in her head. In her mind, she punched him and kicked him and did what she had been wanting to do for years. She got to finally fight back against this person who wasn't listening to her words, who ignored her as she told him "no." All the while, she was holding the pads in her hands.

Suddenly, she was crying. She couldn't stop crying.

"I felt this rush through my vocal cords and my therapist said 'Jane, why are you crying? What do you need to do? What do you need to say?' and I said 'Help me. I need to ask for help.'"

She needed help. But it never occurred to her that she could ask for help. Not when she was being violently raped and there were three other people in her house at the time. It was almost impossible for her to ask for help seven years later, when she was thinking about hurting herself because someone else committed a felony with her body.

"That was my big breakthrough with EMDR. It hadn't occurred to me that I wasn't the only one who could have saved myself. It hadn't occurred to me that anyone else could save me or that it was anyone else's responsibility to save me. I thought it was all on my shoulders—me alone—and that's how it had to be. When clearly, that's not how it has to be. That's what therapists are for, that's what friends are for. So, yeah, that was awesome."

Jane did a total of seven sessions of EMDR. She plans to go back to it, when finances allow. When I ask her why it worked, why these strange-sounding exercises help with emotional healing, she admitted she doesn't really know. She didn't have any distinct sensation at the time while wearing the headphones or holding the pads, but afterwards she noticed a definite emotional shift.

"There is less of an urgency surrounding the memory because I don't feel a current threat, and I definitely used to. I am out of that constant loop."

She also became more self-aware, and she's more vocal about communicating her needs and asking for help. "I think the world would be such a better place if people would communicate more. Just being able to recognize in myself a resistance to asking for help, helped me get in tune with that. I don't know how it worked, but it worked for me."

EMDR did what it claims to do, which is help people put their trauma in the rear-view mirror. It's not about pretending it didn't happen, but rather about realizing that the events of the past don't define you. You are right here. Right now. And you have choices.

Something to Try: Put it Down

I teach a memoir writing class, and my students unfailingly want to write about their most difficult moments. The suicide of a parent, a miscarriage, the abuse they suffered in childhood, their struggles with addiction. We cry together in my classes, but afterwards, everyone feels lighter. When we write the story down, we set it down. We can move on.

Writing about both the facts and the emotional impacts of a traumatic event can be incredibly healing.[113] Writing has been found to strengthen the immune system and actually improves issues like asthma and rheumatoid arthritis. It can lessen the symptoms of depression and result in a 50% drop in doctor visits.[114]

When giving my students prompts for writing, I like to tell the story of the two wolves—you might have heard it before. There is a Native American tale that tells of a fight going on inside each one of us. It's a fight between two wolves. One wolf represents greed, guilt, resentment, ego, envy, vengefulness and anger. The other wolf is all about joy, love, kindness, hope, empathy, truth and peace. So which wolf is going to win this brutal battle for our souls? Simple. It's the one we feed.

I love that story. But with an awareness of the amount of hubris it takes to amend a Native American fable, I'll beg your forgiveness and then do just that. Because that can't be the end of the story.

Okay, so you are feeding the peaceful wolf, but you still have a pissed off, dark wolf on your hands. Oh, and by the way, now he's starving. He's lurking in the background, becoming even more disruptive because he's being shunned while watching his brother, the peaceful wolf, enjoying his Puppy Chow. You still need to deal with that other wolf somehow.

So, I agree, I won't feed him. What I will do instead is honor him by writing about him. That's how I pay my respects. We need to acknowledge the worst in ourselves because that is still part of our divine make-up. It's a vital part of the lesson plan for How to Live with Yourself 101. We don't indulge that wolf or obsess about him and slip him leftovers under the table, but we don't chase him into the night with a flaming stick, either. That just makes him stronger and more likely to turn around and bite our faces off.

I acknowledge the presence of the dark wolf and pay attention with kindness. I write about him with courage and honesty because he's not actually evil. He's scared. He's lonely. He's uncertain. When that wolf isn't banished, he is heard. He's transformed. When he doesn't feel threatened, he'll lie down at your feet and give you a break.

Set a timer and write for fifteen minutes. You can write about whatever you want—it's totally up to you. But spend a little time thinking about these two wolves, and consider writing about them. You can write about your peaceful wolf, or your less peaceful wolf, or about how they interact with each other. This writing is just for you, you never need to show it to anyone. Feel free to write the truest things you can think of, even when they're ugly. It doesn't matter if you think you are a terrible writer and you can't remember the difference between there, their, and they're. When you are done, read it through and then you can burn it or rip it up or keep it in a little box under your bed with the lost socks. If you have a trusted person, and you want to share it, that's cool, too. The opportunity to build emotional connections though writing is one of my favorite things about putting words on paper.

But whatever you chose to do with your work, you'll feed that joyful wolf, and the scared wolf will take his place, submissive, at your side, where you can reach down and scratch his ears once in a while.

* If you have another form of creativity that feels better to you, do it. Paint about your wolf. Dance about him. Woodwork about him. Knit about him. Just make some sort of art and honor that puppy.

Chapter 9: One of These Things Just Doesn't Belong

As a child, I didn't spend much time in a classroom — unless you count trailers/dimly lit offices on various film sets, which most people don't. What existed of my formal education was mostly me flipping through a textbook for twenty minutes during lighting set ups for the next shot. So when I retired from my acting career, finally got my GED, and found myself in a real-life college classroom at the age of twenty-nine, what I wanted was to simply sit quietly and learn everything that I could cram into my formal-education-starved-brain.

What other people wanted me to do was interact. Like, with other people. Professors at the University of Virginia were fond of making their way through the lengthy attendance list and calling on people randomly: "Lisa? Can you explain the difference between the distribution of a population and the sampling distribution of a statistic?"

Lisa would freeze. Lisa would possibly cobble together some words that didn't make any sense when they were in that order. Several times I just sat there, paralyzed and unable to say anything. Tears filled my eyes and I just shook my head violently until the professor took pity on me and moved on to another victim.

UVA was brimming with students who had dominated high school. Most of my classmates were on the traditional path. They could have been carbon copies of one another, and I mean that as a compliment. Their parents had paid their tuition and bought them the prerequisite pastel polo shirts and black North Face jackets. These kids had actually gone to high school. They had academic awards. They knew about MLA style parenthetical citations and how to do keg stands. All I knew was how to cry on cue and do an Eastern European accent.

I was the weird one, the one who would have stood out in a classic game of One Of These Things Is Not Like The Others. THAT ONE! I imagined people would yell, THAT ONE WHO USED TO BE AN ACTOR AND IS TEN YEARS OLDER THAN EVERYONE ELSE AND SEEMS UNABLE TO RESPOND TO A SIMPLE QUESTION! THAT WEIRD, AWKWARD, ANXIOUS ONE WHO NEVER GRADUATED FROM HIGH SCHOOL! SHE IS THE ONE WHO DOESN'T BELONG! HER!

Trying to cope in this ocean of normalcy meant one thing: I spent my mornings in intense intestinal distress. I'd got to school an hour early, because being late made me even more anxious. And then I'd hang out in the bathroom and ride out a panic attack, doubled over with piercing stomach cramps, bracing myself on the cool grey walls while I hyperventilated until I was dizzy and occasionally vomited.

I always chose the bathroom in the library, because at least I got to walk through a library. Seeing all those books provided a little glimmer of happiness to my morning. As I passed through the main hall, I saw other students chatting with each other and sipping soy lattes. They could do this. They could chat in the library, while I only used it as a pass-through to the Puke Place. Maybe they got a little nervous before a final exam, but most of them seemed to have no problem keeping their English muffins down. They had actual friends and some of them were even laughing, for God's sake. Laughing.

One day, I had just made it to the stall closest to the window, my personal favorite because it had better light and a little more elbow room. I was there so frequently that it had started to feel like my office. As per usual, my hands went numb. I hyperventilated and got tunnel vision. I could feel the blood draining from my face and I had to lean against the wall to stay upright. My heart was pounding and I was both hot and shivering. I threw up.

As I stood up from my customary kneel, I hitched up my jeans that had gotten uncomfortably loose since I was not keeping much food in me, and that's when my iPod jumped out of my front pocket and into the toilet.

My iPod. My only friend. His headphones signaled others to leave me alone. He played calming music with titles like "Women's Karmic Spa," the music I most needed to hear as went into battle with Introduction to Italian. And there he was, my sweet iPod, sinking to the bottom of the puke-filled toilet. I stood there for a moment, staring into the bowl. That iPod was getting me through my days. So I went in.

It was pointless to plunge my hand into the toilet. My iPod was already ruined. But life in general was feeling pretty pointless by then. Everything was broken. Every day I felt like I was fishing around in vomit for something that would never work again. But the fact that I went in, the fact that I was still trying, was oddly encouraging.

At that moment—up to my elbow in a toilet in the library —I realized this was all getting a little beyond me. I felt like I did the night I ran to my neighbors' house in my socks. I needed help again.

My Introduction to CBT

As I sat on the crinkly paper of the exam table, the nurse breezed in and flipped open my chart.

"So, what brings you here today?"

She was sturdy and no-nonsense with just a hint of softness, so you knew you could confess any humiliation and she wouldn't make a horrified face. I knew her from previous medical visits; she had given me a variety of shots before my trip to South Africa and had nodded sympathetically when I couldn't shake that phlegmy cough over Christmas. How could I explain what had brought me here now? How could I put into words the crushing darkness that had coated my life? I wasn't even sure what I wanted, other than to lay myself at someone else's feet. I was waving a white flag of surrender and hoping for mercy.

I considered telling her about diving into the library's vomit bowl, but those were details I hadn't even told Jeremy. We had only been married a year, and I was still attempting to be sexy and mysterious for him. There was nothing sexy nor mysterious about that particular truth. My new label of *wife* didn't seem nearly as alluring as *fiancée* had been, and on top of it, I was a wife who was a weeping pile of anxiety, paralyzed by philosophy homework, incapable of making the simplest decision about what t-shirt to wear. I didn't want to appear even less desirable by putting the iPuke image in his head. So I told him I ruined my iPod by accidentally dropping it in the sink while the tap was running and then quickly realized that lying about my anxiety was a really bad sign.

"I'm stressed," I told the nurse. As the words tumbled from my mouth, I wondered how they could be simultaneously accurate yet entirely inadequate.

She nodded at me again and jotted down some notes. She prepared to take my blood pressure, the cuff doubled over my scrawny arm.

"You've always got such nice low blood pressure," she preemptively praised me as she pumped air into the cuff. It's true. It's a family thing, on my dad's side. We've all got the blood pressure of a recent corpse. The nurse's eyes got wider as she noted the numbers skyrocketing.

"Oh. Oh my. Your pressure is quite high today, actually."

"Yeah, that's why I'm here!" I accidentally yelled. "I'm stressed."

She smiled one of those smiles they must teach you in nursing school, the smile that means you are being an asshole of a patient but they will care for you anyway because they are better people than you.

She patted my hand. "The doctor will be here in a moment, honey."

As soon as he opened the door, saying, "Lisa, how are you today?" I started crying.

"I'm not okay. I need help. My stomach hurts and I just want to sleep all the time. My panic attacks are bad. Really bad."

Dr. Z is too attractive to be a doctor, but they let him be one anyway. If I had known he was that good looking when my insurance company included his name on a list of doctors who accepted my plan, I would have skipped down to the next name. It's easier to talk about your rash with someone whose cheekbones are not quite so chiseled. Still, he was my doctor and he seemed to know what he was talking about, so I managed to get past his perfectly coiffed hair and confess what had been going on. He handed me one of those cheap, scratchy tissues.

"Well, we just did a physical for you recently and everything with your blood work looked good. Have you had issues with this sort of thing before?"

I nodded. "I've had panic attacks and anxiety since I was a kid. I've dabbled in depression." For some unknown reason I made depression sound like some sort hobby, like painting watercolors.

"I had a therapist back when I was in my late teens after my parents split, but then I moved and I haven't seen anyone since. I've been dealing with it on my own, but I just can't anymore. I'm really anxious, or depressed, or both—I don't even know."

I rambled on about college and my favorite stall for my panic attacks. We talked about lifestyle stuff, diet, sleep habits and exercise. Those were all pretty much garbage for me at the time, and I promised to try improving them.

"In the right circumstances, there is the medication option. At least in the short term, we can see if it gets you to a better spot. I'm going to write you a prescription for a beta blocker that should help with the panic attack symptoms. If you want to try that, you can just take it as needed. But I also think you should look into CBT. Do you know what that is?"

I shook my head and my tears fell, seeping into the exam table paper and creating tiny, wrinkly lakes of suffering.

"My personal belief is that there is not a person on the planet who wouldn't benefit from counseling. Cognitive behavioral therapy helps you to identify inaccurate or negative thinking so that you can respond in a more healthy way. You'll work on identifying the relationship between thoughts, feelings and behaviors. It's very effective for anxiety and depression."

"Yeah. Okay." I'm not sure that I could actually hear him over my weepy hiccups, but I caught the words *healthy* and *effective* and I was in.

He wrote down a phone number for me.

"I'll give Louise a heads-up and tell her to expect your call. But you should know something, in the interest of transparency. This CBT therapist is my sister. But that's not why I'm recommending her to you. Louise is the only person in town who is doing CBT for anxiety, and studies are showing it to be the most effective treatment. I just don't want it to seem unethical that I'm referring you to a family member."

I wanted to tell him that I had no problem with that, and that if his "sister" just turned out to be him in a wig and heels, I'd be fine with it, as long as *someone* was going to help me.

About a week later, I met Louise for the first time. Too exhausted by my self-inflicted panic to be nervous about my first session, I mostly felt relieved to no longer be dealing with this alone anymore. Now I was her problem.

Louise was in her mid-thirties, with glasses that made me trust her. She wore clothes that were professional but chill, with just the right chunky belts to suggest a certain hipness. I'd spend the next two years with her, almost every week, and I'd never really know much more about her than this initial superficial assessment. Meanwhile, she'd be on a first-name basis with each one of my deepest demons.

We started with basic information, she asked questions about my birth control pills and seasonal allergies and family health history. My eyes wandered around the room as she scribbled notes about the various alcoholics in my family. I found her office comforting, even though it was painstakingly deliberate in its pleasantness. It was generically warm with lots of light and plants that were probably plastic. There was a framed piece of art above the couch that featured a tea pot. Louise asked me about the frequency of my panic attacks.

"Well, it's like...um..." I rubbed my eyes and stalled for time. Would saying it out loud mean it was true? Was she going to think I was crazy?

"I'm having panic attacks kind of a lot, like....three or four times—"

My voice caught in the middle of my sentence, the way it does when I'm nervous. It's like the words were grabbed out of my throat and they took most of the air in the room with them. It was going to sound horrible to say it out loud like that. Maybe this initial therapy session was like a first date and I shouldn't be too honest, lest she pretend to go freshen up and duck out the back door instead, leaving me alone with the bill.

Louise nodded encouragingly. "Three or four times...a week? Month?" She tried to help me finish my thought.

A week? A month? That sounded like a vacation. That sounded like a glorious and unobtainable ideal. That would be like having a Pegasus stabled in my garage for when I wanted a fanciful romp on a Wednesday afternoon.

"Oh. No. I'm having panic attacks three or four times a day."

"Okay." She smiled at me and nodded, looking thoroughly nonplussed, and made a note. I assumed she just had a good poker face and her note indicated that I was a helpless case and she was going to request to have me removed from her very pleasant office.

Panic: A Brief History

Pan was the Greek god of the wild.[115] He was a satyr, one of those half-man, half-goat things, like Mr. Tumnus from the Narnia books. Pan was a talented flautist, and quite liked to chase the ladies (and lady-goats as well, if a shockingly graphic statue in southern Italy is to be believed).[116] However, Pan's affections were rarely returned as he was not very cute, and was a troublemaker who often scared people by screaming at them. During wars, he caused fear and confusion in the enemy, which was mildly helpful, but he was still kind of a twerp about it. It is from this pesky fellow that we get the word "panic" — literally *Panikos*, "of Pan."

Pan still gets around. I'm one of approximately six million people in the US who suffer from a panic disorder.[117] And yet pretty much everyone who deals with this feels alone. Panic attacks are bad, even worse than being chased by a horny little goatman, but it's the self-imposed isolation that's really kryptonite for us. (Remember "The Yellow Wallpaper" and the Rest Cure? Remember chewing on the bed and ripping down all the wall coverings? That's what isolation does to us.) Being open and honest about our issues is the first step in getting a better handle on what we're dealing with.

Panic Attack or Imminent Death? A Handy Checklist

A panic attack is defined by having four or more of the following symptoms at the same time. (If you have less than four of these, you have what is whimsically termed "free floating anxiety," which sounds like a charming fairy-affliction but it's not.[118])

- Shortness of breath
- Heart palpitations
- Trembling or shaking
- Sweating
- Choking
- Nausea
- Numbness
- Dizziness
- Feeling of being out of touch with yourself

- Hot flashes or chills
- Fear of dying
- Fear of going crazy or being out of control

Panic: The Science Stuff

So, as you can tell from my bathroom stall chronicles, I would totally win at Panic Attack Bingo. Let's get technical and see what was really going on.

During the panic attack, my Amy the Amygdala activated my sympathetic nervous system and my adrenal glands went into overdrive, flooding my body with stress hormones. That made me feel like I was shot with a taser, and the resulting jolt caused feelings of terror. It all happened so quickly that my brain's frontal lobes didn't have time to process it and let me know my body was registering danger.[119] It's like seeing a car running a stop sign out of the corner of your eye; you might slam on the breaks before you can consciously think, *hey, look, there's a Volvo coming.*

So my adrenals drenched my body with the stress hormones cortisol and adrenaline.[120] That caused an increased heart rate, shallow breathing, sweating, muscle contractions, shaking and coldness as blood rushed to my core to help me run away faster from all the danger that isn't actually there. This also left my face pale. The fuzzy vision was a result of a lack of oxygen to my brain.

Sounds kind of like a heart attack, right? The body and mind are intrinsically connected, which means it can be tricky to discern which one is actually having the problem. Almost 40% of patients referred by their doctors to cardiac outpatient programs have psychological, not physical, conditions.[121]

While a panic attack can feel an awful lot like a heart attack, there are a few things that indicate a cardiac issue:
- Pressure in the center of the chest that tends to radiate along the shoulder
- Constant pain, pressure, fullness or aching in the chest
- Pain in the arm or upper body
- Fainting more often occurs with a heart attack than panic attack

But if you are not sure, even a little bit, 9-1-1 is *always* the safest call. I really don't want you not to call an ambulance if you're actually having some heart issue, and your last thought is: *Damn Lisa for making me assume this was just a panic attack.*

Are you having a panic attack right now?
- Is someone with you? Tell them.
- Are you alone? It's okay. We'll get through this. A panic attack is time-limited; you will outlast this sensation. Most are over within about ten minutes.
- You are not dying. Even though it feels like you're going to die, you're not. It's just Amy triggering too many stress hormones. It doesn't feel good, but you can handle it.
- Take a deep breath, put your hand on your belly—stick it way out—give yourself a big fat belly and breathe deep. Slowly exhale, suck your belly in. Get all the air out. Repeat.
- Count your breaths. Aim for four counts in, hold for two, four-counts out.
- Ride the panic attack like you're surfing a wave. Don't fight with it. Just notice what your body is doing. Observe without judgment. Is your neck tense? Are your hands tingly?

- Remember that thoughts are just thoughts. They don't control you. They don't own you. You are the master of your life, your thoughts are just flickering ideas. If you can see your thoughts, you are separate from them. You can choose to disregard them if they are not serving you.
- Get fresh air. The colder the better. No fresh air available? Grab an ice cube. Hang on to it. Sometimes it feels good on the back of the neck.
- You are okay. You will be okay. You've gotten through hard things before. You'll get through this, too.

Carly: Panic Attacks and Preppy Rich Boys

Carly has one of those jobs that requires an extensive education and pants with real waistbands. The kind of job where one might use the phrase "mission-critical performance metrics" a whole lot. I find those jobs impressive and intimidating because I could never do them.

Carly's social anxiety problems officially began in October 2015. It was an emotional time: she was ending one job and returning to an old employer. She went out for what was supposed to be a fun evening with her husband and his friends. She was feeling a little insecure already, since she got a "rich kid" vibe from his friends (one of them was practically Blane from *Pretty in Pink*). They were lovely people, she says, but they "have different politics, different backgrounds, lots of differences."

Those differences were about to send her into a panic attack. She felt self-conscious, fat and dorky. The claustrophobia of being at a concert in a small, crowded venue just took over. Her heart rate increased and she started to panic. She escaped to the bathroom and sobbed in a stall for twenty minutes; she felt like she couldn't breathe. Carly started obsessing about all the reasons she didn't belong there and ignored concerned texts from her husband. She couldn't face him. And why had he married her at all? He could have done so much better than her. She was nothing more than "an albatross around his neck."

Then she began the game at which all of us anxious people excel: beating the shit out of ourselves. She was already dealing with the first arrow of anxiety, the one she couldn't avoid. But then she grabbed another arrow of her own volition, and took aim right at her heart.

"This was a date night for us. When you have kids, a night alone and away is supposed to be fun and special...and here I was, bawling in the bathroom at a concert, barely able to catch my breath."

A panic attack was a new experience for Carly, but when she thinks back, anxiety had been lingering beneath the surface for a while. When she was single, it had been easier to manage. She would spend one or two weekends a month not interacting with anyone, except for a phone call with her mother. She could bolt from social situations whenever she wanted. She had a habit of dating "unavailable, uncaring shit-heads" so they wouldn't care if she went silent for a while. But now, she's married with kids and feels like she's falling behind with everything. While the anxiety was always there, now it's "unbearable. It's unleashed. Like a monstrous, nervy blob."

Carly used to handle her anxiety by drinking a lot in social situations. But what she realized is that alcohol actually worked against her.

"I'm so unbelievably insecure that I expend an insane amount of energy every day just controlling my insecurity. When I drink, that façade comes down, and the insecurity is just there. All my failures, all my flaws. Just sitting there. All ugly and stuff."

Things started to change when Carly began to see her husband as an ally against her anxiety. Eventually, she got honest with him and explained that she was having panic attacks. Now, he's there for back-up. She doesn't need him to fix or coddle her, but he can help. He can support her and redirect their social interactions when necessary. She's learned to accept her anxiety, speak up about how she feels, and manage it the best she can. Carly knows she's not alone.

Carly's panic experience was classic. Let's look at what happened to her, step by step:

The Making of a Panic Attack[122]

1. **Initiating circumstances.** Going to a bar, hanging out with rich-kid-Blane-guy who made her feel insecure and uneasy.

2. **Increase in physical symptoms.** Feeling claustrophobic, couldn't catch her breath, felt like she was going to cry.

3. **Internalization, focusing on symptoms.** She was ruining date night, she was a burden, why couldn't she just be okay?

4. **Catastrophic interpretation.** Wondering why her husband had married her at all.

5. **Full-on panic meltdown freak-out.** Sobbing in the bar bathroom, ignoring texts from her worried partner.

When I say I've gotten my panic under control, it clearly doesn't mean that I'm this Zen master all the time. It just means I'm getting better at noticing this process and slowing it down. I usually recognize the panic around stage 3. I've gotten better at knowing what triggers me, and I can often stop it before it gets to 4 and 5. Even for those people whose panic attacks seem to come out of absolutely nowhere, understanding the process is helpful. With increased awareness of early physical signs, it's more likely that the process can be eased or stopped.

Breathing exercises, grounding techniques and even silly-sounding things like counting your fingers, can help get panic under control before you reach that sobbing-on-the-floor point. (See more examples at the end of this chapter.) Stepping back in the moment can offer a space to recognize what's happening — and that just takes practice. Once you can see that Amy the Amygdala is having another temper tantrum, it's easier to say, *Oh, Amy is at it again*, and not be completely swindled by her freak-out. You can respond with kindness and compassion.

Funny, You Don't Look Anxious

With her impressive job and dry-clean-only pants, Carly doesn't seem like the anxious type. I know how that feels. I've had people say to me, "It seemed like you had a great time at that party... You don't really have anxiety, it can't be that bad...You do talks in front of big crowds at colleges... You teach a writing class." I think they mean well. They're trying to be encouraging or something. But this is painful to hear. It's like saying to someone who is in remission from cancer, *Oh, good for you! It must have been one of those easy cancers.*

I work my ass off to not let my anxiety rule my life. I've spent enormous amounts of time, energy and money on therapy, books, meditation classes, yoga classes, soothing music and various potions that are supposed to turn me into one of those chill people who says the right things and never breaks into stress-induced flop sweat. And still, before I go to a party, I whimper in the front hall while Jeremy holds my hand and says supportive things in an endless loop. I put myself through hell. But the important part is that I don't stop there. I keep going, because who wants to hang out in hell? The more comfortable I get being uncomfortable, the more cool things I get to experience.

I shouldn't be surprised that sometimes people think I'm exaggerating my anxiety. I hide it, shove it down, the way many of us do. I'm pretty good at faking it. Being an actor for eighteen years seems to have stuck with me; I'm a decent liar when I need to be. I can laugh lightly and pretend I'm having fun, even when I'm brimming with terror inside. I'll compliment your earrings and inquire about your cat. I'll walk to the podium and make a joke. I'll put on my social mask and look like a completely different person than the one who was shaking while trying to put on her shoes just before leaving the house.

We hide our anxiety because we imagine people are pitying our weak, fragile little souls. But it's just the opposite. Every time we're out in public or riding an elevator or making a phone call—whenever we're facing our anxiety—we are brave as fuck. We're looking straight at the thing that most terrifies us.

We're facing down a thousand clowns with chainsaws every time we accept an invitation to lunch.

We're standing alone in the middle of the woods with a serial killer on the loose when we speak up at work.

We're swimming in shark-infested waters with a rib-eye around our necks when we go to the dentist.

So please remember next time you see someone who looks just fine, holding a plate piled with mini quiche and chatting pleasantly with her spouse's boss's sister-in-law, you don't know what it took to get her to that party. You don't know how many nights she spent staring at the ceiling, making mental lists about what she was going to say in this moment. The effort might have been brutal.

There is nothing weak about someone who is dealing with anxiety.

We are warriors.

Jackie: "I've got to start breathing."

Jackie is my neighbor's cousin. We've known each other casually for a couple of years; we smile at each other politely over pool party barbecues and across the table covered with martinis for girls' nights. I've been to her art openings and watched her explain the inspiration behind the vibrant paintings that hang on the wall. But with all the polite smiling, nothing was ever said about this affliction we share. There is no secret handshake for those of us with panic attacks. No one wears ribbons to indicate being a survivor of our own minds.

Maybe we should.

"I start thinking *I need to make this amount of money by this time, and how am I going to do it*? I start spiraling down with all these negative thoughts, start working against all the positive stuff I've built up. So, I can be in a really good place and I start thinking, *but three months from now I've got nothing*. The anxiety takes over and emotions are haywire and I can't breathe. I have no control. Of anything. My abdomen gets tight, I'll start crying and I guess...I'm scared. How will I sustain myself? It usually happens when I'm lying in bed or I'm in the shower. And I'll just have to ball up or brace my hands on the shower walls and I'll say, *Get a grip. I've got to get a grip. I've got to start breathing*. I'm then in a depressed or emotional state for half a day. Maybe longer."

I was only the second person Jackie had ever told about this. She always assumed that she needed to deal with it alone.

"I feel the way I did the first time I told anyone that my mother was an alcoholic. I thought I was the only person who had this problem. People judge you for it, they look at it as a weakness. It's not a weakness, it's just an issue."

Jackie had inklings of her anxiety as a kid. She'd get stomach aches and didn't want to go to school. "When you're twelve and thirteen, you just want to fit in. It's a horrible time of life. You want boobs, you don't want your skin to break out... I wanted to stay in my room and hide."

Her first panic attack was in Safeway on Christmas Eve, about twenty years ago. (What the hell is it about grocery stores?) She had to grab her two-year-old son, abandon the cart and get out of there. "Holidays are hard. I'll be honest: I don't like them."

The debilitating stress migraines started in her twenties, mostly around financial issues. Since Jackie got divorced, her money concerns have increased and the panic has intensified.

"I'm going to tell you something." She plucked a Kleenex from the box on the coffee table. She gestured to my iPhone and said, "I know it's recording, I'm okay with that." I was using a recorder app that looked like a 1980s cassette player with its tape reels slowly turning. "I've often thought, if it gets that bad, if I'm in a place where I can't take care of myself, I'll just do something about it. I'll end it all." She stopped and dabbed her eyes. "I won't ever really do that...but it's a thought that I have. When I'm in that place, I think I could do it, because life is pretty frigging tough. But it won't ever happen."

I nod in a way that I hope is supportive and try to figure out how to express with my body language that I've been there, I get it, and I'm not afraid to sit with her in this pain. I think I just nod. Suddenly a smile cracks across Jackie's face.

"I have those thoughts about ending it all and then I think — but then I'd have to come back and start over again. It's not worth it to start over again." And we snicker at the image of both of us being reincarnated as dung beetles, being forced by the universe to come back for a do-over of life because we didn't learn how to cope with it all this time around.

At the end of our interview, we hug and she tells me she feels lighter, having shared. It was hard for me not to go into amateur therapist mode. I wanted to give her a list of books to read, breathing exercises to try, offering all kinds of unsolicited advice. But instead I just hugged her tighter.

A few days later, Jackie sent me an e-mail saying she had just gotten an unexpected real estate bill and owed more than $3,000 in taxes, due immediately. "I mentioned panicking about financial stuff and it literally shows up in my mailbox." But Jackie had a new perspective on it and didn't fall into familiar patterns.

"I'm happy to say that I did not succumb to panic. Mild to moderate irritation and some curse words, but I handled it with gratitude: I'm grateful I have a home to live in."

Jackie and I didn't talk about gratitude — she came up with that herself. I just gave her some space to share the burden she'd been holding so tightly. She was able to talk without the fear of judgment, and that made all the difference. Jackie didn't have control over the situation. The bill was not something she could change (what with the inevitability of death and taxes), so she looked at what she was capable of changing about her own experience. She could adjust her perception of it. She could change her mind. She could acknowledge that this was going to put her in a financial crunch and she'd be strapped for a while, but she wasn't going to be out in the street. For the mere fact that she was not homeless, she chose to be grateful. Since the situation couldn't be different, she could save herself the emotional distress of panicking about it. And when she saw the reality clearly, without fighting with it or piling on the story about how she was always going to be financially vulnerable, she suffered a lot less.

Something to Try: Gratitude Journal

Gratitude sounds like some dippy emotion, but its effects on the mind and body are profound. Gratitude has been shown to reduce the frequency and duration of episodes of depression. Grateful people report better physical health, lower blood pressure and stronger immune systems. They even get better sleep.[123] Essentially, gratitude magnifies positive emotions and crowds out the miserable ones. Imagine being jealous and grateful at the same time—it just can't happen. If gratitude is the focus, the other stuff dissipates on its own.

How do we become grateful? It seems a little intangible, like you are either grateful or not, you're a morning person or not. But gratitude, like so much of life, is a practice.

It's easy to be grateful when we get a promotion or the weather is perfect for the baseball game. Where gratitude gets interesting is when you can be grateful for the crappy things. Because no one ever said, "Everything in my life went perfectly and that's why I'm so great." Challenges cause us to go beyond our everyday selves and become extraordinary. That's worth being grateful for, too.

That old saying is true: It's not happy people who are thankful, it's thankful people who are happy. If you roll your eyes at the term "Gratitude Journal," you can call it a List of Today's Awesome Shit.

Before bed, jot down five things that happened during the day that you are grateful for. I'll be honest, there are going to be days when it's hard to come up with five. It feels easier to list the top 105 things that make you want to cry. We are so used to focusing on the things we want to change, but flipping that upside-down can be powerful.

On hard days, my list might look like this:
1. I'm breathing
2. I'm not in solitary confinement in a high security women's prison
3. I wrote
4. I did a little bit of yoga today
5. My husband brought home pizza

That is a totally legit list. Eventually, you'll go through your day looking for things to write in your Awesome Shit Journal. If bedtime isn't a feasible time to write, I have a big vase that I keep in my living room. Every once in a while I'll scribble something on a scrap of paper and I'll throw it in there. When I need a boost, I'll look at the scraps. I'm always struck by how minor the things are. *I'm grateful that my friend texted me to check in. I'm grateful that the power stayed on in that big snowstorm. I'm grateful that we cuddled on the couch and watched* Arrested Development. Writing those little things down helps me remember to acknowledge them in the moment.

Helping others is another slam-dunk way to feel gratitude for your own life. It's been shown that gratitude isn't just about the reward — it doesn't only light up in the reward center of the brain. It also has to do with deeper things, like connection, morality, and taking the perspective of other people.[124] When you act in service of others, gratitude, confidence and compassion come with the territory. Of people who had volunteered in the past twelve months, 78% reported feeling less stress, and 96% felt enriched purpose in life.[125] Even people who were elderly or dealing with chronic health conditions felt better when volunteering. Those of us who struggle with anxiety or depression often feel disconnected from others and wonder about the purpose and contribution of our lives. Whether it's playing with furry friends at an animal shelter or just stopping by to check on your lonely neighbor, giving to others has unlimited benefits.

It's easy to be a naysayer, to find fault, stew in negativity and dwell on the things that went wrong. That's playing life to the cheap seats. But things begin to shift when you help others, write thank-you notes, and try to find opportunities for growth or moments of gratitude — even in situations that involve tax bills.

Chapter 10: SSRI Nation

I am not at all equipped to tell you whether or not you should consider medication for your mental wellness. But since drugs have this bizarre dual distinction of being the first solution presented by many medical practitioners, and an option that is mired in shame and stigma—we need to talk about them.

I had a little green bottle of beta-blockers that lived on my kitchen counter for years. Those were the pills that Dr. Z had given me when I was having multiple panic attacks a day. Something about seeing that bottle on the counter, standing at attention and willing to come to my aid, was very reassuring. When I was really struggling, I would cradle the bottle in my hands. I felt legitimized. Comforted. There were meds for this stuff, therefore, I must not be the only person who has felt this way. If there were meds, this anxiety of mine was real and it was like having an ear infection or high blood pressure.

Aside from beta blockers, there are other types of medication that are commonly prescribed for depression and anxiety. SSRI anti-depressant medications, like Zoloft or Paxil, are intended to slow the re-uptake of serotonin, so that happy chemical can stay in your synapses (gaps between the nerves) a little longer before getting absorbed back into the nerve cells. This can improve the communication between the cells in the brain. Those medications take a while to kick in, usually three to four weeks, but some people find that it makes their anxiety and depression more manageable.

Benzodiazepines are tranquilizers, like Klonopin, Valium or Xanax. They enhance the effect of the neurotransmitter GABA and can have sedative effects. These can be highly addictive, so they need to be taken with great care.

Every time I stood in my kitchen, cradling my bottle of pills, I felt reassured, and then I put it down without taking any. This is not because I thought there was shame in taking medicine or that it was a moral failing of some sort because I absolutely do not. Sometimes medication is the right answer. But much in the same way that I have never been on a cruise, I've never taken medication for my anxiety. I have no disdain for medication—or cruises—it's just that I've always been curious about going a different way. I wanted to focus on behavioral changes first and see how that worked for me. Drugs were my back-up, just one part of my mental health plan. Having the meds available helped me get a foothold on the anxiety so I could explore other options.

For some people, drugs work beautifully. Some say that it helps immensely, and they are pretty sure it's just the placebo effect, but they're fine with that. For others, medication doesn't work at all. The British Medical Journal found that Prozac, Zoloft, Paxil and other SSRIs don't have a clinically significant advantage over placebo, meaning that you could be taking a daily dosage of maple syrup and it would be just as helpful for your depression.[126] And then sometimes pills work for a while and then they're not effective anymore, leading to the notorious "Prozac Poop Out".[127] And then there are the reports that getting off of Paxil is as hard as quitting heroin.[128] As my friend said after watching someone come off anti-depressants, "that's some serious tweaking." In other cases, the anxiety and depression is so overwhelming and all-encompassing that meds can be really helpful for taking it all down a notch—just for the short term. Drugs can allow someone to get a handle on the anxiety and it can truly save their lives. The hard emotional and behavioral work that needs to be done is extra-hard when you are sitting at the bottom of a proverbial well (or a literal well, I suppose), so medication can offer a leg up.

So, do meds work?

Yes and no and sometimes. Like I said, it's complicated.

Whatever your view and experience is with medication, one thing is very clear: the stigma around this issue needs to go away. It doesn't make any sense to say that taking a pill to manage cholesterol levels is normal but taking a pill to manage serotonin levels is a weakness. We all need to decide for ourselves what we need to stay alive.

Medication: A Brief History

Human beings have been stressed ever since we tiptoed out of the cave to see what was making that rustling sound. And yet it was not until the 1920s that doctors began diagnosing depression, and in the 1950s they started identifying anxiety.[129] Before that, of course people had these issues, just under different names: melancholy, nerve troubles, hysteria, neurasthenia and my personal favorite: irritable heart syndrome.[130]

In the 1880s, pharmacists sold tonics and elixirs like Moxie soda to help with "nerves and exhaustion" and cure "softening of the brain."[131] These tonics did little other than separate struggling people from their money. Fast forward to the super-rad 1980s, and social anxiety disorder as we know it became an official thing.[132] It was differentiated from General Anxiety Disorder (GAD) in the DSM, the Diagnostic and Statistical Manual of Mental Disorders, which is pretty much the bible of mental stuff.

When it became possible to identify and diagnose anxiety, it could be billed to insurance, and drug companies could more easily make money off the meds. Enter drugs that can be helpful, but also wave hello to the complicated relationship between patients and Big Pharma. With one in ten Americans taking antidepressants, there are major profits to be made off the backs of those who suffer from mood disorders.[133] But with staggering statistics—like 23% of people with social anxiety attempting suicide—someone needs to do something.[134]

When Miltown hit the market in 1955, a lot of people thought it was the solution to all their problems. Miltown was an anti-anxiety pill that still stands as the fastest-selling pharmaceutical in US history.[135] Think about that for a second. Bigger than birth control. Bigger than Viagra.

Labeled the "peace pill," Miltown was a minor tranquilizer, in the same general category as Valium and Xanax. An enthusiastic marketing campaign helped boost sales, and Miltown had lots of fans, including famous ones who pushed its popularity through the roof. Celebrities talked openly about how much they loved it, and Milton Berle joked that he was thinking about changing his name to "Miltown" Berle. Everyone from movie stars to housewives started popping the little peace pills. The drug took off like a fad, akin to acid wash or Pokemon Go, just in mood-altering, chemical form. Miltown's popularity started to fade in the 1960s when people realized that one of the side effects was psychological dependence—which is even scarier than a four-hour erection.

Miltown represented an important cultural moment in America when pharmaceutical companies realized something: people want to feel better. The door opened to a whole host of helper pills like Paxil and Lexapro. These days, daytime television is inundated with ads featuring actor portrayals of formerly-depressed people smiling gently while making pancakes with the kids. And that is a great result—who doesn't want to giggle with a friend on a park bench? But it's the same thing as the moisturizer that claims to make you sexy, or that sparkly necklace that will prove your love once and for all. It's selling you. It's not that it's wrong or that it definitely won't help, but it might not leave you as carefree as that woman glazing a bowl. And by the way (as they'll mention in the lightning fast disclaimer)—she might not be able to have an orgasm anymore.

Medication is often the first line of defense against anxiety and depression. Access to meds is important, but we need to understand what drugs do and don't do. We need to see the whole picture: the side effects, the possibility that they might not work, and the fact that no one who takes medication is weak. This is another chance to balance two opposing realities. On one hand, if you had heart disease, would you refuse treatment because you didn't want to take drugs? On the other hand, as Taylor Swift has taught us, Band-Aids don't fix bullet holes. So if you want the pills, take them. If you want to find another path, take that.

Your life, your rules.

Charlotte: Medication and Milkshakes

"I can give you the list of medications I've been on. Do you want to hear the list?"

I nodded.

Charlotte looked slightly up and to the left while counting off on her fingers. "Wellbutrin, Serzone, Seroquel, Lithium, Depakote, Celexa, Lexapro, Effexor, Pristiq, Lamictal, Lyrica, Equetro, Cymbalta, Provigil, Valium, Xanax, Klonopin, Trazodone, Beta blockers, Ambien, Sonata, Abilify and Adderall."

In case you weren't counting, that's twenty-three drugs Charlotte just rattled off the top of her head.

"I might have missed some."

Charlotte realized there might be a problem after her first suicide attempt. She was in graduate school and had just defended her master's thesis, which went very well. But instead of celebrating, she went home and took a bunch of opioid pain killers—a class of drugs that includes morphine. It was "dumb luck" that she didn't die. It turned out the pills had expired and she vomited in her sleep. So she survived her own attempt on her life and she is still here to meet me in a coffee shop crawling with hipster men sporting elaborately groomed facial hair.

"I had the impostor complex," she told me. "I thought I was basically a not very clever girl from a rural part of the United States and who was not meant to be at this level. I couldn't handle the stress of knowing I was an imposter. I couldn't deal with what I thought was the inevitable shame that would come when people finally found out I wasn't very smart. I woke up the next morning, having thrown up at some point, and I thought *okay, this is a big deal*. But I kind of thought that I might want to try again, so I didn't tell anyone what I had done."

Charlotte is unequivocally one of the smartest people I've ever met. While many people can put together interesting sentences while in conversation, Charlotte speaks off the top of her head in cohesive and perfectly constructed paragraphs. She is brilliant, but the distorted thinking that comes with anxiety and depression can become so entirely convincing that we don't bother to question it. A friend of mine refers to breaking this habit of presumed worthlessness as "finding out the sky is actually red." We become completely convinced by our repetitive, negating thinking, and after a while, we can believe pretty much anything—including the BS that we are stupid after successfully defending a master's thesis.

For a while Charlotte assumed that being miserable and having a low opinion of herself was just part of the deal for women, a result of the failed feminist revolution. Eventually, she came to a revolutionary notion of her own: "I learned that I didn't deserve to feel like crap." And yes, she knew there were Syrian women being bombed out of their houses, but Charlotte still needed help anyway. She went to therapy, admitted to the overdose and had a couple of stints in the hospital where she was assigned a security guard who told her she shouldn't kill herself because there was so much to live for, particularly NASCAR and milkshakes.

He had a point. At least on the milkshakes.

Charlotte was diagnosed with major depressive disorder, also called MDD. Then her doctors added on general anxiety disorder (GAD) as well. Then they decided it was "atypical depression" because she had these days when she would quickly swing from *I'm fine* to *I'm going to go to the store and buy a gun*. It was hard for her doctors to categorize.

"It's just this weird depression. I call it WD and the diagnostic code is 666." She and I laugh really hard, noting that if we can't laugh at our diagnostic codes, we really are doomed.

Charlotte took a variety of medications, but the problem was that none of them worked for more than three months before she got sick again. When that happened, she felt she needed to act like she was okay—or at least that she was going to be okay soon—for the sake of other people. With cancer, people understand that the disease can go into remission, but a full on "cure" is rare. Sometimes there are relapses; good days and bad days. With depression, not so much. Sometimes it feels like there is an expiration date on people's empathy.

"The person taking the drug and the people around them think they're going to take the medication and they're going to get better. It might take four to six weeks but they're going to get better. For some people that's true. Some people take medication for a year or two and they are done. And some people will be on it for the rest of their lives. For some people, the first one isn't going to work, and the tenth one isn't going to work. And that is something we don't understand. It's a crappy thing to say to someone who feels that bad, someone who is willing to drive their car off a bridge because they just want it to stop. I wouldn't want to say to someone *hey, I've been doing this for seventeen years and it's still not totally fixed.* That's a hard thing to hear and it's not always true for everyone."

It's pretty much understood with other treatments that they might work, or they might not. Cognitive behavioral therapy is incredible for some, overwhelming for others. Yoga can be emotionally transformative, or it can just be some stretching. But since medication is prescribed by a doctor, we might have the expectation that it's going to be the thing that will definitely fix it forever. But even with pills, there is no magic pill. And while this is not great news, having realistic expectations can be really helpful in moving forward. Because it's much worse to expect that something will "cure" you, and then when it doesn't, you feel guilty, like you couldn't even do that right.

Charlotte's medications have caused her an impressive array of side effects, including gaining thirty pounds in a couple of months, being so numb she couldn't cry at her aunt's funeral, and the destruction of her thyroid gland—which caused her skin to peel off in sheets. But she's still here. She is alive. She has a job and friends and hasn't driven off a bridge. So it's worth it.

"When you get the right medication, together with eating the right things, sleeping enough and exercising—those four things together let you do the work you need to do in therapy. Medication helps you do the work of therapy."

I asked Charlotte about something that keeps coming up in these conversations: We feel empathy and understanding for other people's struggles and would never judge them, but we brutally condemn ourselves. We hold ourselves to this standard that would be completely bonkers to place on anyone else.

She nodded. "I feel like a colossal failure. But if I were someone else, looking at my life, I would think, you have a disability, you have an illness that is extremely serious. You are not a bouncing circle on the Zoloft commercial. You are not a little sad. This was a life-or-death situation and it makes sense that your path through life has been a little different."

And that is compassion. You've heard that whole "charity begins at home" thing, right? Meaning, yes, do big important things for the rest of the world, but also, don't be a douchebag. When we start to extend that same compassion to ourselves, maybe that can ripple outwards and become part the social construct. Maybe we can begin to change the way our whole culture feels about mood disorders. Because right now, we're still terrible at talking about it.

"Cancer used to be this deep dark secret and I think mental illness still is. When someone is diagnosed with cancer, there is a huge support network that gets mobilized. My friend had breast cancer, and as soon as she was diagnosed, we organized her meals and someone to help her clean, all of this stuff. That doesn't happen for someone with depression. There are a lot of reasons for that, but really, it's that people don't get it. Or they don't understand how much it can affect your life. If we could have the same kind of enmeshing social support for people with depression and anxiety, that would be wonderful and make a huge difference. If you survive cancer, people tell you you are so brave, but if you say 'I survived two suicide attempts,' no one is going to tell you you are brave. But the reality is, you get up every morning and go about your life and that is not an easy thing."

Something to try: Look at That Body

It's pretty clear that thoughts trigger physical reactions — that's why lie detector tests are a thing. The emotional brain creates physical sensations. The stomach flips in circles, muscles tense, head aches, heart pounds, breath becomes shallow, voice changes. Anxiety is physically exhausting. Since our bodies are highly attuned to our emotions, sometimes it's easier to notice the physical stuff than the mental stuff. We just have to pay attention.

Sometimes the negative voice in our head becomes constant background noise, like the teachers on the Peanuts cartoon. But the messages still get through, and the body doesn't lie. It usually knows the deal before the mind does. Many of us, whether we have anxiety or not, are disassociated from our bodies. We live in this body every day, but we only notice when it's not working the way we want it to. Paying attention to the body offers a bunch of clues to what is going on in the mind.

For me, when I'm anxious, I hold all my tension in my legs. My tense, aching quadriceps and hips cause me to wonder if I'm always going to feel this pain forever and it makes me sad, which causes me to tense up my legs. See the problem?

Body scans can stop this cycle. A body scan can be a preventative; it's awesome as a pre-bedtime routine (insomniacs, take note), or it can be something you do in a moment of impending stress, like before a speech or important phone call.

Body scan meditation

It's preferable to do a body scan lying down for ultimate relaxation magic, but you can do it seated if that's more comfortable for you. A scan involves sweeping through the body with the mind, checking in with each region of the body, and relaxing it. Notice any sensations. Is there heat? Tension? Soreness? Lightness? We're not judging what we feel; we're just noticing. Observing. And then moving on.

Try to spend at least twenty minutes on the scan. Start with the toes. Put all your focused attention into your toes. Notice how they feel. Imagine you are breathing all the way down into your toes.

Now move to each section of the body one by one, relaxing each part...

- Toes
- Feet
- Calves
- Knees
- Thighs
- Hips
- Belly
- Chest
- Entire spine

- Fingers
- Hands
- Arms
- Shoulders
- Neck
- Jaw
- Face
- Mind

If you can take more time, do the right side, then the left side. There are many guided body scans you can download for free online. It can be really lovely to have someone lead you through it. Check out any of the body scans recorded by Jon Kabat-Zinn. Also watch any of his videos. And read any of his books. He's incredible.

Chapter 11: The Gate Swings Both Ways

I kept thinking about a conversation I'd had with my Veteran friend Nate, during the yoga retreat. His PTSD was bad, the anti-depressants weren't working, and he was going three days without sleeping at all. Even though he was against cannabis, eventually he tried it. He found that it helped. It didn't make him a zombie like the prescription meds did, it just offered him a chance to stop the spinning thoughts and use his brain differently.

"It's not that I want to forget, but I need a reprieve. When it's quiet, all those bad thoughts come back. But when I smoke, I think about life, philosophy, physics, and whatever else. Cannabis gives me a break and I can think about other things. And it allows me to sleep. You know the thing about cannabis, right? Why it was made illegal?"

I did not.

In the early 1900s, just after the Mexican Revolution, there was an increase in immigration from Mexico and people brought awesome things to America like Mexican culture and tamales and also "marihuana."[136] This plant seemed new to Americans but really it wasn't, since cannabis existed and was used in over-the-counter remedies at the time. It was just a foreign-sounding name. But just like immigration today, along with these newcomers came increased concern and overblown stranger-danger. Horrific crimes were attributed to weed and those who smoked it. Making marijuana illegal created grounds on which to search and deport Mexicans. Based on prejudice and fear, we demonized a plant that had previously been legal and used as medicine.

"It doesn't make sense because I can drink all the alcohol I want, which studies have shown is not good. It's impossible to overdose on cannabis, but I live here in Texas, where I could do the legal opiate route or I could be a criminal and do the weed thing."

I had read some studies about cannabis for anxiety relief, but I mostly glossed over them. I'd never smoked pot before. (I know, that's is a fairly bold statement for someone with my former-child-actor status, but it's true. All kinds of drugs were always fairly available to me on sets, so they never seemed all that illicit and intriguing.) Since I have no strong feelings for or against cannabis, I honestly never gave it much consideration. But it became hard to ignore how many articles were popping up from reputable sources, saying it could be effective for people with anxiety. It made me wonder. Was weed going legit?

People are closely watching a study underway by researchers from Johns Hopkins University and the University of Colorado, examining the effect of cannabis on the symptoms of PTSD.[137] It's a real scientific study, with various phases and placebo controls and multiple sites and everything. This isn't just some slacker guy in his mom's basement: it's Johns Hopkins, for God's sake.

But this is contentious because the federal government is still pretty sure that marijuana is not medicine and that it has a high likelihood for addiction and abuse. So I did what any anxiety-ridden faux-journalist would do. I booked a flight to Colorado.

Welcome to Boulder

The first thing that happened to me in Boulder was that I got carded. I was only trying to order a martini, but the server was eyeing me.

207

"Can I see an ID really quick?"

I laughed and just sort of looked at her. And then realized she was serious. I dug my wallet out of my purse and explained that being carded at age thirty-seven is surprising.

I don't think the carding had anything to do with my age; I think it had to do with the look on my face. I felt guilty. I felt sneaky for even *being* in Boulder. Had I really flown all the way to Colorado to do drugs? Shouldn't I just be "saying no" like everyone told me to in the '80s? Even though I was a fully-grown person in a place where cannabis was completely legal, my inner good girl was clearly betraying me.

Admittedly, this experiment was a strange choice to make. I had decided to not go the prescription medication route for my anxiety, and here I was flying to another state to try a different form of drug. But I was intrigued by the relief that many of the Vets had found while smoking. I wanted to know what that experience had been like for them. I was also less concerned about the potential side effects of weed compared to an SSRI and I wouldn't have to wait weeks for it to get into (or out of) my system.

There's a lot of drama surrounding cannabis, lots of opinions and mythology, held over from the *Reefer Madness* era. A recent study published in the journal of the American Medical Association found that cannabis use does not, contrary to prior claims, cause mood disorders.[138] But the issue of whether it is addictive or if it leads to other addictive behaviors is uncertain. I could show you ten studies telling you that cannabis use is associated with an increased risk for several substance use disorders and then show you ten more arguing the exact opposite with just as much compelling evidence.

"I feel obliged to tell you that our house is a total happy and chaotic shit show," my husband's friend told me. It was a warning. She had offered me a home base in Boulder and I had accepted, mostly because the entire notion of staying at her house sounded terrifying. I would be staying with near strangers in a house I'd never seen in a town I didn't know. The situation was guaranteed to spike my anxiety to an uncomfortable level—which was perfect for testing out the anti-anxiety properties of cannabis. If marijuana could chill me out in an unfamiliar "chaotic shit show" environment, there might really be something to it.

I had only met Tara a couple of times, and when I showed up at her house I was introduced to her husband, four young kids, two dogs, two cats, plus the nanny and a family friend who hung out in the kitchen a lot. I stayed in their playroom. A five-foot long, hand-drawn shark watched over me as I slept. One of the cats methodically kneaded my belly and drooled on my chest as I lay on the pullout couch.

I didn't know where the light switches were, and the first time I used the toilet it didn't flush properly and I thought I would die. I don't have children and I'm not adept at socializing with them. I asked a medium-sized kid about school and got so nervous I couldn't remember the word for "recess." The words I could remember were mostly curse words, and while I abstained from the worst ones, things like *damn* and *hell* were determined to spew out every time the five-year-old walked into the room.

As an only child, who spent most of her life hanging out with adults on film sets, this was all foreign to me. I was surrounded by normal family life with its abundant hair brushing, knee bashing and the inevitable tornado of kids carrying yowling cats around. It was loud and busy, and closed doors didn't seem to carry any meaning, as their son came in the playroom looking for some dinosaurs and got a pretty good anatomical education while I struggled to get my t-shirt on. The whole family was sweet and kind; they assembled bookcases while practicing the cello, they offered me homemade waffles and showed me endless prank videos on YouTube.

And it all sent my anxiety through the roof.

It was perfect for my experiment.

"Cannabis Can Be an Exit Drug"

Since my personal knowledge of marijuana was close to zero, I needed to be educated. I made my way to Root, a medical cannabis facility in Boulder, and its sister store, The Farm, which is the "adult use" facility. (They prefer the term "adult use" to "recreational," I suppose because the latter conjures images of four wheelers, and that is definitely not the vibe they're going for.)

In November of 2012, Amendment 64 was passed in Colorado, allowing consumers to legally purchase marijuana buds, extracts, and edibles. The Farm grows all the "craft cannabis" that they sell. They pride themselves on producing a clean, potent, natural product for anyone — as long as you are twenty-one and over. If a customer has a medical marijuana card prescribed by a doctor, they pay slightly less through Root, since the taxes are lower for medical dispensaries. Along with the good old-fashioned flowers for smoking, there are oils, beverages, capsules, tinctures, candies, chocolates, baked goods, lotions, transdermal patches — and the list goes on.

I had made plans ahead of time to meet with Casey Cook and Randall Tickles, who were waiting at Root to talk to me about what they do. Casey worked on the medical side of the operation. He's a young guy with a serious passion for helping people, but he admitted to having some reservations when he started working in the cannabis industry.

"At first I was really skeptical. Okay, so medical cannabis, they just say that so they can get access to it. But working in this medical facility you see so many people with legitimate needs, whether they are fighting cancer, they have MS, or they have children with neurodegenerative diseases. It was an eye-opener for me, and that's why I've stayed in it. I'm helping and it's an interesting field to be in."

Randall worked at the adult use facility, and he had a similar story. When he was younger, he started growing cannabis illegally, mostly because he had family members who had a medical need and didn't have access. He truly feels that this is a medication that has been stigmatized and withheld.

"Part of what we do every day is change those stigmas. We have these intelligent conversations and we can show you that even though Casey and I do sell cannabis, we do use cannabis, we are still very professional, very intelligent individuals. The reason that I am here is to help people, to forward the movement of cannabis and to end cannabis prohibition. I think that when anyone comes into one of our facilities, they leave without the stigma. We can show them that this is more than what they think it is—more than what they've been told it is."

Casey agreed that the stigma is disappointing but it's to be expected. "People only know what they have been told and the agendas behind all those messages can be frustrating. But I try to focus on the fact that we are moving forward. Every year there are more states that come online, and we get to be the face—in a small way—of that movement. We can have those preconceived notions corrected."

Part of the stigma is about who uses marijuana. It's all slackers, right? Kids who are flunking out of school, draining both society and a six-pack of Bud Light Lime? Nope. At the medical facility, more than 70% of patients are forty-five or older. Everyone from grandmas, to real estate agents, to teachers, to people who work in psychiatric facilities are using cannabis. And yes, there are some college students, too.

(By the way, Randall cautions that you should never use cannabis with other medications. It's not going to have the effect you're going for because the first medication is already changing the way your brain is working. So, no mixing. Seriously.)

When people come into The Farm, Randall always asks, "Are you prone to anxiety?" The percentage of people coming to the medical operation specifically looking for anxiety relief is pretty low, around 10%, but it's a lot higher on the adult use side of things. That affects the strains he'll recommend. Some strains can cause feelings of anxiety and paranoia; those are generally the ones with higher THC content. THC is tetrahydrocannabinol, the chemical responsible for most of marijuana's psychological effects. Randall is likely to steer people with anxiety towards a strain with a higher CBD level. CBD stands for cannabidiol—a compound of molecules that counteracts the effects of THC and can reduce nausea, vomiting and seizures, among other things. When people talk about the medicine of cannabis, CBD is what they mean.

It's all about getting the right combination for each individual. Everyone experiences cannabis in different ways, but each strain of the plant will have a specific genetic make up—generally that make up will cause the same basic effects for most people. Randall says this is particularly useful for those who are looking to reduce dependence on other medications.

"Cannabis can be an exit drug. It helps people get off of their opiates."

This is a significant switch from what we've all heard: pot as a gateway drug. But guess what? The gate swings both ways.

This is exactly what my Vet friends were talking about. Veterans with PTSD are often treated with opioids for their physical and emotional pain.[139] Those are drugs derived from opium, including morphine, and go by brand names like OxyContin, Vicodin, Percocet and Demerol, among others. It's not just Vets who are on these meds, more than 650,000 opioid prescriptions are dispensed on the average day in the US,[140] more than two million Americans are currently abusing prescription opioids, and 16,000 people die every year from opioid overdoses.[141] (Our friend Charlotte was almost one of them.)

How many people have died from cannabis overdoses? Zero. It can be argued that taking accidents into account, the number of fatalities due to pot is higher than nil. But it's hard to judge exactly what role cannabis plays in accidents because plenty of accidents happen when people are not high; I fractured three vertebrae in my spine while stone cold sober. However you want to look at it, the number of fatalities from pot is nowhere close to opioids.

It seems that this "exit drug" phenomenon is proving true all over the country. In 2013, when seventeen states and the District of Columbia implemented medical marijuana laws, the savings due to lower prescription drug use was about $165 million dollars. The results suggest that if all states had implemented medical marijuana programs, the savings to

Medicare would have been around $468 million dollars.[142] So it seems that people are actually using cannabis as medicine, not just as a chance to get high and eat Cheetos. And what was the cultural impact in these places that legalized? Did society lose its collective, pot-crazed mind? No. As Casey said, "There aren't riots in the streets and people sleeping on the sidewalks. There aren't people walking down the streets smoking joints and passing it out to kids like everybody thought would happen."

Later that day, I went to do some shopping at The Farm. At the door, they checked my ID to verify my age—just like the bartender did when I wanted a martini—and gave me something that looked like a poker chip. This was my stamp of approval and it meant I could shop anonymously; there would be no tracking of my name or order.

I went into the gallery to browse. It was nice. Really nice. It felt like Whole Foods: clean and bright with a side of organic hippie. There were glass counters displaying all kinds of paraphernalia like lighters, vaporizers, bongs, logo t-shirts, hats, mugs, and pens. A sign publicized the "Glass Artist Of the Month" and displayed his work. Ferns and dracaena plants grew on every shelf and corner of the store. It was busy; lots of people were milling around or reviewing the cannabis menu while relaxing on the perfectly retro couches in the waiting area.

When it was my turn, Randall escorted me back to the Flower Room, a locked space beyond the gallery. There was a row of cash registers, the wall behind them lined with every cannabis product imaginable, from glass jars of cannabis flowers to tinctures and baked goods. Randall took on the role of my "budtender" and we discussed what kind of experience I was looking for. I explained the experiment I wanted to conduct: I would partake, then go out to a dimly lit, crowded bar that represented all my worst anxiety fears and observe how I was feeling.

Randall brought over small clear jars, each of which contained about five or six tight little buds. They were beautiful. I've watched people buy pot illegally, a quick exchange of crumpled bills for whatever dusty crushed-up mess was in a Ziploc. Now that I've seen all the various strains, that entire concept seems absurd to me; it's like going to a restaurant and asking for something to drink. They might bring you Red Bull or chamomile tea or whiskey. Every variety of marijuana is different, and each carries different effects.

The buds smelled more like tea than the skunky stuff I was expecting. I shoved my nose in about fifteen different jars; some types were sweet, others a bitter turn-off. Randall says "the nose knows"—if it smelled gross to me, that was my body rejecting that strain. I ended up settling on an indica-dominant strain called Rocky Mountain Blueberry that smelled like a cup of fruity tea. The description said it could make me feel euphoric, relaxed, and creative. My anxiety was still raging from Tara's house and the non-locking doors, so euphoric, relaxed, and creative sounded ideal.

I paid in cash (because of federal laws, dispensaries can't use an FDIC-insured bank or credit/debit cards), and Randall packed the little white plastic vial containing the buds into a childproof package. "You're all set!" he said, sounding very much as if we were done. I looked up at him, feeling like a stupid little lamb. I pointed to my purchase.

"Umm. I...I don't know what to do with that."

"Oh!" He ran off to get me a lighter and a "one-hitter"—a cigarette-looking ceramic thingy.

"Okay, you said you've never smoked a cigarette before, right?" I nodded pathetically. I was tempted to explain that I'm fun in other ways: I have multiple tattoos and kissed two different boys in one day and I've swum in hotel pools where I was not a guest.

"You've seen someone smoke, though, right?" He said this without the slightest hint of a patronizing tone and I was grateful. He explained what I should do, how to get the flowers into the one-hitter and how to smoke it. I pictured Katharine Hepburn with a cigarette.

Yes, I would be the Katharine Hepburn of cannabis.

Smoking With the Law

Thomas was like my own private pot guide. He lives in Colorado and is a strong proponent of legalization so he was knowledgeable about the marijuana industry. He's been smoking since eighth grade. He's now a lawyer, working at a prestigious law firm, so it's hard to imagine that the weed is standing in the way of a productive life.

Thomas prefers edibles to smoking. He tends to stop by the 7-Eleven on the way home to grab a few things after work. He doesn't know exactly why it works, but he knows that being high helps a lot of people get back to something that feels like normal to them.

"Results are so individualized. But that's not really a 'respectable' answer. Science needs to be certain and there is no telling until you try it. There is a lot of hit-or-miss."

One of the challenges of cannabis tourism in Colorado is that while it's legal to buy, there aren't many places to smoke it. You can't smoke on the street or in a hotel room. I wasn't going to take it back to Tara's happy shit show play room and light up with the four kids.

So Thomas drove us to a secluded area, up to a peak with a beautiful view of mountains that looked like they should have the words "wish you were here," printed over them. As a stunning testament to my privileged existence, I didn't think twice about smoking marijuana illegally in a public space. The fact that Thomas looked like a life-sized version of a Law School Ken Doll was also helpful, so I only took the briefest look over my shoulder before I dug the package out of my backpack and tossed it on the picnic table.

Thomas expertly opened it up, not stumbling even a little on the childproofing, and examined the contents. He crushed up the flowers and packed the one-hitter. He explained what I should do, how I should inhale and pause.

"Do what's comfortable. But it's going to be a weird sensation."

He tried to explain how to hold the one-hitter and the lighter, but after watching me fumble he decided to just hold it for me so all I had to do was inhale. I was nervous. This was it. This was the moment, at age thirty-seven, when I would go from being someone who had never smoked marijuana to someone who had. I was losing my pot virginity. It felt significant, though I couldn't explain why.

He flicked the lighter. I inhaled and felt the heat singe my lungs. I held. And then exhaled.

"Oh, that's not...terrible." I coughed.

Then we just sort of waited for something to happen. And waited. After about twenty minutes, I still wasn't feeling anything, so I took another hit. Now that one *was* actually terrible. The burn really got down deep into my lungs. I hacked a cough that made me curl my toes.

"You okay?"

I shook my head. "That was fucking gross. It's in my teeth, is it supposed to be in my teeth?"

Thomas laughed at me. "That's why I like the edibles."

We moved on to the big test: Dark Horse Bar, which seemed to be specifically created to overwhelm me. They actually pride themselves on having an atmosphere that is "sure to boggle your mind and gratify your senses." I found the place to be much more boggling than gratifying, since it was crowded, loud, hard to see, and there were things hanging from the ceiling, like sleds and musical instruments and license plates, threatening to fall on us at any second.

We sat at a long table in the middle of the bar, which was sunken down with raised seating all around us. I hated that most of all. It felt like I was in a fish bowl; there was no chance for me to have my back to a wall (my preferred "gunslinger" seat) so that I could see the whole room. There were people, oh so many people, behind me, on all sides—people above and to my right were yelling and throwing darts. They spilled beer and laughed really loud and screamed and hugged their friend who'd just arrived and the staff yelled orders over the loudspeaker and I startled every time. I waited for my anxiety to melt away. I waited for something to happen. Anything. But I felt no effect. I was exactly me. I was exactly my good old anxious, uncomfortable self.

I wondered if I was just not noticing the high, the way that a drunk person will enthusiastically claim sobriety. But that night when I retired to the playroom with the hand-drawn shark and the princess castles watching over me, my quadriceps cramped. When I get anxious, I tuck my legs up and it leaves them tense and painful. My jaw was locked up, too, it ached and popped when I yawned, another physical manifestation of my anxiety.

I couldn't sleep, so I stared at the ceiling and wondered what had happened. Did I do it wrong? I had heard that you don't always get high the first time—was that it? Or was my social anxiety so ingrained that it would not be thwarted by anything so silly as a psychoactive substance?

The next day, Thomas decided we needed to kick it into high gear.

"You need to do a bong hit." A bong, I learned, cools the smoke so that it's easier to inhale. He took me to Cedar House.

Cedar House was Thomas's friend's place and it looked like something out of a frat house movie. There were half-eaten pizzas on top of a pool table, Christmas lights hanging from the ceiling, and a ripped Bob Marley poster taped to the wall. There were also various young men, strewn about in various levels of consciousness. They had a bong sitting on the coffee table. Thomas' friends welcomed me warmly, and only laughed a little bit that I was so inexperienced in the ways of the weed. They were excited to initiate me.

"You're company, so I'm going to clean the bong for you."

I thanked them and felt bad that I hadn't known we were coming here. I should have brought some sort of *thanks for getting me high* host gift. I'd be smoking my own stuff, but they were going to the trouble of cleaning the mold out of the bong, after all.

As they took care of the housekeeping, I sat on the floor and watched a millennial roll off a futon. Someone, acting as his alarm clock, had just kicked him as a reminder that he had to be at work in five minutes. He untangled himself from the Mexican blanket and landed on the floor with surprising stealth. As he pushed the hair out of his eyes, I realized he was already completely dressed in his Chipotle uniform.

"Efficient," I commented, as he grabbed his hat and stumbled straight out the door.

With the newly sanitized bong in hand, a guy whose name I didn't catch showed me how to use it. Rather, he attempted to explain how to hold the lighter and the amount of smoke I should allow into the chamber, and upon seeing my bewildered face he proceeded to do the whole thing for me, so once again my only job was to inhale.

That time, something definitely happened. Not really something good, but something. Within ninety seconds, my hands started to shake. My heart raced. It felt very much like the beginning of a panic attack. I knew this could happen, so instead of freaking out I just took note of the sensations and after about fifteen minutes, the shaking stopped and I settled into a friendly fog. It was nothing dramatic; I felt much like I did after I had the martini a couple of nights earlier. A little slow. I felt like I had to grasp around in the dark to find my words. My arms felt heavy, like they were filled with warm pudding.

Thomas' friends passed around a joint as they bantered about Tito's, Snapchat, and a beta fish who resorted to suicide. I just sat and listened. As usual, I hovered on the edge of the conversation, feeling no desire to jump into social interaction. I was slightly less anxious about being in a stranger's house, but I still felt very much like myself—only with a shockingly dry mouth.

At one point, I looked down and noticed that I had fallen into a strange quirk I have. I was using my index finger on my thigh to write down what people were saying. It's hard to keep up with every word, but I write quickly and catch most of it. I do this most often when I am watching TV; it's a mindless tic. A way to stay in the moment without having to personally engage. When I am a little divorced from reality, when I've sunken into an empty-headed place, it happens. And here I was, post-bong hit at Cedar House in Boulder, writing on my leg.

A little later, Thomas was telling me a story and I completely lost track of what he was saying. It was like our call dropped out for a minute and when I came back, I wasn't sure what he was talking about. That was exactly what I didn't want. The last thing I need is more isolation; I already feel like I'm likely to float away during social interactions, so having an even more tenuous connection was unnerving.

I was attempting to follow a lively debate about who had watched *Space Jam* the most times, when a group of very well-dressed people wandered into Cedar House. They looked shockingly out of place, stepping over discarded solo cups in their pencil skirts and suit jackets. I wondered if I was having some sort of semiformal hallucination, but they were all real. It was eventually revealed that they were dressed up because they were coming from a funeral. One of their friends had fallen off a fifth-story balcony and they had gone to pay their final respects.

I suddenly sobered up. I stopped writing on my thigh.

The next day I boarded my flight back home. I couldn't help but feel a little disappointed. I had been expecting...something. I had hoped cannabis would turn me into one of those women who felt free to toss back her head and laugh loudly in public, someone who could socialize effortlessly, in awe of a rainbow. But that didn't happen. Nothing terrible happened, either. I didn't have a five-hour panic attack, end up in the ER or bust through that proverbial gateway and turn into a cocaine-snorting fiend. Admittedly, a wider range of test stains and experiences would have been ideal, because, just like finding a medication, a therapist or the right style of yoga practice — there is trial and error involved. It takes time because everybody is different.

I have no doubt that cannabis is helpful for some. If people want to use it to reduce other dependencies and deal with their pain, sleep disorders, PTSD or whatever else, I believe it should be legally accessible. Add in the increased regulation to ensure that more people are engaging safely (not to mention producing revenue streams that get put back into public works), and I can absolutely see the benefit.

But personally, I don't think I'm destined to be the Katharine Hepburn of cannabis after all.

Something to Try: Everything

Remember in the beginning of the book when I told you to not self-medicate with recreational drugs? I still think that's good advice, most of the time. But with everything, there are exceptions. I am certainly not going to tell you to go grab some cannabis-laced gummy bears, but what I will recommend is getting out of your comfort zone. I've had so many people tell me they have "tried everything" in an attempt to feel better. I ask if they have tried meditation, or CBT, or dietary adjustments and they say well, no, they haven't actually tried any of that.

What they have tried is really, really wanting things to be better. And I get that. It can be overwhelming to imagine what could actually help. It can also be scary because what if we try something and it doesn't work? My Colorado adventure, by most accounts, was a failure. I tried something and it didn't really go the way I had hoped. But the experience helped me check something off the list. It taught me what works for me and what doesn't. It was a worthwhile failure, as most failures tend to be. So don't discount something just because it might not work.

Likewise, remember that sometimes the things that can help are tiny and don't require some dramatic gesture and a plane ticket. Maybe we can start taking a fifteen-minute walk after dinner. Maybe we should get a pet. Maybe we could turn off the T.V. just five minutes earlier so we can journal before bed. Little adjustments might not cure massive problems, but they can start to move us in the right direction. Since our troubles feel so gigantic, it might seem like those steps are too minor to count. But try to be open to the grace of small things.

Remember when we made that Start, Stop, Continue list at the end of Chapter 1? Now that we are getting close to the end of this book, and you've gotten some new ideas, revisit that list. Has anything changed? Can you add to the list?

Make a list of things you want to:

Stop: What habits or patterns are feeling unproductive and detrimental?

Start: What do you think you might like to start doing?

Continue: What seems to be working?

Chapter 12: "Cauliflower is the new kale," and Other Obnoxious Things

I'm touchy about food. I think it's because I've been a vegetarian since the age of three and so I've had a lifetime of being teased, mocked, and coerced about my food choices. Backyard barbecues are a hotbed of harassment and hamburger pushing. I was publicly shamed by a waiter in Paris because he found my lifestyle choice to be morally corrupt, even though it was conveyed to him in pretty decent French.

So when people try to dictate what I should or should not eat, it triggers some major four-year-old temper-tantrum style rebellion. Therefore, reading about processed sugar and its effects on anxiety and depression was pretty bad news for me. The American Journal of Clinical Nutrition found that a high glycemic index score corresponded to an increased risk of depression.[143] It seems that high glucose levels trigger a hormonal response that reduces blood sugar; this biological response can trigger or worsen mood changes, and cause fatigue and other symptoms of depression. Sugar also causes inflammation, and inflammation in the brain exacerbates anxiety and mood disorders. When blood sugar levels swing, it can trigger cortisol and adrenaline, which can set off anxiety and panic attacks.

I couldn't ignore the research any longer, so I reluctantly decided to see what would happen if I quit sugar for just a little while. (Just to be clear, I'm talking about refined sugar. I don't mean fruit or even carbs that are turned into sugar in our bodies. I mean the stuff that's in doughnuts.) It seemed to be a straightforward experiment and I had no excuses to not try it, but this was not a lighthearted endeavor for me. I love sugar. I love cake and pie and chocolate. I really love icing. So I whined for a while about how I really *couldn't* give up sugar because what good is a life without cookies? I was about to find out.

I committed to eliminate processed sugar for ten days. I know some people start with cutting out fruit and grains, too, but seriously? Forgoing gelato was going to be painful enough.

The first few days were terrible.

Day 1: Thought about sugar constantly. Had a semi-erotic dream about crème brûlée.

Day 2: Got mad at the internet for having photos of macaroons. Considered cancelling internet service but was too sweaty, itchy, and annoyed to figure out how to contact my provider.

Day 3: Drove past Ben & Jerry's and decided that Karamel Sutra had been the only good thing in my life.

Day 4: Started to feel a little more clear-headed. Meditation practice was easier. Felt a little less puffy. Still forced my husband to stand in the closet while he ate a small piece of dark chocolate, so I couldn't smell it.

Day 5: Woke up in a great mood after an amazing night of sleep. Didn't crash mid-afternoon. Dealt with a stupid situation with surprising ease. Said "no, thanks!" to the offer of a peanut butter brownie and only felt a tiny bit stabby…

That ten-day detox hasn't stopped yet. As of this writing, it's been more than a year.

I wondered what life would be without cookies, and I found my answer. Life is less teary all the time, less emotionally volatile, less like the slightest affront will send me directly under the covers. But I wasn't immediately willing to give sugar all the credit. It might have been a coincidence, right? Maybe I was just feeling good. Maybe those sugar studies only applied to other people and I had a particularly robust sugar tolerance due to the fact that when I was a kid I used to eat white sugar and margarine on crust-less Wonder bread. But I stayed strong even as I gazed through the window of my favorite bakery with the longing of an unrequited love.

One night I made a healthy dinner with lots of bright, beautiful veggies in a teriyaki sauce, then proceeded to cry when Jeremy asked me a question about an article I had written. That night, when I wasn't having nightmares about dead bodies floating in water, I was awake ruminating with dark, obsessive thoughts. I sobbed in the morning while trying to brush my teeth and then yelled at my husband for trying to hug me. Why was I so upset? Because I was miserable, my life was a mess, and I was a failure.

Somewhere, in a tiny back corner of my brain, this seemed odd. I checked the ingredient list on the bottle of teriyaki sauce. It read: soy sauce, sugar. Sugar was the second ingredient. When I showed Jeremy, who was still recovering from being yelled at before 6:30 am, he said, "Well, at least we know it's not psychosomatic."

Okay, maybe my tragic mood really was because of the sugar. I hadn't woken up sobbing in a long time. Nothing in my life had changed, except the Teriyaki Factor. I no longer needed a study to tell me there was a connection between my food and my mood, and I couldn't pretend it didn't matter anymore. We see this all the time in kids: they eat candy, then become completely unhinged and crash in a weepy pile on the floor. Why would we think it's any different now that we're taller?

Even with all this logic, I still had a problem: If I gave up sugar, I wouldn't be fun anymore. Sugar is celebratory and the edible representation of enjoying life. But I had to face the fact that sobbing uncontrollably is not fun. Yelling at my husband is not fun. No one thinks I'm super fun when I'm whimpering in a corner.

I met with Cecily Armstrong, a certified nutritionist and holistic health counselor, to learn about the food/mood connection.[144] We met at a yoga studio, which was helpful. There is something about just being there that encourages me to make healthy choices — it's probably all that tea tree oil and Lycra. The other motivational factor was Cecily herself; the woman is downright shiny. She's in her mid-forties and has great skin and toned arms and you just want to be like her.

I dug my bare feet into a yoga mat and complained that there are too many options out there. Everyone has contradictory opinions on what to eat and which foods are going to kill us. Juicing, Paleo, gluten-free, kombucha, ultra-low carb — it's exhausting. It creates a sense of apathy because we've got info overload, and P.S., we're hungry.

"What we've done with food is really scary. It's easy to feel incompetent when you are standing in front of the yogurt section trying to differentiate between three hundred kinds of yogurt. It's so hard to know what's right, and it's easy to make decisions that maybe twenty years ago were the right decisions based on the information we had at the time. Like, low fat, sugar-free is the way to go, but now when you look at it, it has artificial color and artificial sweetener and weird fat-removed milk that was thickened with artificial thickener, because it doesn't act like yogurt, because it's liquid."

Cecily pointed out that people have different ancestries and so our bodies are going to respond to food differently. We don't need to listen to the crazy claims of the latest fad diet; we have to try on things and listen to the cues our body is giving us. We need to pay attention to what really feels good. That doesn't mean what feels good when you eat it, because raspberry cheesecake feels pretty damn good in your mouth. But think about how you feel an hour later. Do you feel nourished and satisfied? Or buzzed and then exhausted? Things change when you outgrow the need for instant gratification.

Food is emotional; we make it our friend or enemy or reward. Rarely do we think of it as our ally in feeling more stable and less emotionally volatile. We use Monster Energy Drinks and Snickers to help us get through the day, but in reality, these things are working against us.

We forget that food is what powers us — not what holds power over us. What goes into our bodies is what we get in return. When I mentioned my issue with wanting to be "fun" and celebrate the fact that it's Thursday with some pecan pie, Cecily said she gets it. But she's started to see things differently.

"I have less personal attachment to the things I thought I needed to have. There were things I thought I needed to be happy, but that happiness was a false happiness. I want to be Happy-with-a-capital-H. Not just the small happy that comes from *oh my mouth is enjoying this*. I want the Big Happy. And the Big Happy for me comes when I'm connected to myself and connected to my life. It's when I can move my body and I don't need to crash in the middle of the day and I can get good sleep at night. Those things come from making good choices around my eating. But until you have that lived experience about how your eating can take you down, it's all just a vague notion. You think *it would be good to give up sugar, but I really like sugar, so I don't want to* and it becomes a struggle, it becomes a war. But when you eat well and feel the stillness in

228

your body, you realize it's a sense of peace. Then it's easier to sustain because you get what you want: the Big Happy. The peace. It's so freeing to be on the other side of it."

Ella: John Mayer Was Right

Ella has had dramatic mood swings ever since she was a kid, just like her mom. But she's never felt ashamed about it.

"I have a mood disorder. I claim it. I tend towards depression. I tell people 'this is how I roll. And it has nothing to do with you.' It's cheesy but you know that John Mayer song, when he's on the doorstep with his heart in his hand or whatever, and she's upset? And he realizes—*it's not me*. He realizes it has nothing to do with him. That's what I tell people. It's not you. This is biochemical."

In high school, Ella asked her therapist to prescribe anti-depressants, to try to balance her out, but her therapist steered her towards holistic remedies first. Focusing on food choices, essential oils, and bodywork. Ella began to notice how easily she could manipulate the way she felt by what she was eating.

"I had been eating my feelings. I was lethargic, bloated, sad, and blah."

By working with a nutritionist and experimenting with her diet, she found what worked best for her: cutting gluten and sugar, adopting a diet low in carbs and high in fat with lots of meat. It seemed pretty straightforward, but making that change required her to completely change the way she felt about food.

"Now I think about food as fuel, not as comfort. What is going to fuel me best? What is the best gas I can put in my tank? It's not about what will soothe me."

The dietary changes resulted in weight loss, but that's not what Ella focused on. She wasn't happy because she was thinner; she was happy because she was happy. She learned how to regulate her emotions with her food choices, so she didn't feel so up-and-down all the time.

"I felt lighter and brighter. I didn't feel like there was a dark cloud, like I was in mud and just slogging my way through it. Instead of thinking *here we are again, nothing is good and nothing is right*, I felt like, *let's go out and see what's up with the world!* Things had a positive spin rather than a negative spin."

And all of that was working great...until life happened. Recently, Ella moved to California for a job. She lost her support network and the depression returned. She started eating the foods that don't work for her, and it began the unhappy cycle.

"The dark cloud wants the carbs."

Once again, Ella feels like she's slogging her way through life. She doesn't know when this cloud will pass. She's got some real stuff going on; there are things she misses deeply about where she used to live. She misses her friends and regrets moving.

So Ella goes to the bakery, which seems like it might help, but she can feel it magnifying her depression. She's in the process of beginning again and trying to get her food on track.

"When I'm depressed, I feel like I can't do anything. And when I'm dialed in, eating well, I can do anything. It's like turning on a switch. Now I just have to duct tape that switch open."

Make a Plan

Cecily says, "Nature is amazing, and the pharmacy of things that can come from your produce section is unreal." (If you don't believe her, google the phrase *beet doping*.) "For anxiety and depression, I always steer people towards trying this, just for a week: a diet mostly based on vegetables and lots of protein. Eliminate wheat, sugar, and the white foods except for cauliflower—so no potatoes, corn, anything grain—and see what you feel. Just for a week."

She recommends keeping a food diary. The Fitbit app is great for that, but there are other free food tracker apps as well. Paper and a pen also works just fine. Write down everything—seriously, *everything*—you eat for a few days. Jot down anything else you notice about your emotions, sleep, any physical symptoms like headaches or puffiness. You'll start to see how many things are connected to what you're eating.

Some foods That Make Anxiety Worse
(you're not going to love this part)

• Caffeine. Yeah, I know, I'm sorry, but it's notorious for triggering panic.

• Alcohol. Again, I'm sorry.

• Nicotine. Smokers say it calms them down, but actually, smokers are more anxious and worse sleepers than nonsmokers.[145] Plus, you know, there's cancer.

• Simple sugars. That means refined white/brown sugar and honey. They break down very quickly into glucose and that can put you into overdrive.

• Simple starches. White bread, refined grains.

• Packaged foods. Preservative chemicals can complicate anxiety.

Now for the Good News: Foods that Support Healthy Moods

• Veggies (especially dark leafy greens and asparagus)
• Fruits (especially avocados, raspberries and blueberries)
• Complex carbs like whole grains, whole grain breads, oatmeal and brown rice
• Nuts, beans, and legumes
• High protein foods. If you eat meat, pasture-raised is best—chicken, turkey, grass-fed beef. Look for local, happy, well-treated meat. If you're vegetarian—beans, lentils, spirulina, quinoa, goji berries, tempeh, nuts, hemp, chia seeds, kale and greens, non-dairy nut milks, sunflower seed butter, avocados and protein powders.
• Fish. Canned fish like sardines, anchovies and wild salmon (BPA-free cans if possible). Pacific salmon, cod, trout, mackerel and halibut. (Keep an eye on those mercury levels.)
• Non-processed foods that look like the things your grandma would have eaten when she was growing up.

These are the food choices I tend to stick with most of the time. I abide by the 80/20 rule. If I'm eating this way 80% of the time, that's a win. That allows me some compassionate wiggle room and the occasional cupcake, because I'm not a monster. But if I have that cupcake and then find myself sobbing in front of the lobster tank in the seafood section at Wegmans, at least I'll know why.

Why does this plan focus so much on protein? Cecily explained that when your body breaks down protein, it leaves behind various amino acids. Amino acids make up a significant proportion of our muscles, cells and tissues. They drive the neurotransmitters and mood/food connection in the body. Your body can manufacture some amino acids, but others have to come from food. Without an adequate supply of aminos, many bodies do not regulate themselves well. Cecily said that when she meets vegetarians and vegans with depression, it can sometimes be a simple shift—either adding in more protein or supplementing with amino acids.

I know this from personal experience. Recently, I was struggling with another bout of depression. Nothing bad had happened but I was sad all the time; I felt hopeless and unmotivated. I sat by myself on the kitchen floor and cried. I was exhausted. I couldn't even motivate myself to get to yoga or pick up a book. The source of my sadness seemed to be nothing other than the fact that I had to live in my own skin.

Upon Cecily's recommendation, I picked up 5HTP, L-glutamine, magnesium, and GABA (remember GABA from the yoga study?) from my local health food store. Within twenty-four hours, it was like the mud was rinsed out of my brain and I could think again. I could feel things normally again. I had energy again.

I only took them for a couple months, then stopped, and found that I felt fine without them. Cecily said you should feel your nutrition, so if you can't tell it's making a difference, you might not need it. Make sure you start just one thing at a time, so you know how it works in your body. If you start, or stop, too many things at once, it's harder to tell what was actually working. (For lots more on amino acids and emotions, check out *The Mood Cure* by Julia Ross.)

I'm not trying to sell you on a supplement program, or tell you that for only seventeen installments of $19.99 you can feel better (call or click now!). I'm just telling you what worked for me. You — and your doctor/health advisor — need to figure out what works for you. You don't have to believe anyone about anything until you try it for yourself.

Alexandra: When Food Becomes the Bad Guy

Alexandra has a lot going on. She's got five kids, she works part time, and she and her husband own a struggling small business that they're trying to sell because it is bankrupting them. It's no wonder she feels on edge all the time. The financial stress alone is overwhelming; some days she can't bear to talk to anyone, so she just crawls in bed and falls asleep for three hours at a time. But she can't do that very often, because even when she's depressed to the point of being non-functional, she is still the mother of five kids. It's simply not an option.

"I cry. A lot."

Alexandra noticed her food issues when depression hit in high school. But, in retrospect, it started a lot earlier than that.

"When I would pack my lunches in fourth and fifth grade, I would put just one can of orange juice in the freezer and then I would pack that. So I had to be thinking about limiting my food way back in elementary school."

Alexandra played basketball in high school, and her coach used to tell her that if she was just a little quicker on her feet, she'd be a better player. She thought maybe if she lost a little weight, she'd be faster. But when that didn't result in more playing time, food became a way to exert some control over her life, her body, and her depression.

Eating disorders can be a chicken-and-egg situation, because it's hard to tell which came first. Depression can lead to an eating disorder, but also the malnourishment of an eating disorder causes psychological changes that are detrimental for the mood.[146]

In six months, Alexandra's weight dropped from 120 pounds to 100 pounds. She went to counseling with her parents and eventually got back to a healthy weight, but she then found herself swinging in the other direction. She started partying, drinking heavily, and was at 165 pounds when she graduated college. Alexandra just couldn't find the balance she wanted. And she still struggles to find it.

"I wish I was normal. I wish I could have a day where I don't think about it. I wish I could just enjoy myself and go to a party or go to a wedding and not worry about it. I just want to be normal."

After her second child, Alexandra had major postpartum depression and went on Zoloft. That helped her to feel more levelheaded, more able to cope with her life. After taking the pills for more than a decade, she wanted to stop, but the withdrawal symptoms were significant.

"Coming off of it is brutal. And there is fear, too, worrying that I'm going to go back into depression or I'll be angry all the time with my kids. I worry about that."

One thing that helps Alexandra's depression is exercise. But instead of it being an outlet for her, a place where she can take care of herself and feel good, it's become another thing that is out of balance. She calls exercise an obsession, and it's starting to interfere with her family.

"Yesterday my youngest was sick—just a cold, sore throat, she felt yucky—and instead of just saying home with her, loving on her, laying on the sofa, and watching a Disney movie, I took her to my mom's so I could exercise."

Alexandra feels like exercise makes her a nicer person and a better mom. It allows her to deal with the bickering of five kids without just yelling at them all the time. But working out also holds her hostage. She's at its mercy. As she was calling her mom to ask her to babysit, she was overwhelmed with feelings of self-condemnation.

"I felt so much guilt, because I couldn't go one day without doing it. I don't like that. I wish I could just keep my pajamas on all day and stay home with her. But I knew if I didn't go I'd be stressed out about it all day. I would be irritated with everybody. If I don't go, I won't be a nice person. I hate that. I hate that I can't just go on vacation, I have to figure out a way to exercise. And everybody has to work around my schedule and that's how we plan our day. My husband has gotten used to it, but I know it's frustrating for him, too."

In the US, 20 million women and 10 million men suffer from a clinically significant eating disorder at some point in their lives.[147] This is hardly uncommon, but it is serious. It can have detrimental effects on all aspects of your health, including a loss in bone density, muscle loss, hair loss and kidney failure. Please don't try to deal with this alone. Professionals can help you find a better way. You deserve to be nourished.

Something to Try: Try Not to Roll Your Eyes When I Say, "Self-Care."

The term "self-care" can seem egotistical and entitled. It might conjure images of self-centered, bonbon-eating sloths. Who has time for this saccharine concept of "self-care" when there are soccer games and dirty dishes demanding attention?

It's time for a re-branding. Let's re-name this practice, "giving yourself a tune-up so you don't totally lose it and ruin the lives of everyone around you." That might be a little too long to catch on. I'll work on it.

For me, self-care goes completely out the window in difficult times, which is precisely when it's most necessary. Self-care isn't selfish. It's a prerequisite for living a life in which you can actually be of use to others. It's like what they tell you on the airplane: You have to put your oxygen mask on yourself before you can help someone else. If you aren't doing enough to sustain yourself, you're useless to the rest of the world. Self-care doesn't have to be elaborate and expensive; you don't have to take yourself on a spa weekend to Santa Fe (of course if you want to, that's fantastic, and please invite me along)

Culturally, we are stuck in this mentality that being "busy" is the holy grail of personhood, so we can't possibly have time to take care of ourselves. We cling to chaos and feel worthy only if we don't have time to sleep. Why do we need to fill every second of the day with stuff? We all have a lot going on: we have jobs and families and side-hustles, Instagram accounts and appointments with the HVAC guy. But when we really look at it, some of this whirlwind might be self-imposed. We didn't have to agree to get dragged into the fights on the neighborhood board. We didn't have to hand-sew the school play costume with only recycled materials. We never wanted to do those things in the first place, but the busyness tends to make us feel important.

When people ask us to pile yet another thing onto our overloaded plate, we can remember that "no" is a complete sentence. "Busy" is not a merit badge. You are still a worthy person if you have time to take a nap on a Wednesday afternoon. We really can sit and read a book sometimes. We can stare out the window. The world will keep spinning all by itself and we'll be more grounded and useful if we take care of ourselves a little. We don't need to justify our place on the planet and remind everyone about how much is going on; you earned your worthiness just by being born. Just like everyone else.

When we ditch the drama, we have time for play. Play is not frivolous. It's hugely important to having a life that feels meaningful. Kids get this. They know that doing something just for the joy of doing it is what makes life awesome. You know what is not at all awesome? Having a meltdown over making the perfect key lime bars with the hand-squeezed key limes for the pool party. (Trust me. I've done it. Not awesome.)

You can play alone or with others. We've seen how vital community is—maybe you want to join a basketball team or start a book club. Find a few people who really like hula hooping or Star Wars and decide to meet once or twice a month. Creating your own playful community is a great way to increase feelings of connectedness and purpose. It doesn't need to this big formal thing. It only needs to be intentional.

Other cultures seem to do a better job understanding the importance of downtime. The Danish concept of *hygge* (pronounced like "hue-gah") means "a quality of coziness and comfortable conviviality that engenders a feeling of contentment or well-being."[148] It's about bliss, gratitude, taking pleasure in simple, gentle, warm and fuzzy things. It's well understood in Denmark that this is a required activity if we want to be productive and balanced in the rest of life. It's a way to create a sense of peace in the middle of whatever is happening, and many believe it's a major reason Danes are so happy. Relaxing isn't lazy when it's planned. So can you tell

Siri to block your schedule once or twice a week for some *hygge* time? Here are some ideas:

- "*Solvitur ambulando.*" It's a Latin phrase that means, "it is solved by walking." So take a walk. Preferably with a dog. (If you don't have one, animal shelters are often happy to loan you a walking companion.)
- Cook your favorite dinner.
- Buy yourself flowers, or some other small treat.
- Take a bath.
- Take a nap.
- Join a sports team or hobby group.
- Sit on a park bench and watch the trees.
- Paint, draw, write, garden, make pottery—you get the idea.
- Living room dance party. (I recommend Ace of Base, but you do you)
- Warm drink + fluffy socks or iced tea + barefoot in the sunshine.
- Watch something hysterical and laugh until your tummy hurts.
- Be in nature and watch a sunrise/sunset.
- Cuddle with a person or animal or warm fuzzy blanket.
- Eat an orange in the shower. (Seriously, if you haven't, give it a try.)
- Play a board or card game.
- Meditate.
- Read.
- Have an orgasm. (Oh yeah, I went there.)

Chapter 13: The Endless, Desperate Quest for the Thing That Doesn't Exist

The options for addiction are extensive: alcohol, gambling, shopping, cocaine, Louboutins—the list goes on. I've never found any of those things too interesting. My addiction is hardcore. My addiction is perfectionism.

I think that if I make everything perfect, then I can finally relax. If things are perfect—my work, my house, my spouse, my life—there is a split-second high when I feel like maybe I have control over all this chaos. Maybe if I teach a perfect writing class in which I don't stumble over my words, or if I cook a perfect dinner for my family, it will inoculate me from feeling hurt or disappointed. Maybe I can save myself from embarrassment or judgment. Maybe everyone will love me and think I have it all together.

It never works out that way.

When I opened up the hardcover version of my first book, *You Look Like That Girl*, I felt something as close to pride as a Canadian is allowed to get. I had accomplished something. My heart danced as I flipped through the eighty-two thousand words that I had painstakingly chosen, one by one. I read the acknowledgements, the names of the people who had loved and supported me through four years of work.

And then I saw it.

A typo.

My heart stopped dancing and fell on the floor in despair.

Combing through the rest of the pages, I found several more typos. I had to physically sit on my hands to restrain myself from e-mailing my publisher and demanding they stop the presses, which would have been satisfyingly dramatic. But since I held the final version in my hand, it was clear that the book had already been thoroughly pressed.

I didn't want to publish the book anymore. I wanted to throw every copy into a bonfire. I wanted forty-eight months of work to turn to ash and disappear. The first time I had submitted a manuscript to a publisher, I was ten years old, but my life-long dream of being a published author was nothing compared to the shame of having typos in my book.

I was mortified and miserable for weeks. I would wake up in the middle of the night and have a flickering moment of peaceful, sleepy reprieve before those typos — those goddamned typos — would come flooding back to me. I cried into my pillow. I had a constant stomachache; every time someone asked me about the book, my face would flush and I'd change the subject. Those typos were triggering my most persistent and excruciating fear: people were going to think I was stupid.

I obsessed about why I didn't catch them. I fumed about my editor, my publisher, my husband — everyone who read and reread the manuscript and didn't catch the errors. There were errors. It wasn't perfect, therefore, it was ruined. That mean voice in my head was right: I couldn't be a writer. I would never do anything as important as being in that movie when I was fourteen years old.

Then, a friend said something horrible and enlightening. I was droning on about the typos, yet again, and she said, "Huh. Sounds kind of like an ego thing."

Ego? EGO? Me, with my pitiful self-image? Me, who always thinks I must be dumb or weird or out of place? How could this possibly be about my EGO?

But she was right.

I didn't need to have my self-esteem boosted; I needed to be humbled. I needed to show a little humility and drop this ego trip that expected I should have super-human abilities. What else could it be if I assumed I should be able to do everything perfectly, even though I didn't expect that of anyone else? Wasn't I saying I was better than them? Did I think I was so amazing that I should never fail like every other human being? It was was a pretty misplaced sense of arrogance, thinking that everybody was watching my every move, noting any shortcomings and discussing them at length to determine my soul's value. I heard someone say once that the problem is not that we think less of ourselves, it's that we need to think of ourselves less often. Ouch.

I was vacillating from this ego-filled arrogance that insisted I *could* be perfect, to pummeling myself with below-the-belt insults for failing unobtainable goals. If I ever talked to someone else the way I talked to myself, I'd be the biggest bully on the playground. Why was I contributing to the negativity in the world by being so terrible to another living creature—even if that creature was myself? Even if no one else knew I was saying such brutal things internally, I was radiating my suffering all over anyone who got within one hundred feet of me. I was a walking toxic waste dump of self-loathing. The world was hard enough without me adding to the pile of pain and disappointment.

I needed another tactic. I needed to show some humility, while being kind and compassionate. I tried to treat myself like I'd treat a friend who was recovering from a difficult disappointment. I surrendered to the typo situation that couldn't be changed. I hardly felt deserving of such kindness, but for the sake of my family, my friends and everyone around me, I worked on neutralizing the war zone I had created by fighting with reality.

I surrendered to the fact that I was imperfect. I took a bath with Epsom salts and lavender at 3pm on a Thursday. I bought a pretty plant and put it on my kitchen table. I took a nap. It felt unusual to be so nice to me, but it also felt revolutionary. I didn't deny the disappointment I felt at finding the typos, but instead, let myself feel it fully so I could let go of it. I read the Serenity Prayer out loud to myself, in a slightly edited version:

God grant me the serenity to accept the typos I cannot change; the courage to change the typos I can; and the wisdom to know the difference.

From First Grade to Stanford

My friend's five-year-old daughter was crying. Sobbing, really. She had just taken her first spelling test and had gotten nine out of ten correct. Having never done that well on a spelling test in my life, I was impressed with her grade. But other kids in her class had gotten a perfect score, and she had not. She missed that one word. She was not perfect, and it was devastating. Humiliating.

At the University of Pennsylvania it's called Penn Face.[149] At Stanford, they refer to it as Duck Syndrome.[150] It's the feeling of needing to appear perfect, even if underneath the water you are paddling frantically, just trying to not drown. This obsession with an impossible ideal of perfection is so common that we're coming up with cute names for it. But it isn't cute. We might try to frame it as simply wanting to do our best, but perfectionism is much more detrimental than that. It can cause or complicate issues of anxiety and depression and is a risk factor that is linked with suicide.[151]

Perfectionism has two parts: one is having unrealistic standards for yourself that you would never have for anyone else. Case in point, I've seen typos in many other books; it didn't make me think the author was a hack. I just thought, *Hey, the editor missed a typo.* But when it came to myself, I couldn't be so forgiving.

The second part of perfectionism is focusing on flaws to the exclusion of anything that might have been positive. The typos in my book completely negated the fact that I had just published an actual, for-real book with a UPC code and a spot on the shelf in Barnes & Noble.

But here's the deal: Your value as a human being is not based on accomplishments or "success." Let's get morbid for a moment and think about the obituary that will be published after your death. What will be the legacy of your short time on earth? It's not going to include whether or not you got that promotion, or said that awkward thing to your neighbor about his mailbox smelling good. It will be about the people you impacted, the authenticity with which you moved through the world and the fun you had while you were here. That's all anyone is going to remember.

Sharon Salzburg tells a story about the Dalai Lama. He was sitting up on a stage, leading an event for more than twelve hundred people. As the translator translated his commentary on some Buddhist text, The Dalai Lama interrupted him.

"That's not what I said."

The translator responded that yes, that was in fact exactly what he said. The Dalai Lama insisted that was incorrect. The translator then showed the Dalai Lama the text. He looked at it, and then burst into laughter, "Oh, I made a mistake!" He was cracking up. At himself. For being wrong. In front of a huge group of people.

That's how I want to be in the world. Because striving for perfection is like being convinced that I can catch that train that left the station an hour ago. It's impossible. I'll be constantly running after something that I'll never get, falling on my face and busting open my lip on the train tracks.

So when we're obsessing in that crazy-eyed way about our mistakes, we can try asking ourselves—Did anything else happen? Are we seeing the whole picture? We don't have to deny that we screwed up, but we can pay attention in a more complete way. We can practice retraining our brains to be kind and compassionate to ourselves and better learn from our mistakes in the process.

Imperfecting Ourselves

There is only one way to deal with perfectionism. It requires a fundamental shift in the way you view yourself and the way you live your life. Not such a big deal, right? Just a complete change in your view of your place in the world. We can totally do that.

Here are some ideas to consider if you want to shift your perspective and squash your perfectionism:[152]
- Are others people's achievements and accomplishments the most important thing to you? Is it all about your friend's money or job title? More likely you enjoy their deadpan sense of humor or the fact that they always know the names of flowers. Maybe those external markers aren't so important after all.

- Recognize that "all or nothing" thinking is rarely reasonable in the real world. The interesting stuff happens in the grey space between.
- There's no easy way to say this: Get over yourself. Take a look at one of those cool photos of the vastness of the universe and remember how small you are—then take a deep breath.
- Practice gratitude and celebrate the little things that go well. Even minor successes deserve to be acknowledged.
- Set realistic goals. As it turns out, publishing a book that is completely and absolutely perfect is not a reasonable goal. Publishing a book that I'm proud of is hard enough, so that's worth working towards.
- Go have some fun. Do things you enjoy that are not tied to your sense of self-worth. This is what hobbies are for. No one cares if you are any good at jigsaw puzzles or mineral collecting. If you enjoy it, that's all that matters.
- It's about the journey, not the destination. Give up the need to win and instead focus on not being a dick along the way—to others or yourself. One of my teachers says, "Yoga is not about touching your toes, it's about what you learn on the way down."
- Remember that your authentic expression will be someone else's inspiration.

Something to Try: Screw up on Purpose

Every time we acknowledge our fear and move forward, we are fundamentally changed by that. We're not the same person after that experience. Practice not being perfect and see what happens. Plan to do something terribly. Draw with your non-dominant hand. Go to an exercise class and fall down on purpose—see if everyone stops to laugh and stare, and even if they do, see if that results in sudden death for you. Misuse a word and see if your friends abandon you. Practice reframing your thoughts, and write them down. Change "I did this wrong because I totally suck" to "This didn't go as I intended, some parts need some work."

When we drop perfectionism, we leave space for possibility and adventure. Sometimes things will go well, and other times they won't, and we'll have to pick ourselves back up. But when we fail, it means we tried. It means we were not paralyzed by perfectionism and fear. Failure is incredibly brave.

The world doesn't need perfect people. The world needs you.

Chapter 14: It's Okay to be Okay

Maybe you're starting to feel a little bit better. There's a dim light at the end of the tunnel. You laughed really hard at that stupid meme the other day. But then it started to hit: What right do you have to be happy? When there is so much pain in the world, isn't it kind of disrespectful to be content? If you're happy, doesn't that mean something horrible is just around the corner? That's how it always happens in movies. If someone is smiling and enjoying a moment, an axe murderer is definitely behind those curtains.

This kind of thinking is known as "catastrophic misinterpretation." I love this term. Catastrophic misinterpretation refers to thoughts that are simply not correct. They are completely, absolutely, detrimentally wrong. Here's why it's okay for you to be okay: Happy, grateful people are good for everybody. It's more effective to help the world from a place of inner peace than to suffer in solidarity. Greatness does not need to come from suffering; it comes out of being awake to the intricacies of life.

It's easy to get attached to our anxiety and identify with it so strongly that we wonder who we are if we're not unhappy all the time. Sometimes we sabotage ourselves because we feel undeserving of joy or success. Or maybe a calm, happy life seems really unnerving after everything that we've been through. Something new, even if it's good, can be so scary that we choose the bad stuff just because it's familiar. But I think you are now awake enough to see that's just Amy the Amygdala talking. You can do better than her.

Let's keep coming back to examine what is real and what is true. Sometimes we're anxious, sometimes we're depressed.

But that is not who we are. Remember that those are just the clouds. We're the sky, and we don't need to cling to clouds.

Pain is Inevitable. Suffering is Optional.

It's taken me a long time to get to this point, but here I am: I'm a happy person. I used to think that contentment was only for frivolous people, but I'm actually very happy being happy. I've become that person who can also feel incredible joy with just a cup of tea and a patch of sunshine. I laugh a lot more. I can feel something close to calm even when the circumstances of my life are hard and messy and unfair. My baseline emotional state used to be at war with the world. Now it's at ease. I am nowhere near perfect, and sometimes I get sucked into the doom spiral and forget everything I've learned — but I'm far more resilient than I used to be. I remember how to get back to happy pretty quickly. I never thought this anxious heart of mine could feel so peaceful.

We all have the power to make different choices. We can think that we are unworthy and everyone hates us. We can decide we are never going to be good enough because of that thing our cousin said to us when we were nine years old. We can blame ourselves eternally for those mistakes we made, the people we cheated on and the lies we told. We can obsess about our bad decisions and the ways we hurt people. We can get ulcers about things we screwed up ten years ago, and we can curse where those decisions have landed us today.

Or, we can forgive ourselves and decide we did the best we could. We can apologize to those we hurt and we can try to do better. We can make a new choice to refocus our attention in better places than on that dumbass voice with the repetitive, negative messages. We can realize that being okay is not just about us, it's good for everyone around us. We can learn to accept and manage the anxiety. We can decide to start over. Today.

We can be powerful in our lives and make the changes that will benefit us, our family, our friends, and the whole planet. The world has enough cynical, broken, mean, angry people who kick the shit out of themselves and others. Those positions have been filled.

We need people who are courageous enough to live well. To be happy. To forgive. To spread joy. To laugh even though there is pain. To laugh *because* there is pain, and we might as well laugh, because the pain will always be there. So let's laugh while we can. Let's understand it's all just fleeting and kind of meaningless. Let's make our own meaning and let's give ourselves a break and stop dwelling on everything we wish were different.

In case you are looking for a permission slip to be okay, here it is.

You have the right to be okay.

You're allowed to be happy.

It doesn't matter what was done to you or what you messed up.

Forgive. And start from right here.

Breathe in, breathe out, and begin again.

My To Do List for the Day

Open your eyes. Breathe.

Lie in bed and take a second to feel gratitude. Your life belongs to you. Whatever awaits, you get to decide how to interpret it. You choose your responses. No one can take that away from you.

Stand up. Stretch. Put on clothes that fit well and feel like you. Wash your face and use a moisturizer that smells nice.

Breathe.

Eat food that makes you feel good, even an hour after you've eaten it.

Go outside.

Text someone just to check in. Use heart emojis with abandon.

Read something beautiful. Scratch a dog behind the ears.

Forgive someone. Then forgive yourself.

Offer a stranger a compliment.

Roll out a yoga mat. Light a candle.

Turn off the TV and put down the phone thirty minutes before you go to bed. Make a list of everything that you were grateful for today.

Kiss someone you love. With tongue, if at all possible.

And at all times and in every way, embrace your weird.

Dear Doctor

Ready to go to see your doctor? Great. Fill out the following letter and rip it right out of this book or download the letter at NotJustMeBook.com.

Hello, health professional,

The person who handed you this is struggling with anxiety and/or depression and is being super brave and asking for some help. This letter is intended to begin the conversation, and offer some preliminary information to help make some changes.

- I've had issues with anxiety/depression before, it's something I've dealt with (off and on) or (most of my life)
  or
- I've not had any real issues with anxiety/depression. It's been mostly fine until _____.

- I've got some stressful/difficult life situations going on (loss, divorce, finances, job issues, moving, etc) such as

_____

or

- I haven't really got anything unusually stressful going on. The anxiety seems to be coming out of nowhere.

- I've been feeling anxious and/or depressed for_____ days/weeks/months/years

I'm having some physical symptoms like (sleep disturbance, intestinal issues, headaches, shortness of breath, chest pain, trembling, heart palpitations, unintentional weight fluctuations). Here are the times and situations in which I have those symptoms:

_____

_____

_____

_____

So far, I've tried the following things to deal with my anxiety/depression:
- therapy
- medication
- exercise
- nutrition
- increasing focus on good sleep schedule
- meditation/yoga
- massage/acupuncture
- something else

_____

- Yeah, I know I shouldn't, but I'm self medicating with drugs/alcohol/food. Specifically:

_____

_____

- Nope, I'm not self-medicating

- I've had this many panic attacks: _____ this frequently

_____

or

- I haven't had a panic attack

Let's discuss what might work for me, but at this point I'd be willing to try the following things as part of our plan:
- therapy
- medication (SSRIs, benzodiazepines, beta blockers)
- exercise
- nutrition plan
- focusing on sleep habits
- meditation/yoga
- massage/acupuncture
- something else _____
- absolutely anything you can think of, because this really sucks.

And here is something that is not covered in the letter but I wanted you to know about:

_____

_____

_____

_____

Additional Resources

Books

The Anxiety and Phobia Workbook by Edmund J. Bourne

10% Happier: How I Tamed the Voice in My Head, Reduced Stress Without Losing My Edge, and Found Self-Help That Actually Works by Dan Harris

Quiet: The Power of Introverts in a World That Can't Stop Talking by Susan Cain

Anything by Brené Brown, specifically *The Gifts of Imperfection: Let Go of Who You Think You're Supposed to Be and Embrace Who You Are* and *Daring Greatly: How the Courage to Be Vulnerable Transforms the Way We Live, Love, Parent, and Lead*

Anything by Sharon Salzberg, specifically *Real Happiness: The Power of Meditation*

Anything by Jon Kabat-Zinn, specifically *Wherever You Go, There You Are: Mindfulness Meditation in Everyday Life*

Anything by Pema Chödrön, specifically *When Things Fall Apart: Heart Advice for Difficult Times*

The Mindful Way through Depression: Freeing Yourself from Chronic Unhappiness by Mark Williams

Anxious Kids, Anxious Parents: 7 Ways to Stop the Worry Cycle and Raise Courageous & Independent Children by R. Reid Wilson

Hardcore Self Help: F**k Anxiety by Robert Duff PHD

Online

Crisis Text Line

— crisistextline.org or text HOME to 741741

Anxiety and Depression Association of America

— adaa.org

Project UROK — ProjectUROK.org

Patients Like Me — patientslikeme.com

National Alliance on Mental Illness — Nami.org

Psychology Today (finding a therapist)

— https://therapists.psychologytoday.com

Guided meditation apps:

Insight Timer

Headspace

Mindfulness

Calm

Acknowledgements

To my editor, Rebecca Faith, for her brilliant edits, lively discussions on meditation philosophy and for knowing that the plural of Lego is Lego. Your guidance and vision brought this book to a new level and I could not be more grateful. And many thanks for connecting me with Christine Herman who confirmed my suspicion that I don't know how to use a comma.

To everyone who came to my speaking events and let me try out this material on them. Thank you for showing up to auditoriums, church basements and conference rooms, for sharing your stories and for laughing when I hoped you would.

To the stunningly talented Serena Love, for her beautiful portrayal of Amy and Cora. You are a wonder.

To Sarah Cramer Shields for her incredible ability to photograph my soul and to Annie Sheehan for being a sparkly light and checking out my chaturanga and my weird fingers.

To Chris Doermann, for producing the audiobook, for wearing Chucks and having twinkly lights and dinosaur stuff in his studio. But mostly, thanks for being cool when I cried during the recording of Chapter 6.

To Dana Wheeles for her technical expertise when I was spending hours swearing at cover templates.

To my beta readers, Claudia Kalb, Lisa Nelson, Dan Willingham, Scott Craven, Dawn McMillan, JenJen Higgins, Brita Frederickson and Cynthia T. Luna. Thank you for finding typos, offering up cool studies and pointing out those places in which I make sense only to myself.

To Carl Salazar for introducing me to my ExBal Veteran family. I love you all. Thank you for letting a vegetarian hang out with you. Namaste, bitches.

To Cecily Armstrong and everyone at HYC. Without my yoga family, I'd still be on the floor of my closet.

To Kripalu and every soul that has ever walked through that place and made it what it is. Thank you for deepening my understanding, offering me a Sangha, and teaching me that I am a teacher. There is a little piece of my heart that will never leave the Berkshire mountains. Jai Bhagwan.

To the entire I-C family, Randall Tickles, Casey Cook, Jaqueline and Anthony Claudia and their amazing kiddos.

To DM, BG, BF, TG, RS, SI, CT, VG, AO, TW, DF, SD, CC, RT, RL, MD, WQ, FT, LD and DD for their support, honesty and courage. You are all changing lives with your willingness to be open and tell your stories. You inspire me.

And finally to Jeremy and his incredibly anxiety-free soul. The yang to my yin. Thank you for showing me another way to be in the world. Thank you for never making fun of me when I cry and thank you for always listening, even when it's Amy who is doing all the talking. You are my home.

About the Author

Lisa Jakub grew up in Hollywood, acting in more than forty movies and television shows, including *Mrs. Doubtfire, Independence Day* and a bunch of terrible movies you've never heard of. Searching for a path that felt more authentic to her, Lisa retired from her eighteen-year acting career at age twenty-two. She eventually found that passionate life she was looking for — as a writer, speaker, writing teacher, and Kripalu yoga teacher. Lisa lives in Virginia with her husband, Jeremy.

Lisa's memoir, *You Look Like That Girl: a child actor stops pretending and finally grows up*, is available now.

Visit the author's website at LisaJakub.net

Endnotes

[1]. National Alliance of Mental Illness - Mental Health by the Numbers. (n.d.). Retrieved February 15, 2017, from http://www.nami.org/Learn-More/Mental-Health-By-the-Numbers

[2] McPhillips, Deidre. "U.S. Among Most Depressed Countries in the World." *U.S. News & World Report*. U.S. News & World Report, 14 Sept. 2016. Web. 05 Feb. 2017.

[3]. The Benson-Henry Institute for Mind Body Medicine at Massachusetts General Hospital. (2017). *From Stress to Resiliency. Bensonhenryinstitute.org*. Retrieved 26 April 2017, from http://bensonhenryinstitute.org/8-about/74-from-stress-to-resiliency

[4] Junger, S. (2016). *Tribe* (1st ed., p. 17). New York: Twelve.

[5] *Suicide*. (2017). *Mental Health America*. Retrieved 7 May 2017, from http://www.mentalhealthamerica.net/suicide

[6]. *New State Rankings Shines Light on Mental Health Crisis, Show Differences in Blue, Red States*. (2017). *Mental Health America*. Retrieved 24 April 2017, from http://www.mentalhealthamerica.net/new-state-rankings-shines-light-mental-health-crisis-show-differences-blue-red-states

[7]. Bernstein, E. (2017). *In Men, Depression is Different*. The *Wall Street Journal*. Retrieved 21 September 2016, from https://www.wsj.com/articles/in-men-depression-is-different-1474305429

[8] Brown, B. (2015). *Rising Strong* (1st ed., p. 6). New York: Random House Inc.

[9]. Bourne, E. (2005). *The Anxiety and Phobia Workbook* (4th ed.). Oakland: New Harbinger Publications.

[10]. Junger, S. (2016). *Tribe* (1st ed., p. 20). New York: Twelve.

[11]. Tasca, C. (2012). Women And Hysteria In The History Of Mental Health. *Clinical Practice & Epidemiology In Mental Health, 8*(1), 110-119. http://dx.doi.org/ 10.2174/1745017901208010110

[12]. Ko, L. (2016). *Unwanted Sterilization and Eugenics Programs in the United States | PBS. Independent Lens.* Retrieved 1 May 2017, from http://www.pbs.org/independentlens/ blog/unwanted-sterilization-and-eugenics-programs-in-the- united-states/

[13]. *The Neurasthenia Rest Cure and Dr. Silas Weir Mitchell.* (2017). *University of Virginia - Historical Collections at the Claude Moore Health Sciences Library.* Retrieved 27 March 2017, from http://exhibits.hsl.virginia.edu/nerves/rest/

[14]. LeDoux, J. (2015). *Anxious: Using the Brain to Understand and Treat Fear and Anxiety* (1st ed., p. 16). New York: Penguin Books.

[15]. Bourne, E. (2005). *The Anxiety and Phobia Workbook* (4th ed., p.33). Oakland: New Harbinger Publications.

[16]. Cain, S. (2013). *Quiet: The Power of Introverts in a World That Can't Stop Talking* (1st ed., p. 112). London [etc.]: Penguin Books.

[17] Stossel, S. (2013). *My age of anxiety: fear, hope, dread, and the search for peace of mind.* New York: Vintage Books, a division of Random House LLC.

[18]. Van der Kolk, B. (2015). *The body keeps the score* (1st ed., p. 16). New York, New York: Penguin Books.

[19]. Duhigg, C. (2017). *Smarter faster better: The Transformative Power of Real Productivity* (1st ed.). New York: Random House Books.

[20]. *NIMH » Any Mental Illness (AMI) Among U.S. Adults.* (2017). *Nimh.nih.gov.* Retrieved 15 April 2017, from https://www.nimh.nih.gov/health/statistics/prevalence/any-mental-illness-ami-among-us-adults.shtml

[21]. Chodron, P. (2012). *Start where you are* (1st ed., p. 34). London: HarperCollins Publishers.

[22].Entis, L. (2017). *Chronic Loneliness Is a Modern-Day Epidemic. Fortune.com.* Retrieved 22 June 2016, from http://fortune.com/2016/06/22/loneliness-is-a-modern-day-epidemic/

[23]. Holt-Lunstad, J., Smith, T., & Layton, J. (2010). Social Relationships and Mortality Risk: A Meta-analytic Review. *Plos Medicine, 7*(7), e1000316. http://dx.doi.org/10.1371/journal.pmed.1000316

[24].Kim, J. E., Dager, S. R., & Lyoo, I. K. (2012). The role of the amygdala in the pathophysiology of panic disorder: evidence from neuroimaging studies. *Biology of Mood & Anxiety Disorders, 2*(1), 20. doi:10.1186/2045-5380-2-20

[25]. McGrath, J. (2008, March 12). Understanding Panic Attacks. Retrieved May 15, 2017, from http://health.howstuffworks.com/mental-health/anxiety/panic-attack1.htm

[26]. Carl Fulwiler, C. (2011, June 6). *The Neuroscience of Mindfulness - Center for Mental Health Services Research Department of Psychiatry UMass Medical School.* http://www.umassmed.edu/globalassets/center-for-mental-health-services-research/documents/products-publications/presentations/wellness/neurosciencemindfulness.pdf

[27]. Cain, S. (2013). *Quiet: the power of introverts in a world that can't stop talking.* London: Penguin Books.

[28]. Cain, S. (2013). *Quiet: the power of introverts in a world that can't stop talking.* London: Penguin Books.

[29]. Van der Kolk, B. (2015). *The body keeps the score* (1st ed., p. 16). New York, New York: Penguin Books.

[30]. LeDoux, J. (2015). *Anxious: Using the Brain to Understand and Treat Fear and Anxiety*. New York: Penguin Books.

[31]. Bourne, E. (2005). *The Anxiety and Phobia Workbook* (4th ed.). Oakland: New Harbinger Publications.

[32]. Boudewyns, P. A. (2014). Flooding and Implosive Therapy Direct Therapeutic Exposure in Clinical Practice. Springer Verlag.

[33].Cain, S. (2013). *Quiet: the power of introverts in a world that can't stop talking*. London: Penguin Books.

[34]. Cain, S. (2013). *Quiet: The Power of Introverts in a World That Can't Stop Talking*. London: Penguin Books.

[35] Wolfe, A. (2017, February 03). *An Expert Take on Performing Under Pressure*. Retrieved February 3, 2017, from https://www.wsj.com/articles/an-expert-take-on-performing-under-pressure-1486147854

[36] Whitehead, N (2016, January 12). *People would rather be electrically shocked than left alone with their thoughts*. Retrieved May 15, 2017, from http://www.sciencemag.org/news/2014/07/people-would-rather-be-electrically-shocked-left-alone-their-thoughts

[37]. Jon Kabat-Zinn [Television series episode]. (2015, April 12). In *Super Soul Sunday*. OWN.

[38]. Lagnado, L. (2016, September 19). Can Meditation Help Pain After Surgery? Retrieved September 22, 2016, from https://www.wsj.com/articles/can-meditation-help-pain-after-surgery-1474299114

[39]. Van der Kolk, B. (2015). *The body keeps the score* (1st ed., p. 16). New York, New York: Penguin Books.

[40]. Newberg, A. B., Wintering, N., Waldman, M. R., Amen, D., Khalsa, D. S., & Alavi, A. (2010). Cerebral blood flow differences between long-term meditators and non-meditators. *Consciousness and Cognition, 19*(4), 899-905. doi: 10.1016/j.concog.2010.05.003

[41]. Van der Kolk, B. (2015). *The body keeps the score* (1st ed., p. 16). New York, New York: Penguin Books.

[42]. Mindfulness meditation training changes brain structure in 8 weeks. (2011, January 21). Retrieved May 9, 2017, from http://www.massgeneral.org/News/pressrelease.aspx?id=1329

[43]. McGreevey, S. (2011, January 21). Eight weeks to a better brain. Retrieved November 6, 2016, from http://news.harvard.edu/gazette/story/2011/01/eight-weeks-to-a-better-brain/

[44]. Hölzel, B. K., Carmody, J., Vangel, M., Congleton, C., Yerramsetti, S. M., Gard, T., & Lazar, S. W. (2011). Mindfulness practice leads to increases in regional brain gray matter density. *Psychiatry Research: Neuroimaging, 191*(1), 36-43. doi:10.1016/j.pscychresns.2010.08.006

[45]. Reynolds, G. (2016, February 18). How Meditation Changes the Brain and Body. Retrieved December 4, 2016, from https://well.blogs.nytimes.com/2016/02/18/contemplation-therapy/?_r=0

[46]. Harris, D. (2017). *10% happier: how I tamed the voice in my head, reduced stress without losing my edge, and found self-help that actually works: a true story.* London, England: Yellow Kite.

[47]. Mrazek, M. D., Franklin, M. S., Phillips, D. T., Baird, B., & Schooler, J. W. (2013). Mindfulness Training Improves Working Memory Capacity and GRE Performance While Reducing Mind Wandering. *Psychological Science, 24*(5), 776-781. doi:10.1177/0956797612459659

[48]. Luders, E., Cherbuin, N., & Kurth, F. (2015). Forever Young(er): potential age-defying effects of long-term meditation on gray matter atrophy. *Frontiers in Psychology, 5*. doi:10.3389/fpsyg.2014.01551

[49]. Thanks to Firas Ali, one of my yoga teachers for pointing this out

[50]. Cain, S. (2013). *Quiet: the power of introverts in a world that can't stop talking.* London: Penguin Books.

[51] Social Anxiety Disorder from the Anxiety and Depression Association of America. (n.d.). Retrieved February 16, 2017, from https://www.adaa.org/understanding-anxiety/social-anxiety-disorder

[52]. Stossel, S. (2013). *My age of anxiety: fear, hope, dread, and the search for peace of mind.* New York: Vintage Books, a division of Random House LLC.

[53] Gallagher, M., Prinstein, M. J., Simon, V., & Spirito, A. (2014). Social Anxiety Symptoms and Suicidal Ideation in a Clinical Sample of Early Adolescents: Examining Loneliness and Social Support as Longitudinal Mediators. *Journal of Abnormal Child Psychology, 42*(6), 871-883. doi:10.1007/s10802-013-9844-7

[54]. Williams, J. M. (2007). *The mindful way through depression: freeing yourself from chronic unhappiness.* New York: Guilford Press.

[55]. Williams, J. M. (2007). *The mindful way through depression: freeing yourself from chronic unhappiness.* New York: Guilford Press.

[56]. Gilson, M. (2009). *Overcoming depression: a cognitive therapy approach: workbook.* New York: Oxford University Press.

[57]. Cook, G. (2012, January 24). The Power of Introverts: A Manifesto for Quiet Brilliance. Retrieved October 26, 2015, from https://www.scientificamerican.com/article/the-power-of-introverts/

[58]. Cain, S. (2013). *Quiet: the power of introverts in a world that can't stop talking.* London: Penguin Books.

[59]. Cain, S. (2013). *Quiet: the power of introverts in a world that can't stop talking.* London: Penguin Books.

[60]. Stossel, S. (2013). *My age of anxiety: fear, hope, dread, and the search for peace of mind.* New York: Vintage Books, a division of Random House LLC.

[61]. Raghuraj, P., & Telles, S. (2008). Immediate Effect of Specific Nostril Manipulating Yoga Breathing Practices on Autonomic and Respiratory Variables. *Applied Psychophysiology and Biofeedback, 33*(2), 65-75. doi:10.1007/s10484-008-9055-0

[62]. Tavernise, S. (2016, April 22). U.S. Suicide Rate Surges to a 30-Year High. Retrieved May 16, 2017, from http://mobile.nytimes.com/2016/04/22/health/us-suicide-rate-surges-to-a-30-year-high.html

[63]. National Center for Health Statistics. (2016, April 22). Retrieved April 4, 2017, from http://www.cdc.gov/nchs/products/databriefs/db241.htm

[64]. Williams, J. M. (2007). *The mindful way through depression: freeing yourself from chronic unhappiness.* New York: Guilford Press.

[65]. Scelfo, J. (2015, August 01). Suicide on Campus and the Pressure of Perfection. Retrieved July 27, 2016, from http://www.nytimes.com/2015/08/02/education/edlife/stress-social-media-and-suicide-on-campus.html?_r=0

[66]. Anxiety and Depression Association of America - Depression https://www.adaa.org/understanding-anxiety/depression 12/16/16

[67]. Depression. (n.d.). Retrieved December 12, 2016, from https://www.adaa.org/understanding-anxiety/depression

[68]. Williams, J. M. (2007). *The mindful way through depression: freeing yourself from chronic unhappiness.* New York: Guilford Press.

[69]. Williams, J. M. (2007). *The mindful way through depression: freeing yourself from chronic unhappiness.* New York: Guilford Press.

[70]. The Invisible Gorilla (n.d.). Retrieved May 8, 2016, from http://www.theinvisiblegorilla.com/gorilla_experiment.html

[71]. Williams, J. M. (2007). *The mindful way through depression: freeing yourself from chronic unhappiness.* New York: Guilford Press.

[72]. Self-Injury (Cutting, Self-Harm or Self-Mutilation). (2016, August 17). Retrieved January 2, 2017, from http://www.mentalhealthamerica.net/self-injury

[73]. first coined about 20 years ago by Michele McDonald

[74]. Iyengar, B. K. (2015). *Light on yoga: the definitive guide to yoga practice.* London: Thorsons.

[75] Thanks, Susan McCulley!

[76]. Iyengar, B. K. (2015). *Light on yoga: the definitive guide to yoga practice.* London: Thorsons.

[77] 2016 Yoga in America Study conducted by Yoga Journal & Yoga Alliance. (2016, January 13). Retrieved February 12, 2017, from https://www.yogaalliance.org/2016YogaInAmericaStudy

[78]. Manincor, M. D., Bensoussan, A., Smith, C. A., Barr, K., Schweickle, M., Donoghoe, L., . . . Fahey, P. (2016). Individualized Yoga For Reducing Depression And Anxiety, And Improving Well-Being: A Randomized Controlled Trial. *Depression and Anxiety, 33*(9), 816-828. doi:10.1002/da.22502

[79] Streeter, C. C., Gerbarg, P. L., Whitfield, T. H., Owen, L., Johnston, J., Silveri, M. M., . . . Jensen, J. E. (2017, March). Treatment of Major Depressive Disorder with Iyengar Yoga and Coherent Breathing: A Randomized Controlled Dosing Study. Retrieved April 3, 2017, from https://www.ncbi.nlm.nih.gov/pubmed/28296480

[80]. Streeter, C. C., Whitfield, T. H., Owen, L., Rein, T., Karri, S. K., Yakhkind, A., . . . Jensen, J. E. (2010). Effects of Yoga Versus Walking on Mood, Anxiety, and Brain GABA Levels: A Randomized Controlled MRS Study. *The Journal of Alternative and Complementary Medicine, 16*(11), 1145-1152. doi: 10.1089/acm.2010.0007

[81]. Jeter, P. E., Cronin, S., & Khalsa, S. B. (n.d.). Evaluation of the benefits of a kripalu yoga program for police academy trainees: a pilot study. Retrieved February 10, 2016, from https://www.ncbi.nlm.nih.gov/pubmed/24016821

[82]. Villemure, C., Ceko, M., Cotton, V. A., & Bushnell, M. C. (2014, October). Insular cortex mediates increased pain tolerance in yoga practitioners. Retrieved March 11, 2017, from https://www.ncbi.nlm.nih.gov/pubmed/23696275

[83]. King, A. P., Block, S. R., Sripada, R. K., Rauch, S., Giardino, N., Favorite, T., . . . Liberzon, I. (2016). Altered Default Mode Network (Dmn) Resting State Functional Connectivity Following A Mindfulness-Based Exposure Therapy For Posttraumatic Stress Disorder (Ptsd) In Combat Veterans Of Afghanistan And Iraq. *Depression and Anxiety, 33*(4), 289-299. doi:10.1002/da.22481

[84] If you'd like to support Expedition Balance, Carl (and I!) would be so grateful — https://www.expeditionbalance.org/

[85]. Van der Kolk, B. (2015). *The body keeps the score*. New York, New York: Penguin Books.

[86]. Van der Kolk, B. (2015). *The body keeps the score*. New York, New York: Penguin Books.

[87]. PTSD: National Center for PTSD. (2012, May 15). Retrieved April 20, 2017, from http://www.ptsd.va.gov/public/PTSD-overview/basics/symptoms_of_ptsd.asp

[88]. Van der Kolk, B. (2015). *The body keeps the score.* New York, New York: Penguin Books.

[89]. Van der Kolk, B. (2015). *The body keeps the score.* New York, New York: Penguin Books

[90]. U.S. military veteran suicides rise, one dies every 65 minutes. (2013, February 01). Retrieved June 24, 2016, from http://www.reuters.com/article/us-usa-veterans-suicide-idUSBRE9101E320130202

[91]. Guntzel, J. (2017, February 01). Beyond PTSD to "Moral Injury". Retrieved May 16, 2017, from https://onbeing.org/blog/beyond-ptsd-to-moral-injury/5069/

[92]. Van der Kolk, B. (2015). *The body keeps the score.* New York, New York: Penguin Books.

[93]. Cole, C. M. (2010). Performing South Africa's Truth Commission: stages of transition. Bloomington, IN: Indiana University Press.

[94] Final report of the Truth and Reconciliation Commission of Canada. honouring the truth, reconciling for the future. (2015). Toronto: James Lorimer & Company Ltd., .

[95] Archibald, L., Dewar, J., Reid, C., & Stevens, V. (2012). Dancing, singing, painting, and speaking the healing story: healing through creative arts. Ottawa, Ontario: Aboriginal Healing Foundation.

[96] Dance/Movement Therapy with Veterans and Military Personnel[PDF]. (2017, May 15). American Dance Therapy Association.

[97]. Van der Kolk, B. (2015). *The body keeps the score.* New York, New York: Penguin Books.

[98]. Van der Kolk, B. (2015). *The body keeps the score.* New York, New York: Penguin Books.

[99]. Van der Kolk, B. (2015). *The body keeps the score*. New York, New York: Penguin Books.

[100]. Van der Kolk, B. (2015). *The body keeps the score*. New York, New York: Penguin Books.

[101]. Van der Kolk, B. (2015). *The body keeps the score*. New York, New York: Penguin Books.

[102]. Van der Kolk, B. (2015). *The body keeps the score*. New York, New York: Penguin Books.

[103]. Bauerlein, V., & Campo-Flores, A. (2016, December 29). The VA Hooked Veterans on Opioids, Then Failed Them Again. Retrieved December 30, 2016, from http://www.wsj.com/articles/the-va-hooked-veterans-on-opioids-then-failed-them-again-1483030270

[104]. Kime, P. (2016, April 21). DEA approves PTSD marijuana study. Retrieved May 14, 2017, from http://www.militarytimes.com/story/veterans/2016/04/21/dea-approves-ptsd-marijuana-study/83356604/

[105]. Van der Kolk, B. (2015). *The body keeps the score*. New York, New York: Penguin Books.

[106] The Nate Update: When he got home after the retreat, Nate started pursuing this idea he had—creating a non-profit in which he takes Vets on fishing trips. He started Reel Vets Fish On and is now the founder of a thriving organization devoted to helping Vets of all skill and ability levels to find community, support, and serenity through daylong fishing excursions. Today, he seems like a different person than the guy I met the first day of the retreat. He has transformed himself by helping others. I am so proud of him, and completely inspired by him.

[107]. Van der Kolk, B. (2015). *The body keeps the score*. New York, New York: Penguin Books.

[108]. Van der Kolk, B. (2015). *The body keeps the score* (1st ed., p. 16). New York, New York: Penguin Books.

[109]. Junger, S. (2016). *Tribe*. New York, New York: Twelve.

[110]. Van der Kolk, B. (2015). *The body keeps the score* (1st ed., p. 16). New York, New York: Penguin Books.

[111]. Talbott, J. (2008). A Randomized Clinical Trial of Eye Movement Desensitization and Reprocessing (EMDR), Fluoxetine, and Pill Placebo in the Treatment of Posttraumatic Stress Disorder: Treatment Effects and Long-Term Maintenance. *Yearbook of Psychiatry and Applied Mental Health, 2008*, 160-161. doi:10.1016/s0084-3970(08)70743-6

[112]. How EMDR can help police officers exposed to graphic images and incidents. (2016, September 16). Retrieved May 16, 2017, from https://www.policeone.com/health-fitness/articles/220251006-How-EMDR-can-help-police-officers-exposed-to-graphic-images-and-incidents/

[113]. Murray, B. (n.d.). Writing to heal. Retrieved October 16, 2016, from http://www.apa.org/monitor/jun02/writing.aspx

[114]. Van der Kolk, B. (2015). *The body keeps the score.* New York, New York: Penguin Books.

[115]. Stossel, S. (2013). My age of anxiety: fear, hope, dread, and the search for peace of mind. New York: Vintage Books, a division of Random House LLC.

[116]. Pan (god). (2017, May 12). Retrieved May 16, 2017, from https://en.wikipedia.org/wiki/Pan_(god)

[117]. Anxiety Disorders. (n.d.). Retrieved October 14, 2015, from http://www.nimh.nih.gov/health/topics/panic-disorder/index.shtml

[118]. Bourne, E. (2005). *The Anxiety and Phobia Workbook* (4th ed.). Oakland: New Harbinger Publications.

[119].Van der Kolk, B. (2015). *The body keeps the score.* New York, New York: Penguin Books.

[120]. Van der Kolk, B. (2015). *The body keeps the score.* New York, New York: Penguin Books.

[121]. Wilson, R. R., & Lyons, L. (2013). *Anxious kids, anxious parents: 7 ways to stop the worry cycle and raise courageous & independent children.* Deerfield Beach, FL: Health Communications, Inc.

[122]. Bourne, E. (2005). *The Anxiety and Phobia Workbook* (4th ed.). Oakland: New Harbinger Publications.

[123]. Emmons, R. (2010, November 16). Why Gratitude Is Good. Retrieved November 4, 2016, from http:// greatergood.berkeley.edu/article/item/ why_gratitude_is_good/

[124]. Hoffman, A. (2016, November 16). What Does a Grateful Brain Look Like? Retrieved January 2, 2017, from http://greatergood.berkeley.edu/article/item/ what_does_a_grateful_brain_look_like

[125]. United Health Group. (n.d.). Doing Good is Good For You 2013 Health and Volunteering Study (Publication).

[126]. Moncrieff, J. (2005). Efficacy of antidepressants in adults. *Bmj,331*(7509), 155-157. doi:10.1136/bmj.331.7509.155

[127]. Stossel, S. (2013). My age of anxiety: fear, hope, dread, and the search for peace of mind. New York: Vintage Books, a division of Random House LLC.

[128]. Stossel, S. (2013). My age of anxiety: fear, hope, dread, and the search for peace of mind. New York: Vintage Books, a division of Random House LLC.

[129]. Stossel, S. (2013). My age of anxiety: fear, hope, dread, and the search for peace of mind. New York: Vintage Books, a division of Random House LLC.

[130]. Stossel, S. (2013). My age of anxiety: fear, hope, dread, and the search for peace of mind. New York: Vintage Books, a division of Random House LLC.

[131]. University of Virginia. (n.d.). Tonics and Elixirs for Neurasthenia. Retrieved March 16, 2017, from http://exhibits.hsl.virginia.edu/nerves/tonics/

[132]. Stossel, S. (2013). My age of anxiety: fear, hope, dread, and the search for peace of mind. New York: Vintage Books, a division of Random House LLC.

[133]. Van der Kolk, B. (2015). *The body keeps the score* (1st ed., p. 16). New York, New York: Penguin Books.

[134]. Stossel, S. (2013). My age of anxiety: fear, hope, dread, and the search for peace of mind. New York: Vintage Books, a division of Random House LLC.

[135]. Dokoupil, T. (2010, March 13). America's Long Love Affair with Anti-Anxiety Drugs. Retrieved September 16, 2015, from http://www.newsweek.com/americas-long-love-affair-anti-anxiety-drugs-77967

[136]. Frontline. (n.d.). Marijuana Timeline. Retrieved December 10, 2016, from http://www.pbs.org/wgbh/pages/frontline/shows/dope/etc/cron.html

[137]. Burke, M. (n.d.). Study: Can marijuana improve PTSD symptoms for veterans? Retrieved September 12, 2016, from http://www.stripes.com/news/study-can-marijuana-improve-ptsd-symptoms-for-veterans-1.427271

[138]. Ingraham, C. (2016, February 17). Study: Smoking pot doesn't make you anxious or depressed. Retrieved September 12, 2016, from https://www.washingtonpost.com/news/wonk/wp/2016/02/17/study-smoking-pot-doesnt-make-you-anxious-or-depressed/

[139]. Spotswood, S. (n.d.). More Opioid Prescriptions Adverse Effects for Vets With PTSD. Retrieved April 15, 2017, from http://www.usmedicine.com/agencies/department-of-veterans-affairs/more-opioid-prescriptions-adverse-effects-for-vets-with-ptsd/

[140]. US Department of Health and Human Services - The Opioid Epidemic: By the Numbers (Rep.). (2016).

[141]. Prescription Opioid Overdose Data. (2016, December 16). Retrieved March 17, 2017, from https://www.cdc.gov/drugoverdose/data/overdose.html

[142]. Schupska, S. (2016, July 6). Not blowing smoke: Research finds medical marijuana lowers prescription drug use. Retrieved September 13, 2016, from http://news.uga.edu/releases/article/medical-marijuana-lowers-prescription-drug-use-0716/

[143]. Gangwisch, J. E., Hale, L., Garcia, L., Malaspina, D., Opler, M. G., Payne, M. E., . . . Lane, D. (2015). High glycemic index diet as a risk factor for depression: analyses from the Women's Health Initiative. *American Journal of Clinical Nutrition, 102*(2), 454-463. doi:10.3945/ajcn.114.103846

[144] Cecily works with clients online as well as in person, so if you're interested, check out http://cecilyarmstrong.com/

[145]. Bourne, E. (2005). *The Anxiety and Phobia Workbook* (4th ed.). Oakland: New Harbinger Publications.

[146] Eating Disorders. (n.d.). Retrieved January 14, 2017, from https://www.adaa.org/understanding-anxiety/related-illnesses/eating-disorders

[147]. Get The Facts On Eating Disorders. (n.d.). Retrieved September 27, 2016, from https://www.nationaleatingdisorders.org/get-facts-eating-disorders

[148]. Altman, A. (2016, December 19). The Year of Hygge, the Danish Obsession with Getting Cozy. Retrieved December 20, 2016, from http://www.newyorker.com/culture/culture-desk/the-year-of-hygge-the-danish-obsession-with-getting-cozy

[149] Scelfo, J. (2015, July 27). Suicide on Campus and the Pressure of Perfection. Retrieved May 23, 2017, from https://www.nytimes.com/2015/08/02/education/edlife/stress-social-media-and-suicide-on-campus.html

[150] C., Langlois . (2015, August 06). Teens & the Duck Syndrome. Retrieved May 23, 2017, from https://psychcentral.com/blog/archives/2013/09/19/teens-the-duck-syndrome/

[151] Flett, G. L., Hewitt, P. L., & Heisel, M. J. (2014). The destructiveness of perfectionism revisited: Implications for the assessment of suicide risk and the prevention of suicide. *Review of General Psychology,18*(3), 156-172. doi:10.1037//gpr0000011

[152] Inspired by Bourne, E. (2005). *The Anxiety and Phobia Workbook* (4th ed.). Oakland: New Harbinger Publications.